MANAGEMENT: PRINCIPLE AND PRACTICE

MANAGEMENT
Principle and Practice

[According to UGC Syllabus for UG, PG and Diploma Courses]

M.U. Qureshi

ANMOL PUBLICATIONS PVT. LTD.
NEW DELHI - 110 002 (INDIA)

ANMOL PUBLICATIONS PVT. LTD.
4374/4B, Ansari Road, Daryaganj
New Delhi - 110 002
Ph.: 23261597, 23278000
Visit us at: www.anmolpublications.com

Management: Principle and Practice

First Published, 2005

ISBN 81-261-2320-6

PRINTED IN INDIA

Published by J.L. Kumar for Anmol Publications Pvt. Ltd., New Delhi - 110 002 and Printed at Mehra Offset Press, Delhi.

Contents

Preface

Tourism and Hotel Industry are the two significant sectors of modern day economy and are complimentary to each other. The new world order has turned the whole mankind into one family or society. Today's world is a global village, where distances have no meaning. Although, tourism and travelling are the two phenomena, as old as the civilized world, yet, tourism evolved into a regular and well-organised industry, during the last century only.

Hotel industry is part and parcel of tourism sector. The tourists are honoured guests and the hotels offer them the demanded hospitality. Hence, the two form a correlated industrial sector, which is growing and flourishing fast, with promises for future.

Extension of education and expansion of knowledge have created a new anxiety, among the members of the new generation, regarding the above said two areas. In fact, the two sectors offer high profile career avenues and good opportunities for aspirants and job-seekers. However, like other disciplines, Tourism and Hotel Management also require proper training for professionals. Hence, a large room for exhaustive and exclusive books on the subject, is there.

This series of comprehensive books has been outlined within the parameters of the syllabi of various universities and institutes, in a broad-based manner, in order to cover all streams of the discipline and for the benefit of students at graduate and post-graduate levels.

The undersigned is confident of a due recognition and proper acknowledgement from concerned circles. Further expectation is that this series of useful books would prove to be practically helpful to the professionals and students equally.

— Editor

1

Introduction

In the new world order, there is an increasingly competitive environment, and many of world's corporations are engaged in a variety of efforts to renew their enterprises: visioning, thinking strategically, building and changing corporate culture, downsizing, and most recently, total quality of an initiative that emphasizes the importance of participatory decision making and high-performance work teams. Managing diversity now explicitly joins the list, although it has always been implicitly a part of the renewal effort. Much of what executives are now doing in their search for enhanced viability implicitly requires a managing diverse capability.

The point to remember is that these various approaches are related, and that one paves the way for the others. This is especially true when we look at managing diversity in relation to total quality. Together, they constitute an integral strategy for renewal.

Total quality is one of the most promising new ideas in the continuing efforts to maximize employee productivity and restore American competitiveness. Most managers would agree that it can be traced to Dr. W. Edwards Demming's work with Japanese industrialists over a period of some thirty years. They disagree on exactly what it involves.

Some managers see total quality as a collection of techniques: quality circles, just-in-time inventory control, employee suggestion systems, participatory management, and continuous improvement. Others see it as a collection of principles: managerial commitment and involvement, dedication to customers, employee involvement, and improved processes.

A broader view holds that total quality is a comprehensive approach calling for a change in the very fabric of the American corporation. Managers who hold this perspective contend that total quality represents, at heart, a cultural change. That means it takes more than trying out some techniques or adopting a set of principles. It demands modifying the fundamental assumptions that control U.S. business.

This broader view has been well described by Andrea Gabor :

> While many companies have come to understand that they must conduct their businesses differently, few have grasped the enormity of the task that faces them. Some companies adopt SPC (statistical process control) in their manufacturing operations only to discover that marketing and sales have been left out of the improvement loop.... Yet other companies spend millions retraining their workers, but neglect to educate managers about their new role in the process. Quality management, Deming style, is a holistic philosophy that must be adopted in its entirety if it is to work at all.

Typically, managers' perspectives on total quality evolve over time as their experience with it grows. First they are fascinated and preoccupied with the mechanics. It takes a whole before they recognize that they are doing is really a cultural or "fabric" change—far beyond the mechanics. A quality manager described his company's progression:

> We were busy with the mechanics of quality. At this point, we were doing the business and quality. There was no integration. We were getting results by doing quality and then going to manage the business.

We needed quality goals that led to business success, and business goals that led to quality success. We needed to integrate business and quality.

Impressive results can be achieved during the mechanical stage, as various "success" stories have shown. Yet successes achieved during this stage can prove to be elusive, or extremely difficult to sustain.

Managers faced with this reality have several choices:

1. Recommit to the same or additional total quality techniques.
2. Adjust their aspirations downward.
3. Reject total quality as unworkable.
4. Expand their understanding of the concept of quality. Managers who recommit must first rethink their resolve.

After re-examining their rationale for moving forward and finding it adequate, they turn to the specifics of the task. "Why," they ask, "aren't we getting the desired results? What are we doing wrong?" Typically, they refine their implementation strategies.

Managers who are less enthusiastic may adjust their aspirations downward. These managers aren't ready to discount quality, but they believe they've achieved what is reasonable, given their company's characteristics and the nature of the effort. So they adopt a piecemeal approach. Some, for example, eliminate the name but keep part of the concept. In this context, some use task forces that operate sporadically to solve specific problems (usually posed by management). Other companies create all-encompassing employee involvement programmes characterized by mandatory participation. Only a few retain the comprehensive notion of total quality as popularized in Japan.

Reasons for rejection of total quality range from ineffective management to perceived cultural incompatibility. One quality circle pioneer, for example, failed to weave the motivation for and commitment to the circles into its fabric. The result: the circles were abandoned after the departure of one of its first quality leaders. Other companies have discontinued quality techniques after deciding that they are not compatible with American culture. Success with the techniques, they believe requires such "Japanese" practices as minimizing the differences in how managers and workers are treated, and fostering job longevity. "That's all well and good for the Japanese," they say, "but Americans just don't think that way."

Managers who have been most successful with total quality are those who, after re-examining their successes, have decided to broaden the concept. Total quality becomes for them not a technique but a comprehensive management philosophy. These managers take a leadership role. They become change agents, not just advocates of a programme.

Some of these managers, however, have discovered that even this is not enough. Total quality's effects remain beneficial, but the benefits begin to plateau as the amount of energy needed to maintain a given level of progress increases. This reality is typical of managerial efforts that don't incorporate consideration of the corporation's core assumptions. It represents the Achilles heel of total quality. Even winners of the prestigious Malcolm Baldrige Prize, for example, haven't achieved holistic total quality. Contenders are judged, instead, on progress with individual quality techniques, and on the intensity and extent of their efforts toward comprehensive implementation. Little, if any, attention is given to whether root cultural assumptions have been unearthed and made congruent with total quality.

This, of course, explains the difficulty in providing "proof" of the link between performance and total quality. Certainly, a business case can be made for progress with selected total quality techniques. But belief that adopting a holistic approach to total quality will pay off still requires leaps of vision and logic, since no company has achieved this level of implementation.

That doesn't mean that the case is implicitly weak. But doer managers with tunnel vision and short-term time frames often have trouble relating to arguments based on vision and logic.

Even managers with broad vision and open minds are concerned about the difficulty of changing core corporate assumptions (roots). They are increasingly eager to explore ways to achieving total quality that can be integrated with other change-oriented initiatives. And that brings us to managing diversity.

Individually, both total quality and managing diversity offer potential for enhancing corporate competitiveness, and both face challenges that inhibit their implementation. When the two are used in combination, the challenges are better managed and the benefits are increased—synergy at its best.

Total quality and managing diversity are similar in perspective and in intent. But they are not equally well understood. Practitioners may argue about the scope of total quality, but they generally agree on what it is. Not so with managing diversity. Many not only fail to differentiate among affirmative action, valuing differences, and managing diversity; they use such terms as "multiculturalism," "diversity," and "pluralism" with imprecision as well. The result is conceptual confusion. Total quality's skills and techniques are also more advanced than those of managing diversity. Yet their commonalties are more significant.

Both efforts are Grounded in Business Rationales : Managers who become excited about total quality and managing diversity are motivated by competitive realities. Corning, Inc.'s experience is an example. In the early 1980s, this company, faced with aggressive competition, reduced profits, and an assertive work force, decided to adopt a total quality initiative. The Corning Quality Management System was developed and a Quality Institute established. Over the years, this participatory effort has shifted in focus but remains true to its goals. Corning managers are excited about the results and have made substantial progress.

Managers serious about implementing managing diversity are attracted by the same kind of reasoning. They see managing diversity as a strategy for competitiveness.

This is not some type of benevolent activity on our part. There is self-interest here. We have to have a culture and environment in which these people can flourish, and that's what we are working toward.

Total quality requires that people be fully involved and committed; managing diversity calls for the empowerment of people who are diverse. This means that *managing diversity is a prerequisite* for full implementation of total quality. In an increasingly diverse work force, total quality's emphasis on empowering people translates into our definition of managing diversity—empowering people who are diverse.

Progressive organizations are beginning to acknowledge this interrelationship. Their managers realize that if total quality is a priority item, managing diversity is also. If total quality is strategic and competitive, managing diversity is too, since total quality requires managing diversity capability.

Implementation requirements for both options are so broad and deep that they require fundamental changes in the way corporations do business. Deming comments on the magnitude of the challenge:

> Even when the management of a company embarks in earnest on the fourteen points for quality, production, and competitive position, advancement will at best appear to be sluggish. One must allow five years for the purchasing department to learn their new job....
>
> Companies with good management will require five years to remove the barriers that make it impossible for the worker to take pride in his work. Many companies will require ten years....
>
> It may be obvious to anyone... that a long thorny road lies ahead in American Industry—ten to thirty years...

Established corporations are highly unlikely to be able to implement either managing diversity or total quality fully without cultural root change. It isn't that they can't secure behavioural change; this can be done by decree, if necessary. The problem is that if behavioural changes are incongruent with the corporation's roots (culture), they will be short-lived—a painful reality for managers familiar with the start-and-stop process of major change initiatives.

Sustainable, long-term *natural* behavioural change requires congruence with the organization's roots. If the culture does not support the desired behavioural change, the culture must be modified. Managers who drive behavioral change on the assumption that the roots will follow are doomed to repeat the cycle. When they relax their efforts they find the oak root saying to the grafted peach limb, 'This is *still* an *oak* tree."

Most managers have little experience with the false starts, ups and downs, ambiguities, uncertainties, and ambivalences that characterize such change. And most of them are uncomfortable with pioneering. That's why they ask this tell-tale question: "Can you tell us about the successes of other companies with managing diversity?"

When managing diversity is integrated with total quality, the most significant implementation challenges that remain with total quality are more successfully addressed. This integration also addresses another important issue: manager overload and the fragmentation that can occur as a result of too many unrelated initiatives. Any new and complex approach takes time and effort. Implementing managing diversity within the context of total quality gives managers and employees a sense of continuity and unified purpose.

Such integration is, however, more successful if the two thrusts are seen as connected but separate. This is particularly true when a relatively well-established initiative such as total quality is paired with a more recent one such as managing diversity.

As American businesses struggle with their overall renewal agenda, appropriate integration between total quality and managing diversity can make the difference between success and failure.

Strategic Management : Policy-makers are often stunned when their carefully laid plans fail badly. One reason is that institutions present fierce resistance to change, impervious even to the authority of presidents.

Even if plans are implemented, projects begun with great promise may easily go awry to become what have been called "great planning disasters." The Concorde was expected to revolutionize air travel, but huge unexpected costs discouraged its adoption by nations other than the developers, France and England. Nuclear power was expected to provide energy "too cheap to meter," yet it has become economically and politically infeasible in the United States.

Sometimes strategies worsen the problems they were supposed to solve or produce the very opposite of what was intended—"fatal remedies." The Vietnam war was fought to contain communism but instead spread it to other parts of Southeast Asia. Forced busing often provokes parents to move or to send their children to private schools, adding to the segregation problem.

Such examples remind us to be a little Humble in our plans. People are resistant, modern societies are complex, and human behaviour is often surprising. But these failures also point out the truth about how change really works, rather than the way we want it to work. It has been traditionally believed that executives can control change, but, in reality, organisations are largely driven by forces beyond them. If we hope to adapt to a very difficult future looming ahead, it is necessary to begin by acknowledging that any institution is actually an inseparable part of a larger environment with a life of its own.

This intimate organization-environment relationship also helps explain what drives the New Capitalism. These concepts have been adopted by only a minority of progressive corporations, while the bulk of business firms, government agencies, and other organizations are failing because they remain attached to values of the Old Capitalism that are deeply ingrained in our culture—growth, power, and profit. Why should anything change?

Worldwide industrialization in an age of less-is-more demands a balanced form of growth; the exploding complexity of the information age is restructuring hierarchies into flexible networks; competition and new employee attitudes require participative decision-making; and political forces are expanding corporate governance to serve a broader range of goals. The key to successful change is understanding these inexorable forces and turning them to the organization's advantage.

The New Capitalism can be thought of as comprising a "metastrategy" that goes beyond strategic planning to make the organization itself a flexible system for adapting to the discontinuities of a new era. Just as the oriental martial arts convert the strength of an aggressor to one's advantage, so should strategic management convert threats into useful strategies. The world moves on regardless of our puny efforts, so we face the choice of either being changed by it in ways we may not like, or changing with it to share in guiding the future.

The need for strategic change is growing acute because the onset of a knowledge-based society is opening up a sharp, gaping discontinuity with the past. One of the newest things today is the very increase in newness—an accelerated rate of change feeding on itself such that the world changes ever faster as a result of earlier changes. Peter Drucker effectively summed up the challenge of planning for this turbulent period that is buffeting institutions.

...one certainty about the times ahead is that they will be turbulent times... the most probable assumption in a period of turbulence is the unique event which changes the configuration—and unique events cannot, by definition, be "planned."

Even our very concepts for introducing change are proving inadequate. Not too long ago, large organizations developed "future studies," "organisational development," and "strategic planning" to bring about change. These approaches continue to be useful, but on the whole the hopeful enthusiasm they once captured has faded because of basic flaws.

When the economic transition began, a few pioneers responded by inventing a discipline for the formal study of the future. Max Ways, editor of Fortune, announced in a 1964 article that "The New Era of Radical Change" had arrived, and later Alvin Toffler popularized this theme with his best seller, Future Shock. Over the next few years the field grew dramatically. The World Future Society short up to more than 50,000 members, 3000 courses on the future were introduced at colleges, and about 400 think tanks offered advice on the future to corporations and other institutions. In 1972 Toffler described how the study of the future had become an exciting new intellectual movement.

Until a few years ago, the word "futurist" was virtually unknown in American intellectual life.... Today the word has leapt into the language (denoting) a growing school of social critics, scientists, philosophers, planners, and others who concern themselves with the alternative facing man as the human race collides with an onrushing future.

Despite this flood of spirited publications, courses, and studies that washed over the past two decades, interest in the future has had little impact on private or public policy. Many corporations and government agencies, such as GE and the U.S. Congress, started programmes in "future research," but attention has wandered recently toward dealing with immediate issues.

Why have Americans been so eager to immerse themselves in futurism as an intellectual field, but so reluctant to put it to practical use before disaster strikes? Part of the problem is that forecasts of the future tend to use elaborate technical methods which are so complex as to discourage understanding, or they rely on sheer intuition which is so speculative that it is considered guesswork. And simple resistance to change has caused much apathy and reality denial.

But the greatest problem has been that the future remains divorced from the lives of people—which usually focus on concerns of the present. The future has been portrayed as a fascinating, rather science fiction type of distant world that lies "out there" waiting to happen, and so we can only predict it using ingenious computerized methods or the vision of gifted Prophets. What is lacking is a more human concept of the future as largely emanating from choices made in the present by people. The future is not an immutable fate waiting to befall us, especially for powerful leaders who control major technical, economic, and political decisions that shape society. As Irving Kristol pointed out, for instance, the behavior of the "economy" is not preordained by some armorphous external force acting on a passive corporation but is to a great extent the result of collective actions taken by executives.

2

Basic Structure

It is very difficult to have an all encompassing definition of management which covers all its characteristics. Management is a vital function concerned with all aspects of the working of an enterprise. Management has been defined in a number of ways. Prof Haimann has interpreted the term "management" in three distinct aspects:

(a) Management as a field of study or a subject.

(b) Management as a team or class of people or a noun.

(c) Management as a process.

Management as a field of study or a subject refers to the principles and practices of management. It entails all the principles and practices as a knowledge and its application in its entirety. This approach, however, fails to give the correct nature of management.

Management as a team or class of people refers to the group of managerial personnel of an enterprise functioning in their supervisory capacity. However, who are the managers and what are the activities that should be treated as managerial, are hard to identify, unless some yardsticks are prescribed. This becomes more difficult specially when those performing managerial activities have different titles in one organisation as well as in different organisations.

Management as a process refers to different processes or steps of management— right from planning to organising, staffing, supervising and controlling. Management in this context has been defined as the process of getting things done by and in cooperation with others.

The Concepts : There are many definitions of management. They emphasize one or the other important aspect of management activity. According to Koontz, "Management is the art of getting things done with people and through informally organised groups. It is the art of creating an environment in which people can perform as individuals and yet cooperate towards attainment of group goals. It is the art of removing blocks for such a performance, a way of optimising efficiency in reaching goals." According to Dalton E. McFarland, "Management is the fundamental integrating and operating mechanism underlying organised effort."

According to George R. Terry, "Management is a distinct process ... performed to determine and accomplish stated objectives by the use of human beings and other resources."

According to Harold Koontz and Cyrill O'Donnel, "Management is the creation and maintenance of an internal environment in an enterprise where individuals, working together in groups can perform efficiently and effectively towards the attainment of group goals." According to W. Jack Duncan, "Management consists of all organisational activities that involve goal formation and accomplishment, performance, appraisal and the development of an operating philosophy that ensures the organisation's survival within the social system."

According to Kimball and Kimball, "Management may be defined as the art of applying the economic principles that underline the control of men and material in the enterprise under consideration."

According to Brech, "Management may be defined as a social process entailing responsibility for the effective planning and regulation of the operations of an enterprise, such responsibility involves (a) the installation and maintenance of proper procedures to ensure adherence to plans, and (b) the guidance, integration and supervision of the personnel comprising the enterprise and carrying out its operations."

There is no universally acceptable definition of management; so much so that Brech has stated, "Exactly what the term means is not always clear and not always agreed." Common to all above definitions is the connection of management to organisational goals. It evaluates the effectiveness of goals accomplished and devises methods for achieving those tasks which are compatible with the demands of the society within which it operates. The most widely accepted meaning of the term "management" is that management is a process by which responsible persons (e.g., managers or executives) in an organisation get things done through the efforts of other persons in group activities. Before summing it up it is essential to quote the definition of management given by the American Management Association. It reads, "Management is guiding human and physical resources into dynamic organisation units which attain their objectives to the satisfaction of those served and with a high degree of morale and sense of attainment on the part of those rendering services."

Salient Features

Organisational Activity: Management is a group activity. Management is to coordinate the actions and reactions of individuals.

Goal Formation: Management has some defined goals before it to achieve.Goals are set considering the actions and reactions of individuals.

Goal Accomplishment and Evaluation: Management also evaluates the effectiveness of goal accomplishments.

Organisational Survival: Managers are expected to use the resources available to them as efficiently as possible to guide the survival of an organisationin the competitive world. The ability to forecast and adopt to change are also important components of management for organisational survival.

Implementation: Action is the creed of management. Policies and programmes are implemented by management.

The Characteristics

Following are certain features which illustrate the wide breadth of scope of management.

Universal Process: Management is a universal process which is applied in all types of institu tions—social, religious, commercial, political, etc. Every organisation and institution whose object is to achieve its objectives and goals through group efforts, needs planning, coordination, direction and control, i.e., management.

An Integrative Process: The essence of management is the integration of human and physical resources in a manner that it leads to effective performance.

Managers apply knowledge, experience and principles for getting the results. Management seeks to harmonise the individual goals with organisational goals.

Dynamic Function: Management is a dynamic function of business organisations. Its functions change from time to time depending upon the circumstances of the business, i.e., changes in economic, social, political, technological and human conditions. Management adjusts itself to the changing atmosphere— making suitable forecasts and changes in the policies.

Social Process: Management is a social process as it primarily deals with emotional/dynamic and sensitive human beings. The major achievement is to win their confidence and cooperation. Thus, making it difficult to precisely define the principles of management. Management principles are constantly influenced by soçial traditions, customs and regulations.

Management makes things Happen: Managerial ability is distinctly different from technical ability. Management is the art of getting things done through people. It implies that under given set of constraints or problem boundaries how positive results can emerge, by taking well defined actions.

Management is a Multi-faceted Discipline: Management has to deal with heterogeneous resources. Their performance depends upon the proper knowledge and skill of various disciplines. Management has grown as a body of discipline taking the help of so many social sciences like—Anthropology, Sociology, Psychology' etc. Due to this, management is also known as a "Behavioural Science."

Management is a Science and an Art: Management is a science because it has an organised body of knowledge which is based on facts and certain universal truths. It is an art because certain skills, essential for good management, are unique to individuals. So many times managers act on instinct. It is also about interactions which cannot be laid down in black and white.

Intangible Force : Managerial ability is an intangible force; it is a social skill which cannot be seen with the eyes but it is evidenced by the quality andlevel of an organisation.

Practical Aspects

All the managers have to perform certain functions in an organisation to get the things moving. But there is never complete agreement among experts on what functions should be included in the management process. However, Koontz and O'Donnell's classification of management functions is best of all and is widely accepted. According to them, "functions of management are planning, organising, staffing, directing and controlling."

Planning : Planning is an indispensable function of management determining the objectives to be achieved and the course of action to be followed to achieve them. It is a mental process requiring the use of intellectual faculties, foresight and sound judgement. Planning virtually pervades the entire gamut of managerial activity. This function is performed by managers at all levels. The managers at the top level in an organisation devote more time on planning as compared to the managers at the lower levels. Planning includes:

(i) determination of objectives,

(ii) forecasting,

(iii) search of alternative courses of action and their evaluation,

(iv) drawing policies and procedures, and

(v) budgeting.

Planning is a prerequisite of doing anything. Planning is a pervasive, continuous and never ending activity. It leads to more effective and faster achievements in any organisation and enhances the ability of the organisation to adopt to future eventualities.

Organising : Organising involves identification and grouping the activities to be performed and dividing them among the individuals and creating authority and responsibility relationships among them. The process of organising involves the following steps:

(i) Determination of objectives;

(ii) Division of activities;

(iii) Fitting individuals to specific jobs; and

(iv) Developing relationship in terms of authorities and responsibilities.

Organising can be viewed as a bridge connecting the conceptual ideas developed in creating and planning to the specific means for accomplishing these ideas. Organising contributes to the efficiency of an organisation.

Staffing : The staffing function has assumed great importance these days because of rapid advancement of technology, increasing size of organisations and complicated behaviour of human beings. The managerial function of staffing includes manning the organisational structure through proper and effective selection process, appraisal and the development of personnel to fill the roles designed into the structure.

The staffing function involves:

(i) Proper recruitment and selection of the people;

(ii) Fixing remuneration;

(iii) Training and developing selected people to discharge organisation a function; and

(iv) Appraisal of personnel.

Every manager is continuously engaged in performing the staffing function Although some elementary functions like keeping inventory, of personnel, advertising for jobs, calling candidates etc. are assigned to Personnel Department. The manage: performs the duties of job analysis, job description, appraisal of performance, etc. In short, the staffing function can be viewed as an all pervasive function of management

Directing : Directing is that part of the management process which actuates the organisation members to work efficiently and effectively for the.attainment of organisational objectives. Planning, organising and staffing are merely preparations of the work, the work actually starts when managers start performing the direct functions. Direction is the interpersonnel aspect of management which deals directly with influencing, guiding, supervising and motivating the subordinates for the accomplishment of the pre-determined objectives.

According to Joseph Massie, "Directing concerns the total manner in which a manager influences the actions of subordinates. It is the final action of a manager in getting others to act after all the preparations have been completed." It consists of four subfunctions:

Communication: It is the process of passing information and understanding from one person to another. A successful manager should develop an effective system of communication so that he may issue instructions and receive the reactions of the subordinates and motivate them.

Leadership: It is the process by which a manager guides and influences the work of his subordinates.

Motivation: Motivation means inspiring the subordinates to zealously work towards accomplishment and achievement of organisational goods and objectives.

Supervision: Managers have tc personally watch, direct and control the performance of subordinates. In doing this they have to plan the work— give them directions and instructions, guide them and exercise leadership.

Controlling : Controlling is visualising that actual performance is guided towards expected performance. It is the measurement and appraisal of the activities performed by the subordinates in order to make sure that the objectives and the plans devised to attain them are being accomplished. Controlling involves following:

(i) fixing appropriate standards,

(ii) measurement of actual performance,

(iii) comparing actual and planned performance,

(iv) finding variances between the two and reasons for the variance, and

(v) taking corrective actions.

Control keeps a check on other functions for ensuring successful functioning management. The most notable feature is that it is forward-looking. A manager cannot control the past but can avoid mistakes in the future by taking actions in the light of past experiences.

The above functions may give an impression that these sections are independent compartments. Management is a continuous process involving the interaction of all functions and departments. These functions are being performed simultaneously and repeatedly. The purpose of separating the functions of management is to ensure that sufficient attention will be paid to each of them. The functions of management are universal. A manager has to perform these functions in the organisation, whatever the level of the manager or the objective of the organisation. Some people raise the question which management function is more important than others. The importance of the functions will vary from task to task but they are all important and necessary in accomplishing any organisational goal.

Form and Nature

The most dependable view regarding the nature of management is that management is science and art, both. Both art and science are not naturally exclusive fields of endeavour but are complementary to each other.

Management as Science : Science is the systematised body of knowledge pertaining to a particular field of enquiry. Such systematised body of knowledge contains, concepts, theories experimentation and principles which are universal and true. According to Chester L. Bernard, "Science explains the phenomenon, the events, the past situations and that their aim is not to produce specific events effects or situations but explanations that we call knowledge. The various concepts and principles of science are developed on the basis of observation and experiments."

Now, let us see whether management can satisfy the tests which we have listed above for science. Management has a systematised body of knowledge pertaining to its field and the various concepts, principles and techniques have been developed through deductive and inductive reasoning. For example, in the area of designing an effective organisation structure, there are a number of principles which serve as guidelines for delegating authority. The unity of command, the consistency of authority and responsibility are some of the important principles which help to decide proper delegation of authority. In the field of management, some of the important techniques related to budgeting, cost-accounting, planning and control are part of a management theory. These techniques are there to help the manager to plan and execute the activities and goods effectively.

But management is not so exact a science as other physical sciences like Physics, Chemistry, etc. The main reason is that it deals with the people and it is very difficult to predict their behaviour accurately. Since it is a social process, it falls in the area of Social Sciences. Management is a behavioural science. Its theories and principles are situation bound because of which their applicability does not necessarily have the same results every time. That is why Ernest Dale has called management a "soft science" which does not have hard and fast rules.

Management as an Art : Art is about bringing out the desired results through the application of skill. It is concerned with the application of knowledge and skills.

Management is one of the most creative art forms, as it requires a vast knowledge and certain innovating, initiating, implementing and integrating skills in relation to goals, resources, techniques and results. As an art, management calls for a corpus of abilities, intuition and judgement and a continuous practice of management theories and principles.

Management is an art because:

(i) The process of management does involve the use of know-how and skills.

(ii) The process of management is directed towards the accomplishment of concrete results.

(iii) Like any other art, management is creative in the sense that management creates new situations needed for further improvement.

(iv) Management is personalised—every man in this profession has his individual approach and technique in solving problems. The success of managerial task is related with personality of the men, character and knowledge.

Thus, we can conclude that management is both a science and an art.

Various Levels

Management is a manifold activity. It is carried on at different levels of the organisational structure. The stages in the organisation where a particular type of function starts is called a level of management. Thus, the term "Levels of Management" refers to a line of demarcation between various managerial positions in an organisation.

The number of managers depends upon the size of the business and workforce. There is a limit to the number of subordinates a person can supervise. The number of levels of management increases when the size of the business and workforce increases. Levels of management are increased so as to achieve effective supervision.

In most of the organisations, there are generally three levels of management: (i) Top management. (ii) Middle management. (iii) Lower management.

Top Levels : In any organisation top management is the ultimate source of authority. It establishes goals and policies for the enterprise and devotes more time on the planning and coordinating functions. It approves the decisions of the middle level management and includes Board of Directors, Managing Director, General Manager, Secretaries and Treasurers, etc.

Middle Levels : It generally consists of heads of functional departments viz., production manager, sales manager, office superintendent, chief cashier, branch managers, etc. They receive orders and instructions from top management and get the things done through lower level management. They are responsible to the top management for the functioning of their departments. They devote more time on the organisation and motivation functions of management.

Lower Levels : It is the lowest level of management and thus has a direct contact with the workers. It includes supervisors, foreman, accounts officers, sales officers, etc. It is directly concerned with the control and performance of the operative employees. Lower level managers guide and direct the workers under the instructions from middle level managers. They devote more time on the supervision of the workers and are responsible for building high morale among workers. The three levels of management may be put as under:

Management

Top Management	Middle Management	Lower Management
• Chairman	• Heads of Departments	• Foremen
• Managing Director	• Superintendents	• Supervisors
• Secretaries	• Branch Managers	• Finance Officers
• Treasurers	• Account Officers	
• Board of Directors		
• General Manager		

Interchangeable Terms

Management and Administration : Management and administration are generally taken to mean as one and the same and are often used interchangeably. But there has been a controversy because of these two terms. There are following three views on the subject of distinction between administration and management:

The Distinction

Oliver Sheldon was the first person to make a distinction between management and administration. According to him, "Administration is the function in industry concerned with the determination of the corporate policy, the coordination of finance, production and distribution whereas Management is the function concerned with the execution of policy within the limits setup by administration." Thus, administration is formulation of policies and is a determinative function while management is execution of policies and is an executive function. Florance and Tead also support this, in their view, "Administration involves the overall setting of major objectives determination of policies, identifying of general purposes laying down broad programmes, major objectives etc. while management is the active direction of human efforts with a view to getting this done."

Incorporated Items

According to Kimball and Kimball "Management is a generic term with wide functions including administration, which is a narrow function." According to Brech, "Management is a social process entailing responsibility for the effective and economical planning and regulation of the operation of an enterprise in fulfilment of a given purpose of task." "Administration is that part of management which is concerned with the installation and carrying out of the procedures by which the programme is laid down and communicated, and the progress of activities is regulated and checked against plans." Thus, first and second viewpoints are exactly opposite to one another.

No Distinction

Other authors like Fayol, Newman Williams, do not make any distinction between these two terms. This viewpoint is gaining popularity these days. It is very difficult to clearly democrate managerial and administrative functions, as the same set of persons perform both these functions. We do not have two sets of people to discharge administrative and operative management functions. Therefore, there is no difference between the two.

In order to avoid any controversy, we can classify management into: (a) administrative management, and (b) operative management. Administrative management is primarily concerned with laying down policies and determining goals whereas operative management is concerned with implementation of the policies for the achievement of goals. But both these functions are performed by the same set of people, according to Spriegal and Lansbugh, "At the higher levels, the managerial authority is concerned more with administrative management and less with operations." As shown in Figure below every manager spends a part of his time in performing administrative management functions and the remaining time on operative management functions.

Thus, administration and management are considered to be one and the same.

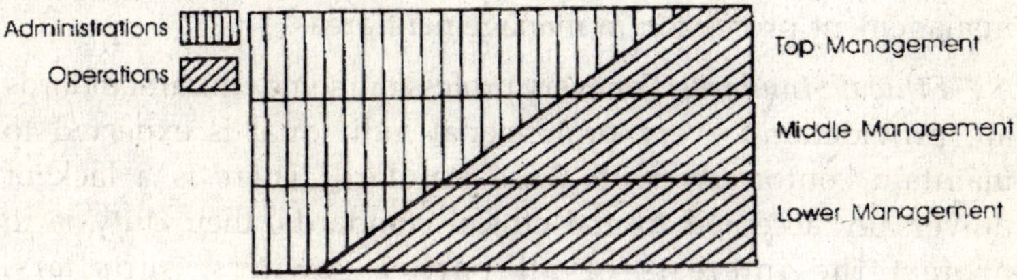

Resolution of management vs. administration

A Profession : The emerging trend of separation of management from ownership and increasing professionalisation of management has led to a debate as to whether management is a profession like doctors, advocates, nurses, accountants, etc. Profession can be defined as an occupation for which specialised skills are required, it is not only meant for self-satisfaction but are used for the larger interests of the society, and the success of these skills is not measured in terms of money alone. According to McFarland, "A profession is a source of livelihood, based on substantial body of knowledge and its formed acquisition the test of success in the service is not the profit earned thereon." A profession has following five characteristics.

Existence of Knowledge: There exists a rapid, expanding body of knowledge underlying the management field. For being a successful manager one has to be alert and study this set of knowledge. A systematic body of knowledge that can be used for professional development has evolved during the last six decades. However, the concept of management is still evolving and new principles are being established continuously.

Formal Teaching of Knowledge: An individual can enter in a profession only after possessing certain knowledge and skills through formal training. To impart management education there are many formal institutes in the world. In India, there are various institutions and universities running management programmes.

Existence of Representative Body: A representative body of professional is needed to regulate and develop the professional activities. Many countries have Management Associations. In India too there is an All India Management Association. These associations manage and coordinate researches and interestsof management profession in management areas.

Ethical Standards: For every profession, some ethical standards are providedand every professional individual is expected to maintain conformity with these standard. There is a lack of universally accepted formal ethical standards, their duty is to protect the interests of all parties—owners, suppliers, consumers,government, etc. In this respect, they are expected to maintain code of conduct.

Reasonable Remuneration: Professionals in management require money to satisfy their needs. However, their success is not measured only in terms of money which they receive by way of rendering their services but bythe contribution they make for the welfare of the society. The management'scontribution by way of integrating various resources into productive unitsis very important for the stability of society.

From the above discussion, it is clear that management has some professional characteristics fully, while others exist partially. Management is a comparatively new field of knowledge and has been developed as a result of rapid industrialisation. It is increasingly being treated as a profession because of the need for acquiring the management skills to solve the complex problems of the organisations. Professional status for management should not be viewed as a matter of definition. The basic elements of professionalisation are important, irrespective of whether they lead to professional status. So we can conclude that management is a profession.

The Implication : The professionalism implies that specialised knowledge will come into existence. Institutions will grow to provide the required specialised knowledge and skill. Consultancy institutions will come into limelight to look into the needs of the profession and also to make the profession serviceable. Such organisation try to coordinate the activities of sister organisations in order to derive advantage of the existence of such organisations. The most important implication of professionalism is the preparation of a code of conduct. This sets morals and ethics for the professionals. It helps in the ethical approach to the problems.

Management, after being professionalised, has become socially responsible. This has helped the management acquire a new role in the business world. Management as a profession plays a role of creator in an economy, particularly when it is in the developing stage.

The Significance : In old times, scale of production was small and there was no economic life. Hence, the role of management was not well-established. But with the advent of industrial revolution, scale of production became very large and there arose various types of complexities in the field of production, distribution and exchange.

There was an urgent and immediate need for effective coordination of human and non-human resources. It required management. The increasing size of business organisations, complex problems of business and advancement of modern technology has resulted in the recognition of management as an important factor of production. Management has achieved an importance today.

Management has the integrating force in all kinds of organised activity. It is not unique to business organisations but common to all kinds of social organisations. Although, organisations other than business do not speak of management, they all need management. It is a specific organ for all kinds of organisations, since they all need to utilise their limited resources most efficiently and effectively for the achievement of their purpose. It is the most vital force in the successful performance of all kinds of organised social activities. However, management has been associated more with business and economic activities. Management has made it possible to organise economic activity in giant organisations like the Steel Authority of India, Life Insurance Corporation, Air-India, Indian Railways, etc.

The factors, leading to the increase in the importance of management are listed below:

(i) To ensure effective utilisation of the available resources.

(ii) To solve the increasing complex problems of business.

(iii) To cope with the research and development.

(iv) To handle large-scale operations.

(v) To coordinate between different levels of work performance in enterprise.

(vi) To meet the problems of competition.

(vii) To inter-link traditional and modern technique of work completion.

(viii) To help the nation in social welfare.

Brain of an Enterprise : All policy decisions are taken by management. Management keeps itself in touch with the current environment and supplies foresight to the enterprise. It helps in forecasting what is going to happen in the future, which will influence the working of the enterprise. The role of management has increased because of the separation of ownership from management regarding corporate (company) enterprise and growth of capital intensive techniques of production. An efficient management can lead a business towards growth and propensity. It provides leadership to the business and helps in achieving its objectives. Management is concerned with planning, executing and reviewing. In short, management involves scientific thinking, deciding, thoughtful organisation, direction and control to ensure better results. Efficient management is equally important at the national level. According to Peter Drucker, "Management is the crucial factor in economic and social development." The development of accounting is virtually dependent upon the quality of management. A capital investment and import of technical know-how and equipment will not succeed if these resources are managed properly. Thus, efficient management is a key to the growth of the economy of any country.

In this chapter we have presented various definitions, concepts, functions, component and levels of management. It also highlighted management as a profession. The important functions of management, viz., planning, organising, staffing, directing and controlling were discussed at great length. The view that management is both science and art was expounded. The various levels of management, such as Top, middle and lower were defined. The distinction between administration and management was presented with concluding remarks that management consists of both administrative and operative aspects.

3

Organisational Management

Taylor and the early systematic management theorists confronted a plethora of detail. In the machine tool industry of the 1890s especially, increasing complexity and specialization required more managers, and thus more coordination among them to coordinate the firm as a whole. High-volume production made difficulties still more extreme. The problems were overwhelmingly managerial, rather than technical. What was needed was some systematic procedure for coordinating and monitoring, and, not inconsequentially, for abstracting the task of management from the details of job performance. Until an appropriate level of abstraction was defined, the problems of coordination were insoluble. In both the performance and the management of routine jobs, some means of transcending the particular individual was necessary. Until this means was found, industrial complexity was limited to what the individual could comprehend, remember, organize, perform, or control. The possibilities for organizational synergy were thereby similarly limited. Organizations needed methods of impounding and retaining the insights of individuals. Some means of replicating acceptable procedures persistently, predictably, and independently of the original discoverers, was necessary.

Systematic Management Techniques

Systematic management techniques, from Taylor's excruciatingly detailed instructions on oiling a machine to Church's accounting systems, were the means to these ends. Taylor sought explicitly to record and codify in order to render the organization less dependent on the memory, good will, or physical presence of any particular employee. Equally, he sought to avoid the necessity of repeated rediscovery of efficient procedures by each worker. Just such a codification of concrete details of task performance is a reasonable description of one sort of "organizational memory." Without resorting to reification, it is apparent that such a mechanism retains the knowledge of how to perform the task. Perhaps more important still, such a recording makes the knowledge accessible to others beyond the original discoverer, eliminating the need to rediscover. Since the task is specified the recording permits supervision of the task to proceed on a different level, by exceptions. Instructions create expectations and demands: this is the way to do it, not some other way; do this, don't spend time experimenting to possibly, fortuitously discover the proper way. Within limits, written instructions create a shared frame of reference and a shared experience—albeit vicarious, for others than the discoverer—of a proper way to accomplish the task.

Once the task itself is specified and can be replicated, managerial attention can shift to a different level of abstraction, treating this particular task and its performance as "given." On one level, this kind of simple replicability is evidence of organizational learning. Successful actions or behaviours can be specified and thus reiterated over time. This is the lower-level, routine learning that March and Simon or Cyert and March were willing to admit: a stored repertoire of successful sequences of action. By permitting the organization to transcend the particular discoverer of the knowledge, and by making it accessible to others, such programmes allow for the synergy (on a rudimentary level at least) are characteristic of organizations. The programme or instructions specify required actions and, implicitly, the means of their coordination. Managerial attention can be freed from the need to coordinate here, and can look instead to coordinating among such sets of specified behaviours. These lower-level learning programmes are so commonplace and pervasive that we frequently dismiss them as trivial, or ignore them altogether. However, they are the essential foundation for the development of higher-level systems. The lower-level programmes create a means of synergy, the shared frame of reference which preserves knowledge. They also create a way of retaining and communicating learning beyond the individual who discovers it, making possible further refinement and more inclusive coordination. And, not incidentally, they substantially improve performance by eliminating the need to rediscover every time what has been learned before. This was Taylor's insight.

Taylor's contributions went beyond the simple recording of procedure, however. In his distinction between planning and performance, he built upon the codification of routine tasks and for the first time made possible the large-scale coordination of details—planning and policy-level thinking, above and beyond the details of the task itself. The initial steps are critical; without them, the manager and the organization remain in undated in details of the task, and abstraction is impossible for sheer want of information-processing capacity. This would not obscure the qualitative difference between the details of the task, and a focus on coordination of them. Taylor tended to focus on the coordination of the tasks of a single workman, or on the relationship among tasks in a single work-flow at most. Nevertheless, instructions on how to coordinate such a group of activities is a step higher, a logical level above the elements themselves. To confuse the two is an error in logical typing, equivalent to confusing the map with the territory, the name with the thing, the receipt with the meal. Thus the "specialty" of records clerks who generate instructions is not the task itself, but a body of knowledge about many tasks. The frame of reference of the clerk transcends the frame of reference of any individual worker whose task is specified. Conceptually, this represents a clear shift to a level of logical abstraction superior to that of the task itself—that is, a more inclusive level. The clerk's perspective includes many tasks, and the technology for codifying them. In generating new sets of instructions, for instance, such questions as, "Does the sequence of actions performed by this worker mesh smoothly with others' actions?" and "Should Worker A notify Worker C when A's task is complete?" illustrate the logical distinction between the level of the task, and thinking about its specification. Another way of drawing the distinction is to note that the clerk's task includes specifying boundary-spanning communications or interfaces which relate self-contained segments; any individual worker need be concerned only with activities within the specification.

The division of labor, specialization, and subdivision of the task encouraging detailed knowledge of a portion of the task in the individual worker, necessarily splits off coordination from performance. This is differentiation by another name. The reintegration necessary for efficient performance is provided by a higher frame of reference, that is, one inclusive enough to contain all the specialized elements. Taylor's methodology provided the means of implementing the specialized knowledge he dissevered, of coordinating it, monitoring it, and assuring that performance was adequate. By specifying the details, management could insure replication of the best practices on the shop floor. By setting up roles and standards, management could be abstracted because the knowledge embodied in standards was accessible to the worker. Since the knowledge was accessible, its ordinary application could be delegated and management could concentrate on exceptions. The procedures and rules for relating various tasks—rudimentary codification of the management task—insured that here too, certain patterns were replicated, independent of their fortuitous rediscovery by each individual. It was no longer necessary to rediscover a right way; one had already been specified. This left management free to concentrate on exceptions, coordination, and new tasks. The details of management were specified; some were delegated (to functional foremen; although Taylor's system was never fully implemented successfully many of the same tasks are separated into different staff jobs today); and a shared frame of reference was specified, guiding performance, perception and interpretation.

Church's further development of thinking about the management task generalized the insights that Taylor had applied to technical details. The accounting methods Church developed provided the means for abstracting management by making possible the description and monitoring of performance in diverse areas or products. The focus is upon how the details of the management task itself fit together; and, on a lower level, how the details of the managed task fit together. The "five great organic functions" of managerial work that Church identified are abstractions about the task of management, approaches to organizing the performance of tasks.

Systems for Planning and Systems for Thought : General Motors and Du Pont offer higher-level analogues to the split Taylor proposed between the performance of a task and its planning and coordination. While there are clearly limits to the usefulness of the distinction, nevertheless it is critical to the management of complex activities, especially when they are combined (as in the modern complex organization of diverse task specialities, products, or areas). Taylor's schematic systematized task details, focused management on coordination, and, by abstraction, freed up management to undertake the overarching tasks of planning and policy. In an analogous fashion, the extensive and sophisticated control systems of General Motors and Du Pont made feasible decentralized management in a complex organization. They thereby also made possible for the first time concerted coordination (that is synergy) and true policy for such organizations. So long as management is overwhelmed by the details of task performance, planning and policy will not occur. March and Simon describe this phenomenon, a Gresham's Law of Planning: routine activities drive out long-range, non-routine activities. In this context, the absence of long-range planning "that makes a difference" is comprehensible, and with it the purely reactive stance of organizations Cyert and March found. That is, until what is routine is systematized and performance replicable without extensive management attention, management attention will necessarily focus on the routine. By the time of Du Pont and General Motors, the specification of task had moved from codifying workers' routine activities to codifying managers' routine activities.

It is through administrative systems that planning and policy are made possible, because the systems capture knowledge about the task, and, at the General Motors and Du Pont Levels, about the logically more inclusive matter of coordinating tasks. The return on assets concepts of Donaldson Brown, the forecasting methods, the systematic relation of demand, production, inventories, and appropriations all represent a methodology for managing, a directed way of thinking that translates a level upwards in a hierarchy of logic and inclusiveness from the single-factory, single-firm management concepts of Taylor and Church. Moreover, any manager who has been exposed to these methods has been trained in an administrative mechanism that explicitly guides perceptions and interpretation. In this, as in Taylor's concrete specifications of a machinist's task, a shared frame of reference is created. The firm is no longer dependent upon the rediscovery of these relations, every time, by each new manager. Instead, the knowledge of Donaldson Brown, Pierre du Pont, John Raskob, or Alfred P. Sloan, Jr., is codified and preserved. It is thereby made accessible to others, for both replication and further development. These administrative systems create a shared pattern of thought, with focus explicitly shifted to the pattern, rather than the specific content. They thus condition the analyses and decision premises of the actors. Specified kinds of thinking are identified. By creating a shared frame of reference, with explicitly directed perceptions—"The relation of finished goods inventory to customer demand should not exceed thus-and-such a ratio when scheduling production", for instance—such systems generalize knowledge far beyond its original discoverer or discovery situation. It should be emphasized here that the kind of knowledge generalized is qualitatively, logically different from the kind of knowledge codified in Taylor's machine-oiling instructions. The focus is on paths or patterns of thought and kinds of thinking, rather than on specific actions.

These systems, in generalizing the insights they codify, also make them accessible to change and refinement. It is no longer necessary for the procedures of a firm to be the work of a single mind. The systems, as Sloan's comments make clear, measure results, leaving the details of task performance to others. Because management need pay attention only to these monitors, patterns among them and over time assume more importance. True management by exception, and true policy direction are now possible, solely because management is no longer wholly immersed in the details of the task itself. Having been guided into replicating the patterns of thought for connecting, say, production and inventory, it is now possible to add the refinements of forecasting demand, and of revising the forecasts or adjusting them in the light of general economic conditions and actual demand. Thus the original relationship, once comprehended, can be changed and shaped, transcended and surpassed. The development of flexible, rather than rote, responses to changing situations grew out of the new attention to the coordinative task made possible only because abstraction focused attention on anomalies in patterns. The systemic relationship among quantitative measures of performance and environmental indicators—substantially abstracted, be it noted, from details of task performance—is what permits control at this level.

Taylor was concerned primarily with individual tasks, or with a single work flow; Church, with the ongoing business of the firm as a whole, and with the relationships of individuals' tasks within that framework, with the coordination of the factory. Du Pont and General Mortors are still more general, abstract and logically inclusive, in that their methods of management relate diverse products typically produced by many factories. For Du Pont, applying accounting methods meant adapting the practices of the steel and traction industries to explosives manufacture, and later to chemicals. For General Motors, the task was adequately systematizing related but distinct products. More importantly for both firms the task was generalizing patterns of thought that would permit decentralization. In both cases, the clear distinction between details of task performance and the coordination of those details, on the one hand, and the overarching coordinative task of relating many tasks (products, divisions, factories) was institutionalized not just in organization structure, but in the administrative systems that controlled information flow and guided critical decision making and analysis. The administrative systems capture the knowledge of how to think about this diversity, how to relate information about it (clearly an abstraction from the things themselves), how to coordinate and manage effectively. The shared frame of reference that is created is more inclusive, and therefore logically superior, to single-firm, single-factory frames of reference. By focusing attention on the abstractions, the systems encourage both replication of established patterns of thought—as relating inventory and production, for instance—and their refinement, keying in economic conditions or actual demand.

Systematic Innovation : The chief accomplishment at Du Pont and General Motors was in systematizing the ongoing business of the large, complex, multidivisional firm. At Texas Instruments, the main task was (and is) of an altogether different nature. The highly changeful environment of modern electronics requires a new set of administrative systems designed to decentralize not only the performance of a routine task in a somewhat turbulent environment, but the decentralization of innovation itself, and with it the fundamental data-gathering of the policy process.

Texas Instruments provides a capsule history of the development of management theory repeated in brief compass. The PCC System institutionalized and insisted upon a fundamental balance in the ongoing business. This might be called the basic task of the firm, systematized in ways that Church would find familiar. Coordinated management of the task required adequate controls, proper attention to the essential elements of product and customer and to the fit between them. With the number of different products and markets, this brought TI to the level of General Motors and Du Pont in the evolution of its management systems.

The OST System is qualitatively different, and constitutes a further distinct logical shift. It is concerned with a higher logical level. Rather than coordinating multiple routine tasks, the OST is focused on generating new tasks which may eventually themselves become routing. Equally as important, it is concerned with generalizing a shared frame of reference, a means of acquiring new knowledge. As a system, the OST generalizes a procedure for acquiring the requisite new knowledge, creating a shared pattern of thought *regarding innovation* in much the same way that Du Pont or General Motors created shared frames of reference about ongoing business. The OST specifies how to proceed, monitor, and evaluate. In so doing, the OST makes it possible for Texas Instruments to acquire not only new products, but new paradigms or identities. Thus TI is not just a geophysical exploration company, but also a military instruments supplier; not just a geophysics and military instruments company, but also an electronics firm, and so on. Recent forays into consumer goods (calculators and watches) are indicative of a major capacity for change.

Learning Hierarchies

In *Steps to an Ecology of Mind,* Gregory Bateson notes that learning, as a communication process, must be subject to the laws of cybernetics. He proceeds to make use of Russell's Theory of Logical Types in a behavioural science context. Thus the concepts of hierarchy, distinctions between logical classes or types, and their importance in guiding analysis suggest new ways of looking at learning phenomena. In particular, accurate class distinctions are essential for a meaningful discussion of learning. Bateson suggests that there are different types of learning, which may be arranged in a developmental hierarchy of progressively more inclusive frames of reference with systematic relationships between levels. Such a hierarchy highlights important distinctions among the administrative systems described above, retaining awareness of their similarities as shared frames of reference accessible to others. Such a hierarchy illuminates these administrative systems as varieties of codified learning.

Taking Bateson a step closer to organizations, Fenwick defines a hierarchy of learning activities in an organization without, however, defining what "knowledge" or "learning" might be in an extra-individual context. Recasting these concepts in the light of the kinds of distinctions necessary to define organizational learning, we can take into account accessibility to others, preservation of knowledge, and a shared frame of reference. Thus we can:

1. Record the specifics of basic tasks;
2. Record the specifics of new tasks, and routinize them when they recur;
3. Generate approaches to analyzing and recording new tasks;
4. Extract the general principles of tasks, going beyond simple replication to efficiency, and possibly to generalized application of the new principles and efficiencies;

5. Develop programmes for approaching new task areas, different from what has been routinized;
6. Evolve training programmes to teach new approaches;
7. Shape or change the organization's mission or paradigm;and
8. Develop approaches for repeated or ongoing paradigm change.

What is the utility of defining so exhaustive a hierarchy? The distinctions facilitate a more precise discussion of organizational learning (as opposed to individual learning), and of organizational learning (as opposed to "mere adaptation"). Each level distinguishes a more far-reaching and thoroughgoing kind of change, with wider impact and longer-range consequences. Finally, this is a developmental sequence. Later levels rest upon the conceptual foundation of earlier levels, as the historical context provided by early chapters emphasizes. Until the managerial technology of Taylor and Church had been developed, the coordination sought by Du Pont and General Motors was impossible.

As Bateson points out, the Theory of Logical Types implies that in such a hierarchy each level constitutes a "meta-communication," that is, a communication "about" the next lower level and inclusive of all elements in it. This is particularly important in the organizational context, where the epistemology of moving from "subjective knowledge" to "objective knowledge"—the hinge between individual and organizational knowledge—turns upon just such a communication phenomenon. A shared frame of reference, relating lower-level elements and guiding their interpretation in order that similar stimuli result in similar results, is dependent in the organizational setting, upon some objective or shared knowledge. That is, it is dependent upon true communication, the sharing of a common frame of reference. This obviously goes beyond simple exchange of noise to shared understanding. The meta-communication, in other words, provides a common frame of reference within which a common understanding can be expected. This may, particularly in the complex organization, be complicated by diversity of interest or speciality, or by organization size or geographic dispersion, for instance. Organizational learning, despite these complications, must be a communication phenomenon. Only through communication does individual insight become accessible to others, and thereby transcend its discoverer, making possible synergy.

A hierarchy of types such as the one suggested provides a means of focusing attention on distinctions between levels, or, in the case of organizations, between systems. What matters is not that there are eight levels here, rather than the three individual-learning levels Bateson defines : "What is important is the developmental nature of the sequence, and the assistance that these distinctions provide, helping to distinguish definitively between rote response in an organizational setting (even a complex rote response) and something more sophisticated. More important still, in delineating the distinction, the hierarchy suggests implicitly the criteria by which "learning" in organizations might be judged, the vocabulary with which such phenomena might be discussed, and the likely direction for systems evolution". On this basis, the already-established data base (Taylor, Church, Du Pont and General Motors, and Texas Instruments) shall be used to make the concept of organizational learning more clear.

Applied Hierarchy

The lower reaches of the hierarchy set out here concern the areas of Taylor's work. While learning to perform any task is learning to perform a "new" task for the first time, the distinction gains importance in an organizational setting. Thus a basic task may be defined as one for which a programme already exists. This is the kind of "knowledge" of "learning" that Cyert and March are willing to countenance in organizations. Taylor's contributions include both specification of particular knowledge (how to oil a machine) and ways to learn new tasks (ways for the organization to record and thereby retain new knowledge, fitting it into is system). The ideas of time and motion study, of noting elemental movements and aggregating them, of adequate description constitute a frame of reference, accessible to others, which specifies how to acquire and preserve new knowledge and expedite its transmission to others.

It is important to underline again the difference between individual and organizational learning. Clearly an individual can approach a task in a variety of ways. What Taylor has outlined is a way to record and transmit organized individual perceptions, making them both accessible to others and independent of the original observer. It is via the specified, shared frame of reference Taylor designates that these perceptions are removed from the subjective to the objective world. Knowledge so recorded and codified is no longer the preserve of the individual. And anyone following Taylor's procedures has gone through a series of guided observations whose recorded output is just such an "objective" record, comprehensible to others trained in the method. Hence the organization is no longer dependent wholly on serendipity or individual talent to create an approach to acquiring new knowledge; one has been specified. These rules provided a limited example of rules for learning. Taylor's metal-cutting experiments and Church's "organic functions" as well are logically superior, because they are more inclusive than the simple recording of observations. The overarching framework is a set of guides for interpretation and for relating many specific tasks. Their focus is extracting general principles and attaining efficiencies. General Motors and Du Pont are to be considered here too, as specifying general principles (abstractions) and noting efficient relationships among elements. Only through abstraction is more general coordination possible. Only through a shared frame of reference, generalized beyond the original discoverer, is such coordination feasible; and with it, something that can meaningfully be described as "organizational" learning.

The upper reaches of this hierarchy, beyond level three, concern just the types of "learning rules" that Cyert and March exclude from their consideration. Bateson's much less detailed hierarchy was intended for discussions of individual learning; but the same distinctions—with some adaptation to take into account the need for communication and extra-individual accessibility—are useful for a discussion of organizational learning. By considering the hierarchy in its logical sense, the problem of "structure" versus "process" becomes clearer, for example. For any level, the given level is "process," subject to change according to the fixed rules specified by levels above. The levels above are, therefore, "structure," and are the "learning rules" that Cyert and March exclude. The advantage of such a hierarchy is that it permits and encourages a richer view of the learning phenomena, and thus provides a more powerful model for considering them. The levels provide ranges of inclusiveness within which to assess the impact or pervasiveness of change. We can choose temporarily to see a certain level as structure, without wholly ignoring the possibility of change there, or in higher levels still, over a longer time frame. Similarly, higher levels correspond to corporate goals; shared frames of reference of far-reaching consequence, changeable only with major effort and over extensive time-horizons. Indeed, such flexibility would seem critical in dealing with learning, which must be a change phenomenon, longitudinal in its development. Thus, while the "learning rules" may change only slowly over time, they are, nonetheless, only relatively fixed. The matter of organization or patterning or arrangement is critical here in specifying rules and their application. The higher levels of the hierarchy are changeable, given the proper focus and time span. They are not excluded nor seen as wholly fixed. It is this distinction that allows a meaningful discussion of morphogenesis, for "change of shape" or re-structuring must also be a long-term developmental phenomenon. Similarly too, in the largest sense, change of mission or paradigm is change of "shape," and can be explicitly included here. Such changes as these require an even longer time horizon and an even more inclusive frame of reference. Buckley's question recurs: "The basic problem is the same: how do interacting personalities and groups define, assess, interpret, and act on the situation?" In light of the foregoing discussion, the question can now be answered, in part at least, by means of the shared frames of reference created by administrative systems and the 'learning rules' they impound. It matters little that the initial insight was an individual's; the codification and communication of that insight, and its translation into a shared frame of reference transcend this origin by communicating the knowledge and preserving it.

Taylor and Church, in providing methods for systematizing or routinizing ongoing business, illustrate level two: routinizing already-learned procedures so that success in what was once a "new" task can be replicated. Replicability, predictability, and thus increased control over the myriad details of concrete task performance were central to one aspect of the work of the systematic management thinkers. Another aspect, that of efficiency and general principles (clearly visible in the writings of both Taylor and Church) is of a higher logical level. The distinction is important, because it determines the criteria on which the procedure is to be judged. Simple replication might well be fortuitous; it certainly smacks of the Black Box with wired-in connections. It is not evidence of "learning" in any meaningful sense. Generating approaches to new tasks is different. A format for approaching new tasks by making possible the continued acquisition of new knowledge repeats a process, rather than its content. It generalizes principles or relationships among elements, guiding thinking. This goes well beyond replication of content. Extracting general principles and generalizing efficiency methods would seem clear evidence of learning, rather than mere iteration. Built into a system in Taylor's work-simplification methods, or Church's management systems, they would be evidence of organizational learning, because they would be accessible far beyond the discoverer. Similarly, the Du Pont and General Motors management information systems and the controls upon which they rest generalize and communicate principles and relationships which are applied to the business of the corporation as a whole (including to new products) to gain efficiencies. Thus, for instance, reducing the cash tied up in divisional bank accounts by arranging for the speedy transfer of funds was a general application of the principle of increasing return by increasing turnover of inventories—including "inventories" of cash.

4

Problem of Communication

"The no. 1 management problem today is communication." This statement by Alvin Dodd, the then president of the American Management Association still remains valid even after passage of the decades. In fact, it is the most important function of management and failure of it may cause distruption and even bankruptcy of business. It is, therefore, the most difficult challenges-for managers to ensure effective communication among the people in the enterprise and outside. To meet this challenge, every manager spends about 80 per cent of his time in communicating.

The Concepts

Simply stated communication means interaction between persons. It includes exchange of information, ideas, emotions and understanding between persons.

In the words of Keith Davis, "Communication is the process of passing information and understanding from one person to another person."

Newman and Summer defined Communication as "an exchange of facts, ideas, opinions or emotions by two or more persons."

In the words of Robbins and Coulter, Communication involves the transfer and understanding of meanings."

McFarland states, "Communication is the process of meaningful interaction among human beings. It is the process by which meanings are received and understandings are reached among human beings."

Robert Albanese defines,"Communication as information flow that transfers meaning and understanding from an information source (sender) to an information receiver."

In the end it may be stated that communication is the process of exchange of information, ideas, feelings and understanding among human beings. It is the process of conveying meanings. It is a systematic process of conveying, listening and understanding something between two or more persons through words, figures, symbols, pictures, body language etc.

Salient Features

The following characteristics of communication explains the nature of communication :

1. Communication is a process of interaction between persons. In other words, it is an interactive process.
2. It is a two-way process. It essentially involves dialogue for its success.
3. It is a social process.
4. It is a dynamic process which is adapted in accordance with the prevailing situation.
5. It involves at least two persons, one of whom is the source or sender and another is receiver of information.
6. It involves exchange of information, opinion, idea, meaning and understanding among human beings.
7. Communication may be intentional or unintentional.
8. It is all pervasive function of management. In other words, it is performed by all the managers and employees across the organisation.

9. The subject-matter of communication is some message expressed through words, data, symbols, body language, pictures, figures etc.
10. It may be oral, written or gestural.
11. It may be formal or informal.
12. It may move downward, upward, horizontally or diagonally.
13. Its main object is to elicit desired response from the receiver.

Aims and Objectives

The main purpose of communication is to affect change in someone, *i.e.*, to influence action or to secure inaction in the overall interest of an enterprise. It enables us to understand others and to make ourselves understand. Without communication we cannot live or work together in an organised way. It is a flux that binds people together in an organisation. The basic purpose of communication is to facilitate and lubricate the organisation. It helps management in planning effectively and controlling efficiently. John G. Clover has outlined the following important purposes of communication :

1. To keep employees informed.
2. To provide employees with orders and instructions in connection with their duties or jobs.
3. To solicit information from employees which may aid management.
4. To make each employee interested in his respective job and in the work of the company as a whole.
5. To express management's interest in its personnel.
6. To reduce or prevent labour turnover.
7. To indoctrinate employees with the will to work and with the benefits derived from their association with the company.
8. To instill each employee with personal pride in being a member of the company.

The Significance

The importance of communication in managing can hardly be over-emphasised. It is the life-stream or life-line of modern business management. No manager can effectively perform his functions without effective communication system. Haimann has rightly stated that "the success of all managerial functions depends on successful communication." Another expert states that, "good communication is the foundation for sound management." In fact, sound communication system is indispensable for small, medium, large and multinational organisations as well. No organisation can exist without sound communication system. Briefly, the importance of communication is being discussed in the following subheads :

Smooth/efficient Functioning of the Enterprise : One expert has stated that "good communication is good business." Another one states that "good managers are good communicators." These statements are testimony of the fact that communication is essential for smooth and successful functioning of an enterprise. "It serves as the lubricant fostering smooth operation of the management process." [*Terry]*

It may be noted that management is the art of getting things done. For this purpose, a manager plans, organises, motivates, controls. Performance of all these functions depends on the successful communication. Peter Drucker has very rightly stated, "The manager has a specific tool: information. He does not 'handle' people; he motivates, guides, organises people to do their own work. His tool-his only tool- to do all this is the spoken or written words or the language of numbers." Thus, it is clear that communication is an indispensable tool for successful operation of an enterprise.

Facilitates Planning : According to Koontz and O'Donnell, "Effective planning occurs when everyone responsible for it has access to complete information affecting areas of planning." In fact, planning requires extensive communication among the executives and the other personnel, who translate the plans into action. Organisational objectives, policies, programmes, practices, procedures and strategies are conveyed to the concerned people in the organisation so that they may strictly follow them. Communication is also essential in executing a planned programme. In the absence of communication, planning may miserably fail.

Facilitates Decision-making : Effective communication system is a prerequisite for making sound decisions. The quality of decisions largely depends on the quality of information. Moreover, effective communication system also helps in communicating decisions to the persons concerned. Implementation of decisions also requires constant flow of communication between managers and subordinates.

Effective Organising : Organising function cannot be performed without effective communication system. Dale Yoder states that "Communication is at the very heart of the process of organising." Organising involves many activities including delegation and decentralisation of authority, assigning responsibility, and establishing relationships among the members of the organisation. For all these activities, manager needs to have communication system in place. George R. Terry opines that "communication is the means by which the act of delegation is accomplished." Similarly, Redfield has candidly remarked "whether a decentralised operation succeeds or fails often depends on the quality of communication." Hence, it can safely be concluded that the success of organising function largely depends on sound communication system.

Effective Staffing : Communication is equally important in the staffing function. Recruitment, selection, induction, training, performance appraisal and so on are the main activities in staffing function. None of these activities can be effectively completed without the help of effective communication system.

Essential for Leading : In the words of Weihrich and Koontz, "Although communication applies to all phases of managing but it is particularly important in the function of leading." No doubt effective leadership requires an efficient system of communication in the organisation. A good leader may direct or lead his subordinates only when an efficient system of communication is present. It brings both the leader and the subordinates in close contact to each other. A leader can make his orders and directives more useful by inviting opinions, suggestions etc. from his subordinates and it requires communication.

Enhances Motivation and Morale : Effective communication system plays crucial role in enhancing the level of motivation and morale of employees. Through effective communication instruction, directions, orders, praise, solutions to the problems etc. can be effectively conveyed. Similarly, suggestions, opinions, ideas, problems, grievances, complaints can also be received in positive mind set by the managers. Such a situation greatly enhances level of motivation and morale of employees.

Effective Control : No manager can exercise effective control of organisational activities without proper communication system. For controlling, manager has to take the following steps :

(i) Convey the objectives, plans, procedures, budgets or other standards for performance.

(ii) Collect the information about actual performance.

(iii) Compare the actual performance against the standard and find out the deviation, if any.

(iv) Finally, to take corrective action to bring the performance as per the standards.

In this process, there should be exchange of information between the manager and his subordinates.

Facilitates Coordination : According to Keith Davis, "Coordination of work is impossible without communication." A manager needs to coordinate among all the departments and individuals in the organisation. He needs to ensure vertical, horizontal and external coordination. This all is impossible without communication system. Through effective communication system, information, thoughts, ideas, opinions etc. can be exchanged and common understanding can be developed. Common understanding brings about unity of action and coordination. William H. Newman has, therefore, rightly stated that "good communication aids in coordinating activities."

Mary Cushing Niles has very aptly remarked that "good communications are essential in coordination. They are necessary upward, downward and sideways through all the levels . . . . "

***Democratic Management* :** In modern times, management of organisations (particularly companies) is done on democratic principles. Owners select or elect their representatives to manage the organisation. Employees, consumers and other stakeholders are given participation in the management of the organisation. They all share information, participate in discussion, consultation and decision-making. All this is possible only when a sound communication system is in place.

***Sound Human and Industrial Relations* :** In the opinion of Robert D. Berth, "It is impossible to have human relations without communication." It is a fact that a large number of industrial disputes take place because of communication gap between the managers and subordinates. But through communication, managers can make the subordinates understand the objectives plans, policies, programmes, rules etc. Similarly, subordinates can also convey their views, opinions, suggestions, problems, complaints, grievance to managers. Thus, communication can promote mutual understanding, cooperation and goodwill. All these, in turn, contribute to sound human and industrial relations.

***Building Image or Goodwill* :** Communication plays a vital role in building goodwill and image of the organisation in the business world and in the society as a whole. Business houses disseminate plethora of information for building their goodwill and image. Information relating to financial performance, sales and export performance, launch of new products, foreign collaboration) award won, social welfare activities etc. are usually disseminated to the shareholders, and public at large. Radio, TV, newspapers, magazines usually contain such advertisements. Press conferences are held and interviews are given by the big business leaders. Public relations executives and managers constantly send press releases in order to build image of the organisation.

***Avoids Illusion and Ignorance* :** According to W.H. Whyle, "The greatest enemy of communication is the illusion of it." During the course of transmission, information may be distorted for many reasons. Sometimes, parties receive no information or incomplete information and remain ignorant of exact inforrnation. Consequently, misundèrstanding, confusion and illusion creeps up in the minds of the concerned parties. In order to remove and avoid misunderstanding, illusion or ignorance, effective communication system is a must.

Good External Relations : Sound relations with the external world to the organisation is also essential in this age. Hence, every organisation needs to maintain relations with customers and their organisations, shareholders, trade unions and trade organisations, competitive organisations, government agencies etc. Exchange of information with all of them is a regular feature of every day working of every organisation.

Facilitates Change : Change is a way of life. Organisations are no exception. Hence, people in organisation discuss the need and scope of change and introduce change. Managers prepare members of the organisation to accept change. This all cannot be possible without effective communication.

The Procedure

Communication process is the sequence of identifiable steps that are necessary to complete exchange of informance, ideas and understanding among the human beings. Usually the basic steps or elements involved in communication process are as follows :

Source of Communication : Every communication has its source. An idea, opinion, thought, information, incident, plan, and so on are the sources of communication.

Sender or Communicator : Sender or communicator is the initiator of the process of communication. He is the person who intends to convey or transmit an information/message to some other person. Sender is usually the source of communication. He initiates the process of communication by defining the idea, coding it and selecting the media for transmission.

Communicatee or Receiver : In order to initiate a process of communication, there should be some communicatee or receiver of the message. He is the person who is to receive, interpret, understand and respond to the message. The communicator, therefore, must properly identify and understand the communicatee in order to ensure effectiveness of the message.

Message : Sender then prepares message to be communicated. Message is the subject-matter of communication. It may be some idea, information, thought or emotion. It may be expressed in written, oral or gestural form.

Encoding : Next step in the communication process relate to encoding of the message. Encoding means transforming or translating the message into some language or code understandable to communicatee *i.e.* receiver of the message. At this step, sender transforms the message into words, data, symbols, figures, pictures, gesturals or other code or language so that the intended receiver may understand it properly.

Channel or Medium : The next step in the process relates to the selection of channel of communication. The sender can choose among a number of media such as face-to-face conversation, telephone calls; letters, e-mail, fax, photographs, meetings, organisation manuals, news releases, press conferences, advertising on TV, radio and newspapers, and magazines. While selecting a medium, sender should weigh its advantages and disadvantages. A sender should always choose a medium which is free from barriers or disturbing influences so that the message can surely and safely reach to the intended receiver and catch his due attention.

Transmission of the Message : After selection of a suitable channel or medium of communication, the next step is to transmit it to the receiver. It is the step at which the message is put into the course of transmission from sender to the receiver. The sender should ensure complete and safe transmission of the message.

Receiving and Decoding : No message accomplishes its purpose unless it is understood by the receiver. Hence, the next step in the process relates to "understanding of the message after receiving it. Where the message has been encoded, decoding should take place. Decoding means translation or transformation of message into an understandable language. But perfect decoding is nearly impossible in our word of many languages and cultures. The chances of successful decoding are enhanced if the receiver knows the language or terminology or code used in the message. It becomes easier, if the receiver understands sender's purpose and background of the message.

Response or Action and Feed Back : The main object of communication is to elicit desired response or action from the receiver of the message. Hence, communication process remains incomplete or ineffective unless it elicits desired action or response. The receiver, therefore, should give feedback of the message. It enables the sender to know whether the message has been successfully received and has created the desired impact. As soon as the feed-back of the response is received, the process of communication is said to be completed.

Expectations

When all the expectations of the receiver in communication process are considered they are sometimes called the Rule of Five in communication *i.e.* (i) receiving, (ii) understanding, (iii) acceptance, (iv) action, and (v) feedback. The communication is regarded effective and successful if these five steps are completed efficiently.

The Pattern

Communication network refers to the pattern of interconnecting lines of communication that exists in an organisation. The type of network depends upon the (i) needs of the organisation, and (ii) attitudes of superiors towards to subordinates.

Various Types

There are basically four types of communication networks found in organisations. They are as follows :

1. Chain network, 2. Circular network, 3. Wheel network, 4. Free-flow or decentralised network.

Chain Network : Chain network of communication is one in which communication flows along the chain of command. In other words, where communication flows in direct vertical line of hierarchy of management it is said to be chain network communication. It is usually two-way communication from top to bottom and bottom to top of the hierarchy of management. But there is no scope of horizontal communication in this network. Figure 19.2 (a) depicts that A can communicate to B, B to C, C to D and so on along with the chain of command.

Circular Network : Circular network of communication is one in which communication moves in circular way. In this network, each individual can communicate with the person on his immediate right or left but not with any other person in the organisation or group. Figure 19.2 (b) shows that A can communicate either with B or E and none else.

Wheel or Star Network : Wheel or star communication network refers to a network in which the members of an organisation usually do not communicate directly with each other. They communicate with other members through one superior or manager *i.e.* hub of the wheel. The manager acts as the central point like the hub of a wheel. All the members of the organisation exchange information, and throught though the hub of the wheel *i.e.* manager. Such a network is also known as 'autocratic network'.

Free-flow or Decentralised or all Channel Network : Free-flow network is one in which lines of communication are not structured. Every member of the group can communicate freely, and frankly with all other members of the group. Thus, there is no restriction on the flow of communication and hence it is a more of a nature of informal network. Figure shows that A, B, C, D or E can freely communicate with each other.

The Categories

Communication may be classified on the following bases :

A. On the basis of organisation structure.

B. On the basis of direction.

C. On the basis of mode of expression.

A. On the Basis of Organisation Structure : On the basis of organisation structure, communication may be of two types :

1. Formal communication.
2. Informal communication or 'grapevine'.

Formal Communication : Formal communication means the communication which travels through the formally established channels. In other words, communication which travels through the formal chain of command or lines of hierarchy of authority is called the formal communication. It establishes the single path of communication which links the various positions. Thus, it is deliberately and consciously established by the management. Members of the organisation are expected to communicate through these formal channels. Formal communication may be upward, downward and horizontal.

The Advantages : The advantages of formal communication are as follows :

(i) It ensures orderly flow of communication.

(ii) It helps in maintaining the lines of authority in the organisation.

(iii) It helps in maintaining direct contact with the subordinates. Thus, facilitates control by superiors.

(iv) It helps in the fixation of responsibility and accountability.

(v) It helps in maintaining discipline.

The Disadvantages : Disadvantages of formal communication are as follows :

(i) It is time consuming. It takes much time to communicate.

(ii) It obstructs free, smooth and accurate circulation of information in an organization.

(iii) It lacks personal contacts and relationship.

(iv) It creates a bottleneck in the flow of information because almost all information is channelled through a single executive.

(v) Organisational distance is a big barrier in the free flow of communication. Hence, there is possibility of distortion of facts when the message passes through various levels.

(vi) The distortion of facts may be possible in upward communication also, since a person working in a subordinate capacity is likely to report to his superior.

Informal Communication/Grapevine : Informal communication refers to the communication which takes place on the basis of informal relations between the members of a group. It is personal communication in nature and not a positional communication. It does not flow along with the formal lines of authority or formal chain of command. It is even not regulated by the formal rules and procedures.

Informal communication channels are not established by the management. Such channels on account of natural desire of people to socialise and communicate with others. In other words, informal communication arises out of social interaction of people. Herbert Simon has rightly stated that "informal communication system is built around the social relationships of the members of the organisation."

Informal communication is sometimes referred as 'grapevine'. It is the primary source of upward communication. It transmits information about what people are doing. It often leads to rumours in the organisation. Keith Davis has identified the following four different networks for transmitting information via the grapevine:

(i) Single strand-In the single strand, one person communicates with only one person.

(ii) Gossip chain-In gossip chain, every member talks with every one else, usually about personal matter.

(iii) Probability chain-In it communication is random.

(iv) Cluster chain-In it messages are transmitted selectively. Grapevine generally operates like a cluster chain. For example, if one tells something to four or five persons, only one or two of them will pass on the information to more than one person. As the number grows larger and the information becomes older, it gradually dies out, because those who know it do not repeat it. This process is called cluster chain because each link in the chain tends to inform a cluster of other people instead of only one person. Grapevine may move in the fashion of a long chain. It should be remembered here that in a cluster chain, only a few persons are active communicator and such persons are known as liaison agents.

The Advantages : The advantages of informal communication are as follows :

(i) Informal communication is faster in speed than formal communication.

(ii) It is more flexible.

(iii) It is dynamic and reacts quickly to the change in the circumstances.

(iv) It works as a powerful and effective tool of communication.

(v) It is effective means of communicating organizational rules, values, morals, traditions and history.

(vi) It supplements or fills gaps in formal communication.

(vii) It helps improve decision-making.

(viii) It satisfies the inner urge or needs of people.

(ix) It may disseminate the tentative view point of management on any important issue.

(x) It may provide feed back to managers on their actions and decisions.

The Disadvantages : Following are the main disadvantages of informal communication :

(i) It carries inaccurate, half-truth or distorted information.

(ii) It spreads rumours and promotes gossips.

(iii) It is difficult to believe on information.

(iv) It is difficult to fix responsibility for the information.

(v) It leads to leakage of secret information.

(vi) It may cause misunderstanding.

(vii) It may mislead people.

Communication on the Basis of Direction : Communications on the basis of their direction can be of the following types :

1. Downward communication, 2. Upward communication, 3. Horizontal communication, 4. Diagonal communication.

Downward Communication : Downward communication is one that flows from top to the bottom of the organisational hierarchy. In other words, when messages are transmitted from superiors to subordinates along with the chain of command, it is said to be downward communication. Such communications may be in the form of orders, instructions, policies, programmes, directives, praise, reprimands etc. According to Katz and Kahn, the major objectives of downward communication are as follows:

(i) To give specific task directives about jobs.

(ii) To give information about organisational procedures and practices.

(iii) To provide information about the rationale of the job.

(iv) To tell the subordinates about their performance.

(v) To provide ideological type information to facilitate indoctrination of goals.

The Advantages : Advantages of downward communication are as follows :

(i) It helps in explaining company policies, programmes, rules, procedures etc. to the subordinates.

(ii) It helps to tie the different levels of hierarchy together.

(iii) It helps an executive to use his authority effectively.

(iv) It increases the effectiveness of upward communication through feedback.

(v) It helps in preparing the people to introduce change.

(vi) It removes misunderstanding and suspicion.

The Disadvantages : Disadvantages of downward communication are as follows :

(i) It is prone to distortions because it passes through various level of the organisational hierarchy.

(ii) It tends to be faulty and inaccurate because of the sender's carelessness, poor communication skills, decoding etc.

(iii) It tends *to* promote one-way or authoritative communication.

(iv) It is time consuming because it passes through various levels of organisation.

(v) Some managers at various levels tend to filter or screen or manipulate messages for their personal ends and gains.

In order to increase effectiveness of the downward communications, following steps may be taken :

(i) The message should be unambiguous and unequivocal.

(ii) It should be specific to time.

(iii) It should be consistent with the duties, responsibilities, capacities and decision-making abilities of the receiver.

(iv) It should be consistent with the organisational policies and practices.

(v) It should be consistent with the organisational goals and objectives.

Upward Communication : When messages are transmitted from bottom to top of the organisational hierarchy, it is said to be upward communication. In other words, when the communication flows from subordinates to superiors along with the chain of command, it is called upward communication. Such communication may be on the form of progress report, problems, suggestions, opinions, ideas, requests, grievances, complaints, appeals, explanations etc.

Upward communication may be of two types :

(i) Voluntary upward communication *i.e.* voluntarily from subordinates. Such communication include opinions, ideas, suggestions, grievances, complaints, appeals.

(ii) Feedback upward communication *i.e.* feedback or response communication from subordinates. Such communications include progress report, follow-up reports, and information reports desired by the superiors.

The Advantages : Advantages of upward communication are as follows :

(i) It provides feedback of information.

(ii) It enables managers to know the progress of the work done by subordinates.

(iii) It allows subordinates to express their problems, grievances and appeals.

(iv) It promotes innovative ideas.

(v) It increases receptiveness of information.

(vi) It promotes feeling of belongingness among the subordinates.

(vii) It enables managers to evaluate the impact of communication.

The Disadvantages : Upward communication suffers from the following disadvantages :

(i) Subordinates may not provide all the information. They may transmit the information which may please their subordinates.

(ii) Subordinate tend to communicate upward the information which is favourable to them.

(iii) Superiors usually do not encourage the subordinates to pass on information to them.

(iv) Superiors may react negatively on some upward communications.

(v) Some subordinates tend distort communication for their personal interests.

Horizontal or Lateral Communication : When communication takes place between persons of same levels or positions, it is said to be horizontal communication.

In other words, when communication takes place between two or more persons of the level or position of the same department or other departments of the organisation, it is known as horizontal communication. Such communication is more of an informal nature. The main object of such communication is to inter-departmental or inter-unit coordination.

The Advantages : The advantages of horizontal communication are as follows :

(i) It facilitates inter-unit or inter-departmental coordination.

(ii) It encourages peers to share information.

(iii) It promotes joint problem solving.

(iv) It develops informal and congenial work environment.

(v) It helps in resolving inter-departmental conflicts quickly.

(vi) It ensures quick communication.

(vii) It helps avoid duplication of work.

The Disadvantages : The disadvantages of horizontal communication are as follows :

(i) Individuals tend to hide information which may prove harmful for the entire organisation.

(ii) Difference in approach and vision of peer may cause distortion in communication.

(iii) The success of such communication depends on the willingness of people to share information.

Diagonal Communication : Diagonal communication cuts across departmental lines. Such communication is in between people who are neither in the same department nor on the same level of organisational structure. It takes place when members cannot communicate effectively through other channels. For example, the cost accountant, who is interested in conducting a distribution cost analysis may ask sales representatives to report directly to him. When sales representatives send report directly to the cost accountant it is diagonal communication. They need not send report first to the marketing manager who may, in turn, send the report to the cost accountant. The flow of communication is diagonal rather than vertical. It helps to save time and to speed up action, though it violates the principle of unity of command.

On the Basis of Mode of Expression : On the basis of mode of expression, communication may be of the following kinds :

1. Written communication.
2. Oral or verbal communication.
3. Gestural or non-verbal communication.

Written Communication : When message is expressed through written words, it is known as written communication. It may be expressed even through groups, charts, diagrams, pictures with or without words. It is, therefore, sometimes the communication in black and white. It may be in the form of letters, circulars, notes, memos, reports, pamphlets, brouchers, hand books, manuals and so on.

The Advantages : Following are the main advantages of written communication :

(i) It ensures transmission of information *in* uniform manner, *i.e.* everyone concerned has the same information.

(ii) It provides a permanent record of communication for future reference.

(iii) It is an ideal way of transmitting lengthy messages.

(iv) It ensures little risk of unauthorised alteration in the messages.

(v) It is the only means of exchanging information at distant places.

(vi) It tends to be complete, clear, precise and correct.

(vii) It provides time to think before communicating.

(viii) It tends to reduce misunderstanding, conflicts, and disputes.

(ix) It is taken as a legal evidence by the Courts.

(x) It is suitable to convey message to a large number of persons at the same time.

The Disadvantages : Written communication is subject to the following disadvantages :

(i) It is expensive.

(ii) It is time consuming.

(iii) It becomes difficult to maintain secrecy about a written communication.

(iv) It is rigid and does not provide any scope for making alterations for inaccuracies that might have crept in.

(v) It is very formal and lacks personal touch.

(vi) It encourages red-tapism because involves many formalities.

(vii) It may be interpreted in a different manner by different people.

(viii) It fails to provide feedback immediately.

(ix) Messages tend to be lengthy when expressed in writing.

(x) It tends to ineffective and unimpressive in case of poor drafting.

Two Shades of Communication

When message is expressed through the words of mouth or spoken words, it is said to be oral communication. It may take place either through face-to-face conversation or through any electronic mode such as telephone, cellular phone, intercom etc. Oral communication may be in the form of one-to-one conversation meeting, group discussion, joint consultation, announcement, group meeting, speech, lecture, radio and TV programme.

A great deal of information is exchanged through oral communication. It is generally preferred over other modes of communication. It is because of the fact that it is regarded as a most powerful and effective mode of communication. Haimann has rightly pointed out that "the human voice can impart the message with meaning and shading which even long pages of written words simply cannot convey."

The Advantages : The main advantages of oral communication are as follows :

(i) It is economical or less expensive as compared to written communication.

(ii) It is quicker and saves in time.

(iii) It is more effective than written communication.

(iv) It establishes a personal touch and leads to better understanding.

(v) Misunderstanding or doubts can be removed then and there.

(vi) Immediate feed back or reaction motivation or response of the receiver can be taken.

(vii) It provides opportunity of active participation *to* the listener.

(viii) It is flexible and the messages can be changed to suit the needs and response of the receiver.

(ix) It is useful means of for conveying messages in times of emergencies.

The Disadvantages : Oral communication is subject to the following disadvantages :

(i) It is less reliable.

(ii) It is influenced by self-interest and attitude of the people.

(iii) It has the tendency of being distorted.

(iv) It provides no record for future reference.

(v) It is not suitable for lengthy messages.

(vi) It does not provide sufficient time for thinking before conveying the message.

(vii) Different perception of sender and receiver of the message may cause conflict.

(viii) It may prove less effective amid of formal relations.

(ix) It has language problems. One may intend to convey something, but due to his way of speaking, it may convey something else.

(x) It involves high cost in case the receiver of the message is at a distant place.

Non-verbal Communication : Communication through postures or gestures of body parts is known as the gestural or non-verbal communication. It is a mode of communication in which anything other than words may be used to transmit message from one person to another. Movement of lips, wink of an eye, the ware of hands, nodding of head, facial expressions, tone of voice, frown on face or any other movement of body or body parts may be used to transmit the message. People also read body language to understand the feelings or thoughts of another person.

Gestural mode is regarded one of the most important modes of communication. It conveys feelings, emotions, attitudes of a person. It also effectively conveys the reactions and responses of the listener of the message.

Selecting Mode of Communication : It is very difficult to say which is a better mode of communication. Both written and oral have merits and limitations. But, in general, verbal communication is more effective mode of conveying ideas, feelings, suggestions, information, messages, etc. However, as a matter of fact, no organisation can depend entirely upon one mode as both are complimentary to each other.

Written communication may be preferred to convey lengthy messages to a large number of persons scattered over distant places and where the information is required to be repeated for purposes of repetition and record. Oral communication may be the only available method to be used to convey emergency messages and where personal touch is required. Oral messages may be supported by gestures, demonstrations, etc. to make communication effective.

Basic Principles

The American Management Association has given following commandments of good communication :

1. Seek to clarify your ideas before communicating.
2. Examine the purpose of each communication.
3. Consider the total physical setting, whenever you communicate.
4. Consult with others, where appropriate, in planning communication.
5. Be mindful, while you communicate of the overtones as well as basic content of your message
6. Take the opportunity, when it arises, to convey something of help or value to the receiver.
7. Follow-up your communication.
8. Communication for tomorrow as well as today.
9. Be sure your actions support your communications.
10. Seek not only to be understood but understand.

A brief description of some of the basic principles of communication is as follows :

Principle of Clarity : The communication message should be clear. It should be communicated in simple, easy and commonly understood language. It is the speaker who makes them meaningful and it is the receiver who interprets them. Therefore, whatever is conveyed should be conveyed in unambiguous clear words.

Principle of Attention : The recipient's attention to the communicated message must be drawn to make the communication effective. The communication is always meant for action. Mere words may not help. An executive should first show the way his men surely will follow. Dale Beach has rightly said, "people think with their heart, not with their mind." Hence a good manager has to decide the time of communication. This decision of time helps him in reducing the effect of man's emotions and moods.

Principle of Consistency : The communications should be consistent with the plans, policies, programmes and objectives of the enterprise. Communications should be consistent among themselves. Inconsistency creates confusion. Better co-ordination is achieved by consistent communications.

Principle of Adequacy : Communications should be adequate and complete, not broken or incomplete. Inadequate communication delays action. It spoils understanding as well as good relations. Efficiency of both the communication and recipient is affected.

Principle of Time : Information should be communicated at the proper time. Wrong choice of time may not have the desired impact on the recipient.

Principle of Integration : Communication is a means to attain the objectives of the enterprise. It tries to get cooperation of all to see that the work is accomplished satisfactorily. As far as possible it should be based on the policy of integration of efforts in order to avoid confusion and help in better understanding. It should help in achieving a genuine spirit of co-operation among the personnel of the organisation.

Principle of Informality : The executive should try to remain informal in his behaviour with subordinates. But in a certain situation, he may bid good bye to informality and become formal in his relations and conduct.

Principle of Feedback : Communication is a two-way traffic. Messages, policies, programmes, directions, opinions etc. are communicated downward. Grievances, complaints, suggestions etc. are communicated upward. Both are necessary in an organisation. Thus communication is also termed as a two-way process. It follows the principle of 'give and take'. It is meant for being communicated. The reactions should be calmly watched, sympathetically received and incorporated wherever and whenever necessary. Oral communication is regarded better as compared to written communication since the former provides more opportunity for feeding back than the latter.

The Difficulties

Every manager makes efforts to ensure effectiveness of communication. However, sometimes barriers to communication cause breakdowns, distortions and inaccurate rumours. Hence, communication fails to elicit desired effect or response. There are several barriers to communication. A few among them are as follows :

Poorly Expressed Message : The most common barrier to communication is its poor expression. Wrong choice of words and phrases, faulty construction of sentence, ambiguous language, lack of coherence etc. are the main causes of poor expression of message. Sometimes, communicator speaks very fast and in haste. Sometimes, he omits certain essential facts. All these create a big barrier to communication.

Complex Organisation Structure : A complex organisation structure is another barrier to communication. Long chain of command, large span of control, several layers of management, confusing relations between line and staff officers etc. create distance between the sender and receiver of the message. Consequently, message tends to be distorted or diluted and ultimately becomes less effective.

Status Barriers : Status or position of a person in organisation may create barriers in communication. A person in superior position, sometimes does not talk freely with his subordinates. In addition, many superiors do not like to listen patiently to their subordinates. Similarly, a subordinate usually hesitates to seek classifications and express his views and suggestions. In such situations, effective communication becomes a distant dream.

Filtering Information : Sometimes, communicator filters or screens information. He tends to convey only that part of information which the receiver would appreciate. For instance, a subordinate tends to pass on information which his superior would appreciate. This practice tends to distort communication.

Semantic Barriers : Semantic barriers means the barrier caused by the meanings of the words or symbols. Different people may derive different meaning from the same words or symbols. Difficulties in communication arise when the sender and receiver of the message use the same words or symbols in different senses.

Language Barrier : Sometimes the language of the sender and receiver of the message is different. For instance, one knows English but the other does not know. Both cannot communicate themselves with each other effectively. In addition, there are large numbers of specialised fields such as systems analysis, computers, operations research, etc., in which technical jargon or vocabulary is used to communicate messages. This factor also contributes to poor communication.

Different Backgrounds : Different individuals often interpret the same communication differently because of their different backgrounds. Thus, when people with different knowledge and experience try to communicate, they often have trouble in getting their meaning across.

Emotional Attitude : Barriers may also arise due to emotional attitude because when emotions are strong, it is difficult to know the frame of mind of other person or group. Emotional attitudes of both, the communicator as well as the communicate, obstruct free flow of transmission and understanding of messages.

Undisclosed Assumptions : Undisclosed assumptions underlie practically all messages. Because of this, the receiver of the message may have some assumptions (regarding the message) which are different from the assumptions of the communicator. This may lead to incorrect action or lack of action on the part of the receiver of the message.

Inadequate Attention or Half Listening : Inadequate attention or half listening to the message makes communication less effective and the message is likely to be misunderstood. Inattention may arise because of over business of the communicate or because of the message being contrary to his expectations and beliefs. The simple failure to read notices, minutes and reports is also a common feature. Whatever be the reason, communication remains only a one-way process and there is no understanding of the message, if the receiver pays little attention to the message. In the words of Joseph Dooher, "Listening is the most neglected skills of communication . . . half listening is like racing your engine with gears in neutral. You use gasoline but you get nowhere."

Barriers due to Lack of Mutual Trust : Communication means sharing of ideas in common. "When we communicate, we are trying to establish a commonness." Thus, one will freely transfer information and understanding with another only when there is mutual trust between the two. When there is a lack of mutual trust between the communicator and the communicate, the message is not followed. Credibility gaps, *i.e.* inconsistency in saying and doing also cause lack of trust which works as a barrier to effective communication.

Resistance to Change : It is a general tendency of human beings to stick to old and customary patterns of life. They may resist change to maintain *status quo.* Thus, when new ideas are being communicated to introduce a change, it is likely to be overlooked or even opposed. This resistance to change creates an important obstacle to effective communication.

Mechanical Barriers : Barriers are created by mechanical system used in communicating messages. Such barrier may arise due to inadequate transmission and receiving equipments, defective instruments, noise at transmission or receiving ends, wrong choice of media etc.

The Strategies

Barriers to communication can be overcome if the following measures are taken :

Clarity and Completeness : In order to communicate effectively, it is very essential to know the 'audience' for whom the message is meant. The message to be conveyed must be absolutely clear in the mind of the communicator because if you do not understand an idea, you can never express to someone. The message should be adequate and appropriate to the purpose of communication. The purpose of communication, itself, should be clearly defined.

Proper Language : To avoid semantic barriers, the message should be expressed in simple, brief and clear language. The words or symbols selected for conveying the message must be appropriate to the reference and understanding of the receiver.

Proper Channel or Medium : To make communication effective, communicator should choose proper channel or medium. A judicious combination of written, oral and gestural modes as well as formal and informal channels should be used for maximum effectiveness.

Sound Organisational Structure : To make communication effective, the organisational structure must be sound and appropriate to the needs of the organisation. Attempt must be made to shorten the distances to be travelled through for conveying information.

Training of Employees : The employees should be trained to understand the objectives, rules, policies, authority relationships and operations of the enterprise. It will help to understand each other, minimise conflicts and distortion of messages.

Empathetic Listening : To communicate effectively, one should be a good listener. Superiors should develop the habit of patient listening and avoid premature evaluation of communication from their subordinates. This will encourage free flow of upward communication.

Participation : The management should promote the participation in communication. Subordinates should be invited to participate in the decision-making process so that co-operation nay increase and communication barriers are removed.

Motivation, Mutual Trust and Confidence : The message to be communicated should be so designed as to motivate the receiver to influence his behaviour to take the desired action. A sense of mutual trust and confidence must the generated to promote free flow of information.

Consistent Behaviour : To avoid credibility management must ensure that their actions and deeds are in accordance with their communication.

Use of Informal Communication : Informal communication help to improve managerial decisions and make communication more effective. Thus, formal channels of communication must be supplemented with the use of informal communication.

Feedback : Communication is not complete unless the response or reaction of the receiver of the message is obtained by the communicator. The effectiveness of communication can be judged from the feedback. Therefore, must be encouraged and analysed.

Gestures and Tone : The way you say something is also very important along with the message for gestures such as a twinkle of an eye, a smile or a handshake, etc. convey sometimes more meaning than even words spoken on written. Thus, one should have appropriate facial expression, tone, gestures and mood, etc. to make communication effective.

5

Theories of Management

Human beings are by nature gregarious. Community or group life has been one of earliest and most enduring features of human existence on this earth. This natural phenomenon of human beings living in groups have generated a variety of groupings such as family, clan, community friendship group, organisations, etc.

Organisations—business or social, dominate our lives. Our activities and behaviour are shaped by these organisations right from birth to death. Everyday of their lives human beings deal with organisation. There is no escape from them. Hospitals, schools, colleges, clubs, societies, local state and central government, manufacturing and trading concerns are some of the organisations we are associated with throughout our life. Our association with some of them are close and long while they are short lived or temporary with some others. The only alternative may be a complete return to nature which very few of us may choose. This association of human beings with organisations dominates in every country irrespective of the ideology and geographical differences.

An organisation needs a system of relationship among functions; it needs stability, continuity and predictability in its internal activities and external contracts. It requires harmonious relationship among people and processes.

All organisations have certain aims and objectives before them for which they strive and do their best to achieve them through their people who run and manage the affairs. In order to define the roles of their members, their behaviour and activities, they develop certain rules and regulations, policies, practices and procedures. Organisations are thus made of objectives, people, systems and procedures.

Different definitions of the organisation make it clear that different scholars look upon organisation from different angles. Some regard it as a mechanism to achieve certain objectives by division of labour, authority and responsibility among its members and coordinating their activities. Some regard it as a network comparison of human relationships in groups. Some others regard it as a system. These different approaches to achieve its objectives are reflected in different organisation theories which have developed certain principles to guide managers in designing the organisation and making it an effective instrument of meeting business goals.

In this block, we discuss different theories of the organisation, i.e., Classical, Neo-classical theory, and Modern Organisation theory,

Classical Organisation Theory

The term "classical" in English language refers to something traditionally accepted or long established. The beginning of the classical organisation theory can be traced back to the heydays of industrial transformation in the second half of the nineteenth century when some perceptive observers felt obsessed with the problem of growing size of the industries. In the beginning, the large scale operations were carried out by the organisations with the help of unskilled and semi-skilled people but later on, the technological development changed the industrial scene completely. Many new economic, social and technical problems sprang up. The need for solving these problems called for the development of organisational forms and management practices which were quite different from the traditional ones. This phenomenon changed the individualistic nature of organisation and management into mechanical nature. This view was current till the first half of the twentieth century.

The classical writers viewed the organisation as a machine and human beings as different components of that machine. Their approach has focused on input-output mediators and given less attention to constraining and facilitating factors in external environment. Workers were considered to be driven by economic considerations who could be solely motivated by economic rewards. While managers were regarded as kind-hearted, rational, intelligent and qualified people. Because an organisation was treated as a machine, it was felt that its efficiency could be increased by making each individual efficient, so that both the organisation's and the workers' interests might be served. Increased human productivity would facilitate the organisation in achieving its goals and objectives while on the other hand workers would get higher wages in return for their increased productivity. Thus, management is to emphasise on the improvement of machine in order to get higher productivity from the people at the minimum expense. The emphasis was on specialisation of performance and coordination of various activities.

Assumptions : The classical theory was based on the following assumptions:

(i) The relationship between workers and management was established through formal communications, defined tasks and accountability and formalised procedures and practices to minimise conflict between them.

(ii) Workers are considered to be driven by economic considerations who can be motivated basically by economic rewards. Money is considered the main motivator.

(iii) The managers were characterised as rational, kind-hearted, intelligent and qualified personnel but they are supposed to deal with the workers firmly in the system.

(iv) The theory assumes that the organisation is a machine and the people its components. In order to make any improvement in the whole system, internal factors were considered and less attention was given on factors in the external environment which may constrain and facilitate the system.

(v) It has been assumed by the theory that both workers and managers are rational. Workers can easily perceive that their interests can be served only by increasing the productivity and getting more wages for higher productivity, on the other hand, management gets the fruits of higher productivity. Management tries to find out best ways of doing a job by introducing new improvements in machines and devoting time to such technical engineering and administrative aspect of organisation which can make the man produce as much as he can with minimum expenses so that workers can contribute more to the organisation and earn more for themselves in return.

(vi) The theory puts special emphasis on error and particularly on the detection of error and its correction after it happens.

(vii) The theory assumes that man is relatively homogeneous and unmodifiable while designing the jobs and in picking the extra pairs of hands.

(viii) The classical organisation theory, in its essential character, is centralised. The integration of the system is achieved through the authority and control of the central mechanism.

Two Streams : Classical theorists were divided in opinion. The two streams are scientific management and administrative management. The scientific management stream of the organisation theory emphasised on the efficiency of lower levels of organisation while administrative stream focused on the efficiency of higher levels. F.W. Taylor is called the father of scientific management approach. Taylor and his followers insisted upon dividing and sub-dividing the tasks through time and motion studies because he was of the view that objective analysis of facts and collection of data in the workplace could provide the basis of determining the best way to organise the work. Thus, they investigated the effective use of human beings in industrial organisations and studied primarily the use of human beings as adjuncts to machines in the performance of routine tasks. The approach taken by this theory is quite narrow and encompasses primarily psychological variables. As such this theory is also referred to as 'Machine Theory' or 'Physiological Theory.'

The scientific management group was mainly concerned with the tasks at floor or operative levels, and these tasks were quite different from other tasks in the organisation because:

(i) These tasks are largely repetitive in nature so that the daily activities of a worker can be sub-divided in a large number of cyclical repetitions of essentially the same or closely related activities.

(ii) These tasks do not require any problem-solving activity by the workers who handle them. Thus, more attention was given in standardizing the working methods.

The second stream is the administrative stream of organisation theory emphasises efficiency at higher levels. It was concerned with the managerial organisation and process. Henry Fayol was the leader for this group. He, for the first time studied the functions and laid down principles of management in a systematic manner for the guidance of managers. The other contributors were Gulick, Oliver Sheldon, Mooney and Reliey, Urwick, Weber and others. The theorists have viewed the central problem as being one where there must be identification of tasks necessary for achieving the general purpose of the organisation and of the grouping or departmentalising, to fulfil those functions most effectively.

These two approaches are similar in recognising the fact that organisation is a closed system, however, there are differences between the two.

Key Characteristics : Scott and Mitchell have pointed out four key pillars on which the classical organisation theory seems to have been built. They are:

1. Division of labour, 2. Scalar and functional processes, 3. Structure, 4. The span of control.

Division of Labour : Division of labour refers to the division of tasks of an organisation into sub-tasks and then allot these sub-tasks or sub-parts to individuals. The allotment should be in such a way that each individual would have a small task so that he can specialise himself in that part with a view to improve the efficiency of the organisation while at the same time, the total of individuals' tasks should add up to the organisation's goals and objectives. The approach rests upon the simple assumption that the more a particular job is broken down into its component parts, the more specialised a worker can become in carrying out his part of the job and the more specialised he becomes, the more efficient the whole organisation will be. This element is the cornerstone among the four elements mentioned above because other three elements are dependent upon division of labour.

The Scalar and Functional Processes : The scalar and functional processes deal with the vertical and horizontal organisation. The scalar process deals with the vertical elaboration of an organisation. In other words, it is the chain of command or the line of authority, along which authority flows from the top (chief executive) to the bottom (first line supervisor) and obligations and reporting from the bottom to the top. Each one in the organisation is told who their superiors are and who are their subordinates or to whom they are responsible and accountable in performing their job.Delegation of authority flows from this line of command. The functional process deals with the horizontal organisation, i.e., grouping of various functions into units and clearly defining the relationship between the various heads of the units. The grouping of functions can be done on the basis of purpose, process, clientele, place and time.

Structure : It refers to the logical relationship of functions in an organisation arranged in order to accomplish the objectives. These relationships are lineand staff relationships. People, departments, divisions and other segments of the organisation that are authorised to determine the basic objectives of the business and assess their achievements constitute the line. The staff is that part of the organisation which assists and advises the line on matters concerning it, in carrying out its duties. For example, in a manufacturing concern, production is a line function while personnel and finance are the staff functions.

The Span of Control : In order to achieve the objectives, the managers are to get the work done from the unlimited number of workers in a large organisation. A manager cannot supervise an unlimited number of people. The span of control refers to the number of subordinates a supervisor can supervise effectively. Wide span yields a flat structure whereas short span results in a tall structure. Graieunas has developed a mathematical formula to show the numerical limitations of the subordinates, a manager can control. If an organisation is designed on the above principle, it will look like a pyramid. At the top of the structure, there is head of the organisation followed by the top executive, executives, middle managers, junior managers and at the bottom the firstline supervisors. Chain of command and line of communication both flow from the top to the botom in this structure. The line of responsibility, however flows from bottom to top. There is no provision of upward communication in this system except in relation to the results of task performance.

Principles of Organisations : The classical theorists have developed certain principles of organisations for the guidance of managers and executives and they claim them as fundamental, essential, inevitable and universal. Though divergence of views exists, there is a considerable degree of unanimity on these principles. Fayol was the first to give principles of administration. He developed a comprehensive list of fourteen principles: (i) division of work; (ii) authority and responsibility; (iii) discipline; (iv) unity of command; (v) unity of direction; (vi) subordination of individual interests to general interests; (vii) fair remuneration; (xi) equity and a sense of justice; (xii) stability; (xiii) initiative; and (xiv) teamwork spirit. These principles are more or less have a considerable degree of unanimity and some of these principles are still applied in organisations.

The Criticisms of the Classical Theory : The classical theory suffers from various limitations. It was put under serious criticisms in the first half of the nineteenth century by the neo-classical thinkers and others. The criticisms are mainly based on the following grounds:

Certain Assumptions are Unrealistic: The classical theory is based on certain assumptions. These assumptions were found unrealistic and hence not applicable to organisations at a later date. The wrong assumptions, found unrealistic are:

Close system assumption : The classical theorists viewed the organisation as a closed system, i.e., it has no environment and hence no interaction with the outside world. They felt that the organisation structure could be created as a house, i.e., step by step. They thought, once the organisation is created, it would run smoothly and efficiently because human beings are rational and they work more for economic rewards. In this way, the model fails to consider many environmental factors which influence upon the organisation and, thus, this assumption leads to incomplete view of actual organisational situations.

Static view of the organisation : The classicists took a rigid and static view of the organisation whereas an organisation is not static but dynamic. The organisation can instantly respond to changes in the environment and adjust accordingly. The environment influences the organisation and is influenced by it. The organisation imports inputs, transforms them and export outputs to the environment. The adjustments are necessary keeping in view the requirements of the organisational environment and its various internal parts. Thus, the best organisational pattern should meet the external and internal requirements and these requirements are ever-changing and dynamic.

Unrealistic assumptions about human behaviour : A major criticism of the classical theory is that the assumption regarding human behaviour was quite unrealistic. Human behaviour is complex in nature and not as simple as was established by the classical theorists. They lack sensibility to the behavioural dimensions of an organisation and make oversimplified and mechanistic assumptions for the smooth running of the organisation, ignoring all complexities of human behaviour at work. They assumed human beings as inert machines who performs tasks assigned to them and ignored their social, psychological and motivational aspects of human behaviour. This assumption of classical behaviourists led the workers to frustration, conflict and failure and thus subordinates man to the organisation.

Human nature under this theory was also wrongly predicted, Mason Haire observed that "there are implicit assumptions about man on which classical organisation theory seems to me to be based. He is lazy, short-sighted, selfish, liable to make mistakes, has poor judgement and may even be little dishonest."

Economic rewards are main motivators : The assumption that people at work can be motivated solely through economic rewards is wrong. Several researches in human behaviour have contradicted this assumption. Hawthorne Experiments brought seven facts to light about several other motivational and maintenance factors that motivate people at work. Such other factors may be formation of informal groups, emergence of leaders beyond the chain of commands, improvement in productivity linked with better status and job enrichment, etc.

Criticism of Principles : The theory was not only criticised for its certain assumptions that are unrealistic in modern industrial world but its certain principles formulated by classical theorists were also criticised. The main criticisms of classical principles are as follows:

Lack of empirical research : Its various concepts and principles are developed by practitioners in management which are mainly based on personal experience and limited observation. They (principles) lack precision and comprehensive framework for analysis. No scientific method was used. Moreover, it is not clear whether these principles are action recommendation or simply definitions. Certain independent specifications are to be made in understanding the meaning of an organisation. The classicists have referred to the advantages of various organisational arrangements, their arguments are one-sided and they offer no objective criteria for selecting one method over other methods. March and Siman observed, perhaps the most crucial failure of the administrative management theory is that it does not conform to the practice. The theory tends to dissolve when put into testable form. Thus, not a single principle is applicable to all organisational situations and sometimes contradicts each other.

Lack of universality : The classical theorists have claimed that these principles have universal application. This suggests that these principles can be applied in: (i) different organisations, (ii) different management levels in the same organisation, and (iii) different functions of the same organisation. The empirical researchers, however suggest that none of the principles has such characteristics. Moreover, there are many principles which are actually contradictory with other principles. For example, principle of specialisation is quite in conflict with the principle of unity of command. The following are certain classical principles which are invariably questioned:

Hierarchical structure : The classical theory is based upon the hierarchical structure that establishes the authority relationship between individuals in an organisation. It refers to arrangement of individuals in superior-subordinate relationship. Today, the institutions of hierarchy based upon position within the organisation is being discounted and the technological specialisation with authority of knowledge is gaining importance.

Unity of command : The classical theory suggests that each person has one superior. This principle has now become outdated. The trend is changing and the organisation seeks help from other members who are not in their chain of command, such as staff personnel. The organisations formally provides such supervision and the members thus, work under multiple command instead of under unity of command.

Excessive Reliance on Strength of the Key Characteristics : The classical theorists have focused excessive reliance on the strength of four key pillars, i.e., division of labour, scalar and functional process, structure and span of control. The neo-classicists who do not entirely reject the principles of classical theory, have attacked these key pillars. Some of the more important points raised by them are:

Division of labour : Division of labour is one of the key pillars of the classical theory but this tenet is criticised on the ground that there is no exclusive basis for grouping products, process, person or place, can always be used. The considerations of expertise and economy warrant different approaches in different situations. Besides, division of labour cause depersonalisation of work at the operative level which results in loss of human relationships.

Moreover, despite the fact that there is division of work among individuals and even though they may work independently of each other, the unit to which they belong specialises in a particular activity and its interdependence causes stresses and strains. Because these individuals and units work for common goals it raises a serious problem of coordination so that work may be done efficiently, cooperatively and harmoneously. As executive of each unit is answerable to the goals set for his unit, he internalises his sub-unit goals resulting in jealously guarded functional segments in the organisation.

Division of labour, moreover, causes several human problems of work. Due to limited repetitive tasks, the workers feel boredom, monotony, psychological alienation, etc. It also fails to utilise multiple capacities of people. The theory ignores human values such as satisfaction of job.

The scalar and functional process : The scalar and functional process raises another problem of delegation of authority and responsibility. It is assumed that the rational personal programme will help in selecting the personnel having capacities matching authority and responsibility in a particular position. But the neo-classicists are of the view that there is no measuring rod for measuring the capacity. Besides, in an organisation, only capacities do not work, there are so many other kinds of overlays which affect decision-making process. Moreover, as March and Siman have pointed out, in most organisational situations, people are not looking for any optional solution but they require 'satisfying' solution, i.e., solution that meet the requirements.

Structure : Classicists have laid down certain principles which, if followed will lay down a neat and perfect organisation structure, but the human behaviour disrupts the best laid organisation plans. Research showed that major conflicts between line and staff personnel in the organisation were experienced because jobs are becoming increasingly specialized have requiring a higher knowledge context. It can be felt if everything had worked in a predetermined way, there would have been no need of specialised control agencies, or organisation structure and it was the only cause for the development of control agencies.

Span of control : The classical approach suggests a narrow span of control specifying the number of subordinates to 5-6 at higher level and 20 at bottom. But the view of neo-classicists favour a wider span of control having a large number of subordinates under one supervisor. According to them, there are several considerations, such as the abilities of supervisor and subordinates, nature of work, time schedules, geographic dispersion, etc. The ability to handle the responsibilities increases with the increase in level of education.

Bureaucratic Behaviour : Weber's 'ideal' bureaucracy, the main constituent of the classical theory, suggests the strict adherence to rules and regulations through mindless application of the letters of the rule. The scope for individual initiative and contribution to the organisation goal is thus limited. The result is red-tapism and observation of rules and regulations becomes the main objective and the objectives for which these rules and regulations are formed, are forgotten. Robert K. Morton has rightly observed that the rules and procedures may take positive values and become ends rather than means to ends and the decision-making tends to become a routine application of precedents with little attention to alternatives not previously experienced. Today when problem-solving ability, innovativeness and creativity are required, the bureaucratic approach appears to be inadequate.

Neglect of Human Factor for Focus on Anatomy of Organisations : The classical theory is devoted to specialisation of different parts of organisation to maximise output with the use of minimum input. The classicists concentrate their views along with the division of labour, organisation structure, grouping of activities and span of control, etc. but not with its effects on the interrelationships. It is a need model and assumes action and communication will flow uninterrupted. They do not envisage the development of informal groups and their leaders who control the behaviour of their members. According to neo-classicists, there is no scope for emotions and sentiments and no conflicts due to elaborate job descriptions, policy specifications, rules and regulations, clear-cut authority and responsibility, etc. under the classical theory. In thisway, it recognises tasks and not the people.

Little Scope for Integration : The theory provides little scope for integrating people with the organisation. The goals are set at the top without consulting the subordinates who are actually, the real executors. The decision-making is highly centralised. The theory concentrates too much of authority at the top as the people at lower level are considered to be the 'inferior lot.'

The various criticisms of the classical organisation theory should not lead one to feel that it is a useless theory and does not offer any guidance for managerial action in an organisation. In fact, still there are many classical principles which are applied successfully in many organisations. It shows that though not much, the classical theory has its validity in designing an organisation. Scott observes, "It would not be fair to say that the classical school is unaware of the day-to-day administrative problems of the organisation. The classical organisation theory has relevant insights into the nature of an organisation, but the value of this theory is limited by its narrow concentration on the formal anatomy of the organisation."

Neo-classical Theory

The classical organisation theory focused attention on physiological and mechanical variables of the organisational functioning in order to increase the efficiency and productivity. But positive aspects of these variables could not produce the positive results in work behaviour and the researches tried to investigate the reasons for human behaviour at work. They discovered that the real cause of human behaviour is somewhat more than the physiological variable. These findings generated a new phenomenon about the organisational functioning and focused attention on human beings in the organisations. These exercises were given new names such as 'behavioural theory of an organisation', 'human view of an organisation' or 'human relations approach in an organisation.'

The neo-classical approach was developed as a reaction to the classical approach which attracted so many behaviourist to make further researches into the human behaviour at work. This movement was started by 'Mayo' and his associates at Hawthorne

Plant of the Eastern Electric Company, Chicago in the late twenties, gained momentum and continued to dominate till the sixties. An impressive account of thinking of human relations has been given by Douglas M. McGregor in his book entitled *'The Human Side of Enterprise.'*

The classical theory was the product of the time and the following reasons were responsible for its development:

(i) The management thinking was showing signs of change because of the improved standards of living and education level. The technological changes were forcing the management to expand the size of the organisation and complexities were increasing. This also led to the fact that the management be somewhat more sympathetic and considerate towards their workers.

(ii) The trade union movement got momentum and made the workers conscious of their rights. It was no longer possible for the management to treat the human beings at work as 'givens'.

These were two main reasons which were responsible for the change of management behaviour from autocratic to the custodial approach which was based on offer of fringe benefits apart from wages to meet their security needs.

Though neo-classical approach was developed as a reaction to the classical principles, it did not abandon the classical approach altogether, rather it pointed to the limitations of the classical approach and attempted to fill in the deficiencies through highlighting certain points which were not given due place in the classical approach. In this regard, there were two schools of thought—one school of thought with writers as Simon, Smithburg, and Thompson, pointed out the limitations of the classical approach to structural aspect only and the analysts called this group as 'neo-classicists'. This school of thought suggested modifications to the classical principles but did not abandon the basic principles. The other school of thought which consisted of large number of writers focused on the human aspect neglected by the classicists. This group was called as human relationists or behaviourists. Both these schools were reactions to the classical theory but failed to suggest or develop any new theory except providing some points of criticism on varying counts. Both of them could be referred as neo-classicists.

Neo-classicists, endeavoured to identify the weaknesses of classicists through empirical research and most of the criticisms of classical theory have emerged through researches. Howthorne studies were the beginning of the series. The other contributors are Roethlisberger, Dickson, Whitehead, Lippitt and White, Coach and French Jr., etc.

Neo-classical approach is based on two main points: (i) Organisational situation should be viewed in social as well as in economic and technical terms, and (ii) The social process of group behaviour can be understood in terms of clinical method analogous to the doctor's diagnosis of human organism. The neo-classicists view organisation as combination of formal and informal forms of the organisation. The informal form was missing in classical approach. They also introduced behavioural science to diagnose human behaviour and showed how the pillars of classical doctrines—division of labour, functional processes, structure and scalar chain are affected and modified by human actions. The main prepositions of neo-classical organisation theory are as follows:

1. The organisation in general is a social system composed of numerous interacting parts.
2. The social environment on the job affects the workers and is also affectedby them. Management is not the only variable.
3. The informal organisation also exists within the framework of formal organisation and it affects and is affected by the formal organisation.
4. There is always a conflict between organisational and individual goals that always increases the importance of integration between these two.
5. People are interdependent and their behaviour can be predicted in terms of social factors.

6. Money is one of the motivators but not the sole motivator of the human behaviour. Man is diversely motivated and socio-psychological factors are more important.
7. Man's approach is not always rational. He behaves irrationally as far as rewards from the job are concerned.
8. Both-way communication is necessary because it carries necessary information downward for the proper functioning of the organisation and transmits the feelings and sentiments of people who work in the organisation upward.
9. Teamwork is essential for cooperative and sound functioning of the organisation.

The Appraisal : The neo-classical theory provides various modifications and improvements over the earlier theory and offers a more humanistic view towards people at work. Neo-classicists have also introduced behavioural science in the study of organisational functioning which has helped managers quite a lot. This approach emphasised the micro-analysis of the human behaviour. The theory has brought into light certain important factors which were altogether ignored by the classicists such as informal group, group norms, informal leader, non-economic rewards, etc. Thus, the approach gives evidence of accepting the classical doctrine though superimposing its modifications, resulting from individual behaviour and the influence of the informal group.

The Criticisms : The main criticisms of the neo-classical theory are as here under:

Certain Assumptions are not True: Certain assumptions on which the neo-classical theory is based do not seem to be true. For example, the assumption that there is a solution to every problem which satisfies everyone in an organisation is not true. Often there are conflict interests among various groups in the organisation that are structural and not merely psychological.

Limited Application: The various formats and structures of organisations given by neo-classicists are not universal. Their application is limited. There is no particular structure which may serve the purpose of all the organisations. It also overlooks some of the environmental constraints which managers cannot ignore and this lapse makes the practicability of the theory limited.

Lack of Unified Approach: The theory lacks the unified approach of the organisation theory. In fact, it is not a theory at all. All that was done in neo-classical theory is simply modification of the classical theory rather than organisational transformation. So, this theory has almost the same limitations as the classical theory.

More Emphasis on Human Aspect: The theory gives too much emphasis on human aspects in the organisation. As the classicists concentrated on structural aspect, neo-classicists concentrate their attention on the human aspect. It ignores the other aspects such as formal structure, discipline, etc.

Some thinkers while criticising the theory have called it bankrupt because it suggests nothing new. Though, the theory has offered valuable contributions to the lore of organisation like the classical theory, it suffers from incompleteness, a shortsighted perspective and lack of integration among the many factors of human behaviour studied by it.

Facts Discovered : Howthorne studies at the Western Electrical Company, Chicago was the main source of inspiration to the neo-classical school. Mayo and his associates carried out several experiments there, by providing better working and living conditions and financial incentives, and they got amazing results. Productivity and efficiency went up considerably. The following facts were uncovered by these experiments:

1. The individual roles as defined and norms established by their social system differ from those of the formal organisation. Workers follow the social norms rather than try to achieve the target management thinks they can achieve even though this would have helped them earn better and as much as they physically can.
2. Non-economic rewards and social sanctions also play quite a significant role in guiding the behaviour of the workers. It is their perception of the situation that matters

and not that of the management. They fear retaliation for violating the group norms. So, they follow group norms and are not motivated by the economic incentive plans.

3. The group plays an important role in determining the attitudes and performance of individual worker. Often workers do not act or react as individuals but as a member of their group. A worker can more readily accept the change in his behaviour if the group of which he is a member changes its behaviour.

4. Informal leader and not the formal leader, i.e., the formal incharge of the group as supervisor or manager, sets and enforces the group norms. Formal leader is proved ineffective unless he conforms to the norms to the group of which he is incharge.

5. There is need for communication between the ranks participation in decision- making and democratic leadership. It explains to the lower participants as to why the management has taken a particular decision. The lower ranks are allowed to share in the decisions taken by the higher management especially in matters concerning them. Thus, suggesting that the management is just, non-arbitrary and concerned with the problems of workers and not only with the work output.

6. Increasing satisfaction leads to increased organisation effectiveness.

7. The management should possess not only technical skills but also effective social skills.

8. People are motivated in the organisation not merely by the satisfaction of lower needs but by fulfilling certain higher level needs.

The above conclusion of Hawthorne Experiments received a wide publicity and they changed the attitude and the thinking of the management significantly. This approach was further persuaded relentlessly by behaviourists.

Systems Approach : We may look at the organisation from two different angles:

1. We may consider the overall picture of the organisation as a unit; or
2. We may consider the relationship between its various internal components.

When we consider the overall picture of the organisation, we consider all the elements—internal and external—and their effects on each other simultaneously. This approach may be called the 'goalistic view' because it tries to reach the goal of an organisation by unifying the efforts of all the elements. For example, when we consider finance, workers and their attitude, technological developments, etc. we are following goalistic view. It serves as a mean-ends analysis which in turn facilitates division of work and helps in judging the extent of success of comparing actual and targeted performance. But it does not answer many problems such as interdependence of elements, organisations environment, interfact, etc. It gives a systematic view when we consider the second approach, i.e., we examine the relationship between each element of the organisation and their interdependence. If we examine employer-employee, customer and organisation, debtors-organisation relationships, we follow systematic view.

The systems approach focused attention on the following aspects:

(i) It integrates all elements for the proper and smooth functioning of the organisation.

(ii) The organisation overall goals can be achieved successfully because it considers all the aspects of the problems deeply and maintains a harmoneous relationship between various elements so that they work unitedly to achieve goals.

(iii) The approach helps in acquisition and maintenance of various resources, i.e., man, material, money, and machinery, etc. for pertaining the smooth functioning of the organisation.

(iv) It allows adaptation to internal requirements and environmental changes in order to survive and grow.

Definition and Characteristics

Definition of System: Kast and Rosenzweig define the system as an organised unitary whole composed of two or more interdependent parts, components or sub-systems and defined by identifiable boundaries form its environmental suprasystem. More simply, a system may be referred as units composed of several interdependent parts. System may be denoted as a grouping of parts and not simply an agglomeration of individual parts. Though each part performs its own functions yet they work towards a common goal. The behaviour of tne entity is a joint function of the behaviours of the individual parts and their interactions. For instance, a human body may be regarded as a system, consisting of several sub-systems, such as circulatory, reproductive digestive, nervous systems, etc. Even though each sub-system performs different and distinguished function, they depend on each other. Similarly, an organisation is composed of a number of sub-systems of sub-systems such as internal organisation, technological, psychological, structural, managerial and environment etc. which are constantly changing and evolving. A change in one may affect the other.

Characteristics of System: From the analysis of foregoing definition and discussion following characteristics of a system emerge:

Interdependence of parts: A system has several parts. Each part is dynamic and affects all other parts. They are interrelated and interdependent. Interdependence of different parts is must in an organisation as a system because of division of labour, specialisation, sharing of limited resources, scheduling of activities, etc. The work of the organisation is divided into various departments, sub-departments and so on, assigning each unit an independent specialised task, which on integration culminates into the accomplishment of overall organisational goals. These parts are interconnected in such a way that a change in one part may affect the other part and in this way, the whole organisation.

A system is composed of several sub-systems: A system is composedof several sub-systems. For example, in a manufacturing organisation,total manufacturing is one system, within which may exist a completeproduction system which again may contain an inventory control system.Conversely, a system or sub-system may form part or container ofother system. For example, an individual who may be a part of onesystem, may also be a part or container for another physiological system.

Every system has its own norms: Every system may be distinguished from other systems in terms of objectives, processes, roles, structures, and norms of conduct. So, every system is unique if anything happens in the organisation,we regard it as an outcome of a particular system and we locate the fault in the system.

Systems are cpen: Almost all systems are open. Open system imports certain factors processes them and exports them to the environment. Organisation is also an open system. It imports matter, energy and informations, from its environments, transforms or converts them into a usable product or useful service and export that product or service to the environment. This process of importing, transforming and exporting goes on indefinitely. Though the organisation exports, they do not import all but retain some energy within themselves for survival and growth. As they are open, they are to absorb shocks and influences from the environment and those that are flexible respond to adapt themselves to the environment situation.

Systems influence and are influenced by other systems: As systems are open, they influence other systems in the environment depending upon its strengths and capacities in relation to other systems. Obviously, the influence of environment, in most cases is greater than the system's over impact on the environment.

The Sub-system

In the previous section, we have suggested that a system is an integrated whole of various sub-systems. An organisation as a system can better be understood by identifying the various sub-systems within it. The levels of systems within a subsystem are called sub-systems and levels of systems within are identified by certain objectives, processes, role, structures and norms of conduct. A system is composed of various lower order sub-systems and is also a part of a super-system. The various sub-systems of the system constitute the mutually dependent parts of the large system, called organisation. These sub-systems interact, and through interaction create new patterns of behaviour that are separate from, but related to, the patterns specified by original system. The interdependence of different parts as characterised by Thompson, may be pooled, sequential, or reciprocal. When dependence is not direct, it is pooled interdependence. For example, an organisation, having sales divisions in different cities making their own buying and selling, but drawing upon its common funds is an example of pooled interdependence. When one sub-system is directly dependent upon another, it is sequential interdependence. Such type of interdependence may be seen in production job or assembly line when output of one sub-system is the input for the other department or sub-system. Reciprocal interdependence refers to the situation where outputs of each unit becomes inputs for another such as in production and maintenance divisions. Thus, system behaviour emerged as one, and since different variables are mutually interdependent, the true influence of alerting one aspect of the system cannot be determined by changing it alone.

The Classification : There are various ways of classifying sub-systems and one may support any of them. Each of the organisation unit may be treated as a sub-system. In other words, each functional unit of an organisation may be regarded as different sub-systems such as production sub-system, personnel or finance or sales sub-systems, etc. Seiler has classified four components in an organisation, i.e., human inputs, technological inputs, organisational inputs and social structure and norms. From these inputs, he has derived, the concept of socio-technical system, Kast and Rosenzweig have identified five sub-systems, i.e., goal and values sub-system, technical sub-system, psychological sub-system structural sub-system, and managerial sub-system. Katz and Kahn have identified five sub-systems. These are: technical sub-system concerned with the work that gets done; supportive sub-system concerning with the procurement, disposal and institutional relations; maintenance sub-system for uniting people into their functional roles; adaptive sub-system concerned with organisational change; and managerial sub-system for direction, adjudication and control of the many sub-systems and activities of the whole structure. Carzo and Yunouzas give three kinds of sub-systems in an organisation as a system, i.e., technical, social and power sub-systems. We shall here discuss these three sub-systems.

Technical Sub-system: The technical sub-system may be referred to as the formal organisation. It refers to the knowledge required for the performance of tasks including the techniques used in the transformation of inputs into outputs. Being a formal organisation, it decides to make use of a particular technology; there is a given layout; policies, rules and regulations are framed; different hierarchical levels are developed, authority is given and responsibilities are fixed; and necessary technical engineering and efficiency consideration are laid down. The behaviour in the organisation cannot be explained fully by technical sub-system, also because there is a fundamental conflict between the individual—a part of the system and the system itself resulting from the expectancies of the organisation and that of the people—regarding the work he has to perform. It requires certain modificationsin the behaviour of the man through the social and power sub-systems.

The objective of the technical sub-system is to make necessary imports from the environment, transform them into products or services and export them back to the environment. For this purpose, it involves decisions, communications, action and balance processes. Through the decision process, three main problems of what to produce, for whom to produce and how to produce are resolved. Decisions are based on information gathered from various sources. Such informations are communicated through the communication process to action centres to implement them. Through balance process, an administrative balance is obtained so that all parts may be coordinated and no one part can dominate all other parts in the organisation. These processes take place on the basis of roles assigned to people according to the requirements of the job. In order to handle the job properly one is given authority from the superiors and is assigned a status matching with the importance of the job and the individual's ability to do the job. Norms of conduct are defined in the well-designed policies, norms, rules, procedures and description of the job. Thus, the arrangement of job in relation to each other, process and authority relations, etc. provide a structure to the technical sub-system.

Social Subsystem: As we have explained earlier, there exists a conflict between an individual and the system itself because people differ very widely in abilities, capacities, attitudes and beliefs, likes and dislikes, etc. People find the formal set-up quite inadequate to satisfy all their needs especially social ones. Gradually they are seen interacting with each other and at times by cutting across the hierarchical and departmental lines, etc. on non-formal matters. Thus, they form groups to discuss their informal matters and display their positive and negative sentiments towards each other. Sometimes, one member gets the membership of different social groups for different purposes and thus social behaviour is patterned.

The interaction between individuals and the group are generally known as informal aspect of the organisation which is the result of operation of socio-psychological forces. Such interaction can be interpreted in terms of mutual expectancies. Informal group expects certain type of behaviour from its individual member and in turn, individual has expectancies of psychological satisfaction, he hopes form the association. In this an individual modifies his behaviour according to group norms and the group modifies its behaviours according to what is expected from it by its members.

Another group of elements in social sub-system consists of status, role, norms and values. Status is a position determined as being important in the interpersonal relationship of the group. Thus, it is a social rank, prestige, sentiments and feelings of a person in comparison with a social system. Some members come to be more highly respected than others while some others born to be followers. Role is a pattern of action, expected of a person in his position involving others. Thus, it describes specific form of behaviour and develops originally from the task-requirements. Different members have to play different roles assigned to them by the group. Norm is that the general expectation demands character for all role incumbents of a system or sub-system. Unwritten norms are followed by the members of the group. Anybody not adhering to norms are reprimanded or punished. Value is the more generalised ideological justification and aspiration. Value guides the behaviour of the members.

Power Sub-system: Power behaviour of the people in an organisation plays a very important role. As the organisation starts functioning, people realise the importance of their job in relation to others in the organisation; the benefits of their experience to the organisation; the benefits of their experience to the organisation; the crucial location of their jobs, their personality characteristics; the fact of their access to the superior authority holder. In this way, they have acquired power to some degree or the other, based on the source of their power that influences the decision-making and regulate others behaviour.

Individual's abilities to regulate the behaviour of others vary. Some persons are more powerful and some others have powerful influence areas than others have. Consequently, a power differentiation based on the amount of power enjoyed (which is again a function of success achieved and attempts made to influence the behaviour of others) develops in a power structure. It gives birth to politicking and people play opportunistic roles. Power minded people have no norms. Generally, norms are decided by the individual's interests and the opportunity of serving those interests and, therefore, sheer expediency is the norm. The power holder enjoys the status in accordance with his abilities to influence the behaviour of others in order to carry out his wishes. This part of the system is known as power sub-system.

All the three sub-systems discussed above have distinct operational field. But, in actual practice, a clear-cut distinction among the three is very difficult to make and disentanglement of one sub-system from the other poses a serious problem. The three sub-systems are intertwined by considerable overlapping. Some behaviour pattern in the organisation are part of two sub-systems; some others are part of all the three sub-systems; some other activities are exclusive to a particular system; and still there are few behaviours which do not fall in any of the sub-systems.

These three sub-systems are mutually dependent parts of the larger system, the organisation. There is interdependence between these parts of sub-systems and the whole organisation. Moreover, organisation itself, is a sub-system of a larger system society and has many other systems in its environment. Besides each part, sub-system or system constitutes environment of the other. As such, each of them influences and in turn, gets influenced by others.

Modern Organisation Theory

Modern organisation theory has its evolution from the General Systems Theory whose inventor and chief architect was Bertalanffy. General system theory presents an integration of different levels of system. It provides a macro view from which we may look at all types of systems.

The modern organisation theory is of recent origin having developed in sixties, and flourished in seventies. The theory presents the answers of several questions remained unheeded to by the earlier theories. The modern theory has an analytical base and has sufficiently relied on empirical research. The theory is a fundamental one, though it presents a new paradigm. It is not simply an extension of the old theories like the classical or the neo-classical theories. Its premises are based upon a conception of organisations as open, organic and probabilistic system. It gives answers to many complex questions ignored by the classical or the neo-classical theorists as pointed out by Scott and Michell:

(i) What are the various parts of the system?

(ii) What is the nature of their interdependency?

(iii) What are the processes which link the various parts of the system and facilitate their adjustment to each other?

(iv) What are the goals of the system?

We shall now discuss how these questions as answered by the modern theorists:

Various Parts

As every system has several parts, so the organisation being treated as a system, must also have several parts. The parts of organisation system may be classified.

Individual: Individual is an important part of an organisation and provides energy to matter and information—the organisational inputs. Individuals in an organisation come together with varied backgrounds, attitudes, motives and sentiments, they interact and influence each other and things in their environment and are also influenced by them.

Formal Organisation: Every system is formal because it lays down certain principles, rules, regulations, procedures, and norms of conduct for its proper functioning. Such rules, etc. may be oral or written. There are also hierarchical levels through which communication flows downward and upward. Organisational charts and manuals also constitutes important parts of formal system.

Informal Organisation: In a formal system, people come together and interact with each other which causes development of certain relations and sentiments— positive, negative or indifferent. These relations and developments steadily result in spontaneous development of informal groups, groups so formed satisfy many of the social needs that remained uncared for by the formal organisation.

Status and Roles: Every organisation has hierarchical levels. It is like a pyramid consisting of layers and every layer has functional segmentation. The number of segments get reduced with the increasing level of the layer in the organisation and at the top only one layer remains that ultimately envelops the entire organisation. Every level and every individual at that level is assigned a role which is played by everybody in relation to those having role relationships. Accordingly, an individual gets certain previleges and prerogatives over others.

Physical Environment of the Work Situation: The technical equipment, technology employed design of machines, arrangement of jobs, etc. constitute the physical environment of the work situation. It provides, implies or embraces the physical conditions under which a person is to perform the work and it affects skills, motivations and perceptions of people ultimately leading to a particular efficiency level.

Mutual Interdependence

The above parts of a system of an organisation work unitedly for the attainment of a common goal. While performing their individual roles, they hardly work independently and to prove themselves productive, they work cooperatively and in collaboration with each other. Thus, these parts interact within and between themselves and such interaction may be interpart interactions and intrapart interactions.

Interpart Interactions: Each part of the organisation interact with all other parts. Individuals interact with informal organisations to get their social needs satisfied which formal organisation fails to satisfy. It makes modifications in individuals and expectations of the organisations. The individual may mould the group according to his point of view and by convincing the group, they can put their viewpoint before the organisation. Thus, each part interact affecting each other and resulting in mutual modification of expectancies. Consequently demands and expectations of individual reconcile for harmonious relationships. The same may happen with organisations.

Intrapart Interactions: Individual performs a very minute part of the total job and even for that limited task he is to seek assistance from others such as mechanic for removing the defects of a machine or for oiling the machine, etc. Thus, the individual's job may be a part of the series of processes involved, i.e., one may be a supplier for raw material for a job while the other depends for raw materials on others. In this way no part can complete his job without the assistance of others and thus their actions affect each other.

Inter-connected System

As we have mentioned earlier no one part works in isolation. They are interdependent and interrelated. The linking processes are decision, communication, action and balance. The interrelationship between the parts effects decisions which conversely explains the relationship through the decision processes. This shows the flow of significant decisions and how decisions are arrived at through socio-metric authority, power, functional communication, etc. processes. All parts make decision and most of them especially the important ones are the product of joint efforts of various parts. Thus, the decision process links the various parts. Through communication process, various parts are able to get, store, retrieve and feed information to the action centres and such centres implement the decisions. So, through action process, decisions are implemented. Different units are controlled, integrated and balanced in order to be sure that no one part dominates the other parts.

The Goals : Every system including the organisational system has certain goals. Leaving apart certain specific goals meant for a specific organisation or part, every organisation or system works towards the attainment of common goals which necessitates interaction, ability, adaptability and growth. Interaction takes place because parts are interdependent and interconnected. Stability is the objective of every system. However, static structure and the simple dynamic of every system do not seek adaptability and growth. The cybernetic system seeks adaptability but adaptability and growth are the objective or characteristics of all open living systems.

The Appraisal : The modern organisational theory has made valuable contributions in the development of the organisational theories. The following are important:

1. The theory has an empirical and analytical base and looks at the organisations in system perspective.
2. It seeks interrelationships and interconnections amongst various organisational parts and seeks an answer to the question arising out of such interdependence.
3. It takes holistic view, i.e., a whole is not a sum of the parts. The system approach does not approve the separate study of different parts and then integrating them to make a whole. It opines that such integration is not possible and the total system should be studied as whole and not in parts.
4. The concern of modern organisation theory is to study the interrelationships between parts and to know how these parts respond to it. Thus, the system approach opened up

vast possibilities for the analysis of innumerable parts and sub-systems within an organisational system and its interaction with its environment.

5. Unlike the classical or the behavioural approaches, modern theory adopts a realistic view regarding the principles of the organisation. The theory suggests as the organisation is composed of several sub-systems, it is quite impossible to prescribe certain principles which are universally applicable or appropriate to all organisations. Such principles are possible only when the system is stable, mechanistic, and effectively closed to intervening external variables. But once we take the organisation as an open system with interactive components, we can no longer think in simplistic and unidimensional terms.
6. .The theory presents an open, organic and probabilistic system of the organisation as opposed to traditional theory's closed, mechanistic and deterministic view. Open system refers to an exchange relationship of the organisation with the environment and its serious dominating influence. Organisations are organic systems because they have adaptability and flexibility to adapt themselves to the environmental situation. Organisations are probabilistic systems because nothing is certain in an organisation, only a probability can be forecasted.
7. The classical approach followed a macro approach and the behaviourists, a micro approach but the modern organisation theory attempts a macro- micro-macro approach of the organisation. Besides, this attempt to comprehend the impact on the organisation to changes in environment has proved a new paradigm which is not merely an extension of old, rather it constitutes a real revolution in theory. It helps us understand the interrelationships between the major components of an organisation its goals, technology, structure and culture.

Though the modern theory has contributed a lot to the organisation, yet it is not free from criticisms. Notwithstanding its contribution to modern thinking, it has not lived up to the expectations, it raised at the beginning. It promised to provide an adequate and comprehensive explanation of the organisation, but this promise does not seem to be fulfilled. It was initially received enthusisastically but the initial enthusiasm could not be sustained for long. It remains fragmented because isolated attempts have been made in this direction and no integration of techniques and concepts into a high level of abstraction was attempted. Its concepts are still evolving. Though critics regard it as an important theory of organisation, but undoubtedly it has not yet developed sufficiently as a theory of explanation in the realm of human behaviour. There is no such transformation in the theory that can eliminate the old and substitute the new.

In this chapter, an overview of various management theories was provided. In depth, the analysis of classical and neo-classical theories was furnished. The key characteristics of classical organization theory being: (a) Division of Labour (b) Functional Process (c) Structure and (d) Span of Control. The neo-classical approach was developed as a reaction to the classical principles, it did not abandon the classical approach altogether, rather it pointed to the limitation of classical approach. Highlights of Hawthorne experiments were also described. The major facts discovered by these experiments include the important role of groups in determining the attitude of workers; need for communication among ranks; increasing satisfaction leads to effective organization and that people in an organization are motivating higher level needs. It also provided an overview of systems approach and the modern organisational theory.

6

Significance of Environment

Every organisation exists and operates within its environment. In fact, every organisation is a sub-system of its total environmental system. Every organisation interacts with its environment, and both affect each other.

Organisational Environment

Simply stated, organisational environment refers to the environment under which an organisation exists and operates. The environment is composed of many factors, forces, conditions, influences and so on.

According to Robert Albanese, "The environment of an organisation may be defined as a perceived set of conditions, influences, or forces external to an organisation that has relevance to the goals and tasks of the organisation."

In the words of Robbing, "Environment is the composition of those institutions or forces that affect the performance of the organisation but over which the organisation has little control."

According to Prof. Keith Davis, organisational environment "is the aggregate of all conditions, events and influences that surround and affect it."

Thus, organisational environment refers to those surroundings, factors, circumstances, institutions or influences that affect the working and existence of an organisation.

Salient Features

Following characteristics of organisational environment highlight its nature :

Dynamic : Organisational environment is dynamic. It is constantly changing due to the change in the factors or forces composing it.

Complex or Dynamic Factors : Organisational environment consists of many factors, forces, conditions, events, influences institutions etc. arising from many sources. These all interact with each other and create new set of influences. Thus, it is complex phenomenon. It is easier to understand in parts but difficult to understand in its totality.

Internal and External : The dynamic environment consists of internal and external environment. Internal environment is composed of the forces and conditions within the organisation. External environment is composed of the forces and conditions outside the organisation.

Geographical Boundary : There is a geographical boundary of the environment of every organisation. Forces and conditions that arise within that boundary usually affect the organisation. However, the geographical limit is determined by the area of operation of the organisation.

Mutual Dependence of Factors : All the factors of the environment are mutually dependent. Each factor affects all the other factors. For instance, social factor affects economic, political, legal, religious, technical and other factors.

Multi-faceted : Organisational environment is multi-faceted. It may look different to different persons. Moreover, a slight change in factors may cause change in the environmental scene. Again, some see a particular state of environment as an opportunity while others may perceive it as a threat.

Affects Organisation : Environment affects all organisations. The profitability, growth, prosperity, diversification, etc. of art organisation largely depend on the environment in which it exists and operates. Moreover, any change in the environment also affects an organisation in several different ways.

Exchange of Resources: Every organisation imports its resources (human, physical, financial and informational) from its environment and export its goods or services to its environment.

Satisfaction of Needs : The basic purpose of every organisation is to earn profits through satisfaction of needs of the environment. No organisation can survive and succeed without achieving this purpose.

Challenges : Every organisation has to face and deal with the challenges posed by its environment. It is a precondition for the success of the organisation. In order to face challenges effectively, every organisation needs to change its plans and strategies according to the change in the environment.

Further Studies

Every organisation needs to study and understand its environment. Survival and success of an organisation largely depends on its ability to understand and anticipate its own environment accurately. Briefly, the need for study of environment arises due to the following reasons :

1. To understand complexities of environment.
2. To obtain information about the changes that are taking place in the environment.
3. To know and understand environmental fluctuations.
4. To know and evaluate the amount of risks associated with the organisation.
5. To understand the mutual effect of the environmental factors.
6. To evaluate the plans under execution.
7. To prepare strategic/corporate planning.

8. To prepare action plans.
9. To obtain information about opportunities and threats for the organisation.
10. To evaluate strengths and weaknesses of the organisation.
11. To make the organisation environmental friendly.
12. To prepare for organisational change.
13. To ensure overall managerial effectiveness.

The Categories

Organisational environment can be classified under the following heads :

Internal Environment : The internal environment means the environment composed of the conditions and forces within the organisation. In other words, internal environment is a result of the internal forces and conditions. It influences the actions and behaviour of the persons internal to the organisation. The main components/ elements of internal environment are as follows:

1. Purpose or objectives of organisation.
2. Counter value system and philosophy of organisation.
3. Policies, rules and regulations of organisation.
4. Nature, composition and structure of management including the Board of Directors.
5. Authority relationships in organisation.
6. Human resources of organisation.
7. Physical assets and production facilities of organisation.
8. R & D and technological strengths of organisation.
9. Finance strength of organisation.
10. Market standing and brand equity of organisation. Internal environment is largely controllable. Hence, managing this environment is not regarded as a serious challenge for managers.

External Environment : External environment consists of the forces and conditions outside the organisation. Such an environment influences the actions and behaviour of the entire organisation. It is beyond the control of the organisation. The components of external environment are being discussed under the next heading.

External Environment

External environment may be classified into two parts :

Micro, Direct-action or Task Environment : The micro environment consists of the factors or activators within the immediate environment of the organisation. Such an environment directly affect the performance of the organisation. It is, therefore, also known as the direct-action environment. The main components or factors of such an environment are : (i) Shareholders, (ii) Consumers, (iii) Trade unions, (iv) Suppliers, (v) Market intermediaries, (vi) Competitors, (vii) Financial institutions and creditors, (viii) Government and government agencies.

Macro, Indirect-action or General Environment : The word macro means large or whole. The macro or general environment means the environment composed of all those major forces and conditions that affect the organisation's activities and behaviour. Such an environment provides opportunities and poses threats to the organisation. The macro environment forces are beyond the control of the organisation. The main components of macro or general environment include economic, social, cultural, religious, political, legal, technological, educational, international and so on. Macro environment is sometimes classified into economic and non-economic environment. Economic factors of macro environment constitute economic environment whereas the other factors of macro environment constitute non-economic environment. The main components of macro environment are briefly described as follows :

Economic Environment : Economic environment refers to the economic factors and forces that have economic effects on organisations. Such environment affects the direction and working of organisations. The main factors and forces of economic environment are as follows :

(i) Economic system, whether capitalistic, socialistic, communistic or mixed economic system.

(ii) Stage of the economy, whether developed, underdeveloped or undeveloped.

(iii) Present state of economic or trade cycle, price level and rate of inflation.

(iv) Economic structure *i.e.,* the structure and sources of national income, income distribution pattern, rate of capital formation, rate and growth of GNP, per capita income, export-import and balance of payment position, stock of foreign exchange, etc.

(v) Economic planning, such as Five Year Plans, annual budgets etc.

(vi) Economic policies including industrial policy, licensing policy, exim policy, fiscal policy, agricultural policy, taxation policy, labour policy, etc. These policies have far reaching effects on organisational environment.

(vii) Economic laws, including the companies law, business laws, FEMA, competition law, banking law, law relating to securities and stock exchanges.

(viii) Other factors including the following :

(a) Disposable income with consumers.

(b) Conditions of resource market *i.e.* money market, human resource market, raw materials market, services and supply markets and so on.

All these economic factors form economic environment of an organisation. These factors influence the performance of all organisations. These factors decide the supply of inputs, their costs, quality availability and reliability of supplies and performance of organisations.

Market or Competitive Environment : Market environment directly affects the success and failure of business organisations. The main components of market environment are as follows :

(i) Customer or client factors such as needs preferences, attitudes, values, bargaining power, buying motives and psychology and so on.

(ii) Product factors such as demand and image of products, features, design, utility and functions of products, product life-cycle, price, differentiation, and so on.

(iii) Distribution factors such as channels of distribution or middlemen, level and quality of customer service, transportation system and its costs, delivery system etc.

(iv) Promotional factors such promotional measures and promotional mix, advising and promotion media and methods and so on.

(v) Competition-related factors such as different forms of competition and competitors, entry and exit of competitors; nature of competition, and relative strategic position of major competitors.

Technological Environment : The single most important factor that has greatly affected modern business organisations is the technological environment. Technological environment is the most dynamic of all the environmental factors. It refers to the forces that help transformation of organisational resources into goods or services. It is concerned with the dynamics of product and process technology, research and development, innovations in product and processes, technological obsolescence and so on. Advancement and change in technology vitally affect the organisation's product lines, plant size and location, costs, profitability, growth and development. The main components of technological environment are as follows :

(i) Technological development, change and rate of change of technology.

(ii) Development of automatic machines operated through computers and robots.

(iii) Research and development in product and production processes.

(iv) Search and use of new sources of energy *e.g.* automatic power, solar power, mind power and so on.

(v) Advancement in communication system and information technology *e.g.* satellite communication.

(vi) Advancement in transport system.

(vii) Advance in packaging materials and packaging system.

(viii) Development of new synthetic materials.

(ix) Research and development in bio-technology.

(x) Speed of transfer of technology between the nations and its absorption.

(xi) Cost of technology acquisition and collaboration in technology.

Political Environment : Political environment has close association with the economic environment. Political environment greatly affects the economic environment and consequently the economic organisations. The components of political environment are as follows :

(i) Political ideology of the government such as democratic, autocratic or military, socialistic or communist.

(ii) State of political development.

(iii) The degree of politicalisation of business and economic issues.

(iv) The level of political morality.

(v) Political stability.

(vi) Efficiency of the government agencies.

(vii) Extent and nature of governmental intervention in the business.

(viii) Government policies with regards to social and economic organisations.

(ix) Political parties and pressure groups.

(x) Structure of the government.

(xi) Centre-state relations.

(xii) Bureaucracy and administrative system.

(xiii) Executive and judiciary.

(xiv) Parliament and its working.

(xv) Foreign policy and relations.

Political environment has a great bearing on the growth and development of business organisations. It establishes an environment which may be pro-business or anti-business. It provides stability needed for long-term business planning.

Legal or Regulatory Environment : Legal environment is an illegal part of the organisational environment. It is closely related with the' political environment. The main components of the legal environment are as follows :

(i) Constitutional framework of the country.

(ii) Basic legal framework regulating the general law and order environment of the country.

(iii) Business laws, including the Contract Act, Sale of Goods Act, Partnership Act, Negotiable Instruments Act, Arbitration Laws and so on.

(iv) Corporate and economic laws, include the Companies Act, Banking Laws, FEMA, Competition Act, Consumer Protection Act, Essential Commodities Act, Trade Marks Act, law relating to Cooperatives, law relating to securities and stock exchanges (SEBI etc.) and so on.

(v) Industrial and labour laws including Industrial (Development and Regulations) Act, Factories Act, Industrial Disputes Act, the Payment of Bonus Act, Gratuity Act, Provident Funds and Miscellaneous Provisions Act and so on.

(vi) Pollution control laws including air, water, social, noise pollution control laws, Environment Protection Act and so on.

(vii) Judicial system and judiciary.

(viii) Taxation system and laws.

(ix) Economic policies such as industrial policy, licensing policy, foreign investment policy etc.

All these factors and forces form the legal or regulatory environment of an organisation. These factors regulate and control the working of all the organisations.

Socio-cultural Environment : Socio-cultural environment influences all organisations. It is the environment of society as a whole. It consists of the following factors :

(i) Demographic characteristics such as population, its density and distribution. Composition of population such as male, female, age, class, caste, education religion etc.

(ii) Degree and rate of urbanisation, rate of rural-urban mobility, income distribution.

(iii) Social values and beliefs.

(iv) Social and religious organisations and their impact on society.

(v) Social traditions, customs and conventions.

(vi) Cultural heritage.

(vii) Family structure and changes in it and family values.

(viii) Standard literacy and education.

(ix) Level of general awareness and consciousness of rights.

(x) Work culture and ethics of members of society.

(xi) Changing life-style and patterns and materialism in society.

Thus, social and cultural environment is the social and cultural fabric that affects organisations and their members.

Customs, traditions, beliefs, value system etc. mostly affect the organisations. With the change in social and cultural environment, life-style and needs of the people change. Therefore, new products appear and new managerial challenges evolve.

Historical Environment : Historical environment consists of the events, thoughts, work-practices etc. that have taken place in the past. Historical environment also influences all the organisations. Past events, thoughts, practices always influence the future organisations. Hence, social or racial clashes, wars, political instability, administrative styles, industrial, social and political movements in the past are likely to influence the future organisations.

Natural or Physical Environment : Natural or physical environment is created by geographical, ecological and physical factors. Weather, climatic conditions, topographical factors, geographical location, natural resources such as mountains, rivers, sea and coastal area, oil and other minerals, live stock, water-level, level of pollution etc. are the major factors that form the natural or physical environment. All these factors and their combinations affect all the organisations.

International Environment : The international environment is very important in the era of globalisation. It mainly affects the organisations engaged in internal business. International environment is the result of the relationship between the countries and their trade policies. Sound international environment may lead to increased flow of capital, technology and other resources, goods and services between the countries.

Managers need to scan and analyse organisational environment.

7

Controlling and Directing

The third step or function in the management process is directing. Planning and organising functions lay the foundation for directing function. Once the plans have been formulated, the organisation structure has been designed and competent personnel have been assigned the task and authority, the function of directing starts. It emphasises working with people by guiding, motivating, leading, communicating and supervising the subordinates with a view to achieve organisational objectives efficiently and effectively.

The Concept

Directing is the process of initiating action according to some plan. It is the process of guiding, supervising, motivating, leading and influencing people for accomplishment of organisational objectives.

According to Haimann, "Directing consists of the processes and techniques utilised in issuing instructions and making certain that operations are carried on as originally planned."

In the words of Koontz and O'Donnell, "Direction is a complex function that includes all those actions which are designed to encourage subordinates to work effectively and efficiently in both the short and long run."

According to Ernest Dale, "Direction is telling people what to do and seeing that they do it to the best of their ability."

In the opinion of Urwick and Brech, "Directing is the guidance, the inspiration, the leadership of those men and women that constitute the real core of the responsibilities of management."

According to Marshall E. Dimock, "The heart of administration is the directing function which involves determining the course, giving orders and instructions, providing the dynamic leadership."

Directing

Thus, directing is the process of guiding, instructing, motivating, influencing and leading subordinates with a view to achieve organisational objectives efficiently and effectively. It includes issuing of orders, explaining procedures to the subordinates and seeing that they do their tasks to the best of their ability.

Characteristics/Features of Directing : The nature or function of directing has been discussed in the following features/ characteristics :

A Function of Management : Directing is one of the most important functions of management. Marshall Dimock calls it the 'heart of administration (management)'. In fact, it is an indispensable function of management because it is concerned with initiating, mobilising, influencing and integrating human resource of the organisation.

Pervasive Function : Directing is all pervasive function. It is performed by all the managers at every level of the organisation. However, the amount of time and effort spent on directing varies by the level of managers.

Continuous Process : Directing is a continuous or on-going process. It is not a one-time activity or one-shot action. A manager never ceases to direct, guide, teach, coach and supervise his subordinates. *[Haimann]*Every manager has to guide, supervise, motivate or lead his subordinates continuously.

Integrating and Connecting Function : Directing is an integrating and connecting function between the other functions of managerial process. *[Haimann]*

Dynamic Function: Directing is a dynamic function. The style of directing depends on the level of subordinates and prevailing circumstances.

Two-fold Objectives : Directing function has two-fold objectives :

(i) To accomplish organisation objectives, and

(ii) To develop managers. Thus, directing aims at not only to accomplish objectives but also to develop future managers.

Performance-oriented : Directing is the process around which all performance revolves. It is the essence of operations. . . . *[Haimann/*Without proper direction, no task can be effectively performed. It is essential for effective performance of tasks.

Wide Scope : Directing consists of many activities and processes. It consists of issuing orders and instructions, explaining procedures to the subordinates. It involves motivating and leading subordinates and seeing that they do their tasks to the best of their abilities.

Core of Human Relations : Directing is the core of human relations at work. It deals with interpersonal human relationships at work. Therefore, sometimes, it is also referred as the 'people' function of management. It involves the study and influencing the human behaviour and relations.

Communication based Function : Directing is founded upon communication system. In the absence of effective communication system, directing function can never be performed.

Importance of Directing : Marshall E. Dimock has very rightly stated that "the heart of administration is the directing function. . . ."

Without directing, management process remains incomplete. It is wrong to assume that good planning and good organising will automatically result in the subordinates performance of the assigned duties. The function of directing deserves equal attention along with other functions. Haimann has observed that "In order to make any managerial decision really meaningful, it is necessary to convert it into effective action which the manager accomplishes by directing." Briefly, the importance of directing is discussed in the following points :

To get the Things Done : Directing is essential to get the things done through others. Without proper guidance, instructions, supervision, motivation, no manager can get the things done as per plans. Theo Haimann has rightly observed that "nothing happens until and unless the car is put into gear and accelerator depressed. Without the issuance of directives, without guiding and overseeing subordinates, nothing or at best very little would be accomplished."

To Initiate Action : Directing initiates action. Through direction managers motivate and influence subordinates to initiate action for accomplishing the objectives. All resources will be utilised only when action is initiated. Planning, organising and controlling functions can be effectively performed when work is initiated through directing.

To Execute Plans and Decisions : In order to execute plans and decisions, directing is essential. Without effective directing, no plan or decisions can be effectively executed. Faulty directing can nullify the effects of best plans and sound decisions.

Helps Achieve Coordination : According to Haimann, "Coordination is a necessary by-product of good managerial directing." In fact, effective direction contributes in coordinating activities in organisation. Directing is one of the techniques of coordination.

Helps Develop Managers : One of the basic objectives of directing is to develop future managers. Through directing, managers constantly coach, counsell, guide and advise their subordinates. This practice helps develop efficient future managers.

Helps Achieve Objectives : Directing helps achieve objectives effectively. Through direction, managers can integrate the individual objectives with organisational objectives. This ultimately helps in accomplishing organisational objectives.

Facilitates Management of Change: Usually employees resist change. But through proper directing, employees can be induced to accept change pleasantly.

Creates Work Environment: Directing is important for creating work environment. Through proper directing, managers can mobilize and motivate employees and influence their behaviour. Hence, they are able to create work environment in the organisation.

Motivates Employees : Through proper direction, managers can motivate employees. In the process of directing, managers can deal with many physical and psychological problems of employees and motivate them.

Stability and Growth of the Enterprise : Effective directing means effective supervision, communication, motivation and leadership. These all contribute to the growth and stability of the enterprise.

Irreplaceable Function : The function of directing is irreplaceable. There is no substitute of directing. Even computer-aided work procedures cannot substitute directing. It shall always remain an irreplaceable function of management.

Essentials for Effective Directing : Following are some of the basic principles of directing :

Principle of Directing Objective : This principle states that subordinates should be given clear understanding the objective of directing. Moreover, subordinates should also be made known of their roles in accomplishing the objectives.

Principle of Harmony of Objectives : This principle states that for effective directing, there should be harmony of individual objectives and organisational objectives. A good directing system should encourage fulfilment of individual objectives while at the same time contributing to the achievement of organisational objectives.

Principle of Unity of Command : This principle states that a subordinate should receive orders and instructions from only one superior. A subordinate should have reporting relationship to a single superior. In other words, a subordinate should be accountable to only one superior. It is necessary because no one can serve two bosses at the same time.

Principle of Direct Supervision : This principle states that managers should, as far as possible, ensure direct supervision.

Moreover, objective methods of supervision should be supplemented by direct personal supervision. *[Koontz and O'Donnell]*

Through direct supervision, superiors can better communicate with other subordinates. Moreover, they can view the problems first-hand and receive suggestions from the subordinates immediately.

The Principle of Leadership Style : This principle states that effective leadership is essential to effective directing. Therefore, managers should adopt an appropriate style of leadership to ensure effectiveness of direction. Managers should vary the leadership style appropriately. The leadership style that is effective for one environment may not be effective for another environment. Hence, manager should adopt an appropriate style in order to illicit desired response from the subordinates.

Principle of Communication : This principle states that sound two-way direct communication system should be maintained to ensure effectiveness of directing. It will provide free flow of ideas, information, suggestions, complaints and grievances between superior and his subordinates.

Principle of Motivation : This principle states that for effectiveness of directing, a manager must motivate his subordinates. A manager should devise and use proper techniques to satisfy the physiological and psychological needs of his subordinates. Satisfied subordinates are ready to accept orders and instructions voluntarily. Hence, managerial task of directing becomes effective and easier.

Principle of Individual Contribution : This principle emphasises that manager should try to maximise individual contribution to the attainment of objectives. Therefore, directing should aim at maximising individual contribution.

Principle of Participation : This principle states that directing can be more effective if manager ensures participation of his subordinates in the process of directing. Therefore, a manager should solicit and consider ideas, opinions, views and suggestions of the subordinates before directions are issued.

Principle of Informal Relations : This principle requires that for effective directing, a manager should develop informal relations with his subordinates. A manager should, therefore, promote and recognise informal groups and their leaders. Informal relations can increase the effectiveness of directing because it is easier to secure cooperation of people through such relations.

Principle of Appropriate Techniques : This principle states that a manager should select and use appropriate techniques of directing. The selection of techniques should be based on the nature of task and the prevailing situation. The technique of supervision should be appropriate to the person supervised and the task performed.

Principle of Follow-up : This principle requires that a manager should follow-up the directing process and make necessary changes in it wherever necessary. It means that directing is a never-ending process. It involves constant coaching, counselling, advice, supervision, and helping the subordinates in their respective activities. This requires continuous follow-up and feed back.

Scope/Elements/Components/Techniques of Directing : The main elements or components or techniques of directing are as follows :

1. Issuing orders and instructions,
2. Supervising,
3. Motivating,
4. Leading, and
5. Communicating

Issuing Orders and Instructions : The first and foremost step in the process of directing relates to the issuing of orders and instructions. A manager is required to issue orders and instructions to initiate, modify or stop any action. These are necessary to ensure proper performance of activities necessary to accomplish organisational objectives.

An order or instruction is, in fact, conveys a decision of a manager. Therefore, the order or instruction must be properly issued. A good instruction should have the following features or essentials :

(i) It should be clear and unambiguous.

(ii) It should be simple and easy to understand.

(iii) It should be brief, concise and complete.

(iv) It should be reasonable and enforceable.

(v) It should be logically convincing and acceptable.

(vi) It should be compatible with the organisational objectives, policies and rules.

(vii) It should, as far as possible, be in writing.

(viii) It should be properly drafted or worded.

(ix) It should be able to secure cooperation.

(x) It should specify the time within or by which it must be complied with.

(xi) It should pass through the managerial hierarchy from top to bottom.

(xii) It should be backed up by feedback and follow-up action or instruction.

Supervision : Supervision is an essential element of directing process. The term 'supervision' is made up of two words : 'super' and 'vision'. Supervision, therefore, means overseeing by some superior of the subordinates at work. Every superior (manager) has to see that his subordinates work as per plans and standards.

Thus, the supervision is the process of ensuring performance of subordinates in accordance with the plans, policies, programmes, procedures, methods, rules etc.

Though supervision is important at every level of management, it is mainly concerned with the operative level of management. A supervisor is usually a first line manager and deals with the rank and file employees. He teaches his subordinates in the ways in which their job can be best performed. He explains them the procedures, methods, rules etc. of the organisation. Moreover, supervisor also looks into the problems and grievances of his subordinates and helps them in resolving the same.

Motivation : Motivating means arousing desires and wishes in the minds of subordinates to do the best for the organisation.

It is a process of stimulating or inspiring individual and groups to do things with utmost zeal and enthusiasm.

Motivation satisfies needs and meets the expectations of the employees. It creates willingness among the employees to contribute more to their jobs. This leads to higher performance. Moreover, motivated employees can readily accept organisational changes. This all helps in achieving organisational goals efficiently and effectively.

It is, therefore, the task of every manager to motivate his subordinates. He must use financial as well as non-financial incentives to motivate the employees. He must make every effort to satisfy intrinsic and extrinsic needs of the employees in order to motivate them.

Leadership : According to Koontz and O'Donnell, "Leadership is the ability of a manager to induce subordinates or followers to work with confidence and zeal." Simply stated, leadership is the process of guiding and influencing behaviour of subordinates to work willingly for attaining objectives of an organisation.

Leadership plays a vital role in management. The quality of leadership usually determines success or failure of an organisation.

There are different leadership styles. Every manager must develop and adopt the style that can best inspire individuals and groups for higher, effective, and regarding performance.

Communication : Communication is the process of exchanging information, facts, ideas, emotions and understanding by two or more persons. It is a systematic process of conveying or exchanging, careful listening and understanding of the message.

Communication is successful only when desired response is elicited. Therefore, every manager must develop sound two-way communication system. Moreover, he must also be responsive the feedback and communications received from the subordinates.

Communication is the fundamental and vital to all managers. It is a basis of action and cooperation. Sound communication system gets ideas and instructions, understood properly, results in increased performance and morale. It helps in coordinating activities in an organisation.

Controlling

Control is the fourth and final principal element of the managerial process. This function intends to ensure that everything occurs in conformity with the plans and predetermined goals are successfully achieved. Thus, this function aims to make things happen in order to achieve goals.

Simply stated, control means checking and correcting activities in order to ensure that things occur in accordance with the plans.

1. According to Massie, "Control is the process that measures current performance and guides it towards some predetermined goals."
2. In the words of Philip Kotler, "Control is the process of taking steps to bring actual results and desired results closer together."

In the opinion of Henri Fayol, "Control consists of verifying whether everything occurs in conformity with the plan adopted, the instructions issued, and principles established."

According to Terry and Franklin, "Controlling is determining what is being accomplished that is, evaluating the performance and, if necessary, applying corrective measures so that the performance takes place according to plans."

In the words of Robbins and Coulter, "Control is the process of monitoring activities to ensure that they are being accomplished as planned and of correcting any significant deviations."

According to Robert Albanese, "Managerial controlling is the process of assuring that actions are in line with desired results."

Thus, control is the process by which managers ensure that performance is in conformity with the plans and goals. It involves setting of standards, measuring actual performance and correcting the performance if it deviates from the standards. It should be noted that function of control is concerned with checking and correcting activities of human beings and not the human beings.

Characteristics/Nature : Following characteristics of control clearly explain its nature :

Managerial Function : Control is a managerial function. It is the task of every line manager. A non-manager is not required to perform control function.

Pervasive Function : Controlling is all pervasive function. Controlling exists at every management level. *[Terry]* Every manager has to exercise control over the activities and behaviour of the subordinates. However, the scope of control varies by level of managers.

Universal Process : The elements' and nature of control process are universal. The control process remains the same regardless of the activity involved or its location in the organisation. [*G. Dessler*] Every control process involves four steps or elements: (i) Fixing standards, (ii) Measuring actual performance, (iii) Comparing performance with standards and detecting deviation, and (iv) Taking corrective action if required. All these steps are involved in every control process.

Continuous Process : Control is a continuous and never ending process. As long as organisation exists, managerial control continues to exist. It is a continuous process of setting standards, evaluating the actual performance and correcting the performance if it deviates from the standards.

Dynamic Process : Control is a dynamic process. It is not static. It involves continuous review of standards in the light of changing situations and ensuring performance in conformity with the standards. Thus, this process is subject to change with the change in the situations.

Positive and Constructive Process : Controlling is a positive and constructive process. The purpose of controlling is positive because it aims at making things happen as desired. Terry and Franklin have rightly alarmed that "Controlling should never be viewed as negative in character .... It is a managerial necessity and not an impediment or a hindrance."

Goal-oriented Function : Control is a goal-oriented function. Objective of controlling is to assure that actions contribute to the goal accomplishment. *[Robert Albanese]* Thus, control is not an end in itself. It is a means to achieve desired results.

Action-oriented : Control is an action-oriented function. It implies taking some corrective action to achieve desired performance. Mere evaluating actual performance is no control. Taking suitable action for correcting the deviation from desired performance is the essence of control. Thus, its essence is in determining whether the activity is achieving the desired results. *[Haynes and Massie]*

It is Forward Looking : Control is a forward looking. It aims at future. It not only aims at correcting the current performance but also provides standards for future performance.

Controlling and Planning are Twins : Control is one function of management and its twin is planning. In other words, controlling and planning are closely related. These functions cannot be separated. Planning and controlling may be viewed as the blades of a pair of scissors. The scissors cannot work unless there are two blades. Without objectives and plans, control is not possible. *[Weihrich* and *Koontz]*

Control not of Men but of Actions and Behaviour : Control relates to checking and regulating actions and behaviour of human beings towards organisational goals. It does not aim at controlling human beings and their freedom.

Control is not Interference : Control is not meant for interfering with others. It does not aim at reducing authority of subordinates. It is simply a means of ensuring actions of subordinates are in line with the desired results.

Wide Dcope : The scope of control is very wide. It covers all the aspects of performance leading to desired results. More specifically control includes the control of quantity, quality, time and cost. Any activity to control these four aspects of performance can be included in its scope.

Aims and Purposes

Controls are intended to serve several purposes. However, the basic purpose is to ensure actions and behaviour in line with the desired results. Briefly, the principal objectives of control are as follows:

1. To direct the activities according to plans.
2. To establish co-ordination between objects, means and efforts of the organisation.
3. To know the progress of the activities on the basis of standards fixed.
4. To find out deviations and try to remove these deviations.
5. To get the knowledge regarding quality cost and time of work performed.
6. To regularise actions and behaviour.
7. To prevent dishonesty and establish order and discipline.
8. To maintain flow in activities of the business.
9. To stop wastage and to minimise the cost.
10. To make decentralisation and delegation of authority successful.
11. To motivate employees.
12. To ensure efficient and effective use of organisational resources.

Importance of Control : Control is an important element of the management process. Without control, manager cannot complete the process of management. He cannot get the things done and achieve desired goals results. Robbing and Coulter state, "Control is important because it is the final link in the functional chain of management activities. It is the only way managers know whether or not organisational goals are being met and why or why not." Briefly, the importance of control is described in the following subheads :

Smooth Functioning of the Enterprise : According to Peter Drucker, "Control maintains the equilibrium between ends and means, output and effort." When there is such an equilibrium, enterprise functions smoothly. In other words, a sound control system ensures smooth functioning of the enterprise. It ensures achievement of long- term and short-term goals by maintaining equilibrium between ends and means and output and effort.

Managing Large Organisations : Modern large organisations have got a lot of complexities. They produce large variety of goods and services. They use automatic and computerised techniques of production. They cover vast geographical market area and use complex distribution network. Thus, their working is influenced by many factors simultaneously. In such a situation, uniformity of actions and behaviour in entire organisation can be ensured only through effective control system.

Maintaining Competitiveness : To become competitive is one thing. But to remain competitive over a long period of time is a big challenge. Maintaining competitiveness requires effective control. Through effective control, managers may use their available resources judiciously and remain competitive.

Attainment of Goals : Control is essential in order to attain organisation goals. An effective control system ensures that activities are completed in ways that lead to the attainment of organisation goals. *[Robbing and Coulter]*

Ensures Success of Planning : Control is the function intended to ensure that everything occurs in conformity with the plans. Thus, control is the essential to the success of planning. Without effective control, no plan can be successful. Terry and Franklin have rightly pointed out that "failure of controlling means sooner or later failure of planning and success of planning means success of controlling."

Facilitates Decision-making : It has been rightly said that executive decisions are primarily control decisions. Control system finds deviations in actual performance from the standard. Managers have to decide how to correct the deviations. Thus, control system facilitates managers to decide about follow up actions.

Delegation and Decentralisation : Control system is essential for the success of delegation and decentralisation of authority. No delegation or decentralisation of authority can produce desired results without proper control system. Moreover, a manager remains responsible even after delegation. Hence for meeting this responsibility, he has to control the actions of the delegate.

Effective Direction : According to Peter Drucker, "The synonymous to control is direction." It means, effective control means effective direction. Through control process management can ensure that actions are efficiently and effectively directed towards objectives of the organisation.

Promotes Coordination : Effective control system ensures unity of direction. This, in turn, ensures unity and uniformity of actions and behaviour. These develop spirit of cooperation among the employees. This ultimately promotes coordination of efforts among all employees and departments.

Enhances Motivation and Morale : An effective control system is vital to the employee motivation and morale. Controlling helps employees to do their work better, to win respect. It serves, as challenge and opportunity to improve performance. Employees never like a situation that is out of control because in such a situation they cannot predict what will happen to them. They become victims of caprice of managers rather than the beneficiaries. *[McFarland]*

On the other hand, effective control system ensures judicious evaluation of the employee efforts and adequate rewards. It safeguards them against raw-deal. Consequently it enhances employer the motivation and morale.

Ensures Discipline and Honesty : Effective control system causes every organisation member to comply the norms, rules and other standards of behaviour and action. Members are not under the temptation of greed of monetary and other gain for doing things violating the norms, rules etc. Thus, the disciple and honesty can be ensured to a reasonable extent. However, it should be noted that control cannot cure habitual dishonesty in all the cases. But management shall be regarded irresponsible if it does not make a reasonable effort to main disciple and honesty among its employees through effective control system. *[McFarland]*

Timely Performance : Control system also contributes to timely performance of activities. Predecided work schedules programmes, time-tables etc. are the controlling techniques that ensure timely performance of the activities.

Detection and Correction of Mistakes : Through control system every action and activity is evaluated against the set standards or rules or plans. Hence, mistakes or irregularities can be detected and corrected at early stages.

Promotes Economy : A Sound Control System can ensure economy in operation. It can help in reducing and controlling overall and per unit cost of production. It is possible because control system ensure efficient and effective use and elimination of wastage of resources.

Organisational Stability : Sound control system plays pival role in ensuring organisational stability. The techniques of control such as plans, policies, rules, budgets, standards or norms of behaviour can greatly contribute to the organisational stability. These can give sound foundation to the organisation and create its own work, culture and build image and goodwill in the society.

Adapting to Changing Environment : Modern business organisations work in an ever-changing environment. Products, competition, technology, consumer likings, government policies, corporate and industrial laws, employee behaviour, social and religious beliefs etc. are changing. Such a changing situation can be managed through adaptive controls. Adaptive controls enable organisations to make adjustments in their objectives, structure, functioning and means in accordance with the needs of the situation.

Process of Control/Control Cycle : Control is a continuous or ongoing dynamic process. It may involve many steps. Usually a control process consists of the following steps :

1. Establishment of standards.
2. Measurement of performance.
3. Comparison of performance with standards.
4. Taking corrective action.

Establishment of Standards : The first step in the process of control is the establishment of standards of performance. It may be noted that standards are the objectives or plans against which actual performance can be measured.

Standards may be in several forms. But they should be tangible, verifiable, and measurable. More specifically, standards should be in quantitative as well as in qualitative terms. The performance standards are generally classified into four categories :

Productivity Standards : These standards state the amount/ number of product or service to be produced during a given time period.

Time Standards : These standards state the length of time to be allowed to make a certain product or perform a certain service.

Cost Standards : These standards state the cost associated with producing a product or service.

Quality Standards : These standards set the level of perfection desired.

Behavioural Standards : These standards prescribe the desired type of behaviour of employees in an organisation.

Standards to be effective, should satisfy the following conditions :

(i) Standards should be fixed in all the key areas of business.

(ii) They should be consistent with the goals and policies of the organisation.

(iii) They should be, as far as possible, expressed in quantitative terms. Such standards can reduce subjectivity.

(iv) They should be precise and tangible so that everyone can understand them easily.

(v) They should focus on achievement of results and not on procedures.

(vi) They should be capable of achieving with reasonable effort, cost and time.

(vii) They should be flexible and capable of being adapted to changing circumstances.

(viii) hey should be set in consultation with the employees.

(ix) They should be objective and based on facts.

(x) They should include the tolerance limits *i.e.* permitted limits of deviation.

(xi) They should be levised from to time.

Measurement of Performance : The next step in the control process is the measurement of actual performance. Actual performance may be measured through personal observation, samples, reports, accounting statements etc. But managers should carefully select the methods and time measurement. Measurement methods may be quantitative as well as qualitative or a combination both.

Again the time of measurement should also be fixed with the most care. Managers should also decide a reasonable time interval for measurement of performance. It should not be so short nor so long. Too short time interval may involve too much expenses whereas too long interval may not detect deviations in performance in time.

To make measurement of performance worthwhile, it should be clear complete, precise and objective.

Comparison of Performance against Standards : The third step in the control process is the comparison of actual performance with the standards. At this step, manager finds out the degree of variation or deviation between actual performance and the standard. Where manager finds no deviation, no further action is required. Then the control process is deemed to have completed.

When deviation is found in the performance, manager has to find out the extent of deviation. If the deviation is within the tolerance limits, manager need not bother. However, if the deviation exceeds the tolerance limits, the manager's attention is needed. In such a case, manager has to take some corrective action.

Taking Corrective Action : The fourth and final step in the control process is to take correction. At this point, manager should find out the cause of deviation. If the cause is beyond the control, manager can do nothing. If the cause is controllable, manager may either (a) correct actual performance, or (b) revise the standards.

Manager may correct actual performance by (i) providing training, (ii) revising compensation plan, (iii) redesigning job, (iv) changing the strategy, (v) changing the organisation structure and so on. When he decides to take corrective action, he should take it immediately. Immediate action corrects problems at once and gets performance on track. Where the deviation has been the result of faulty and unrealistic standard, manager should revise the stand.

The above stated four steps constitute an effective control process. This control process is basic and universal. It essentially remains the same regardless of the activity involved at the level of manager.

Principles of Control : Late Profs. Koontz & O'Donnell and many other experts have laid down certain principles of control. Some of the basic principles of control are summarised as follows:

Principle of Objectives : This principle states that control must contribute to the achievement of objectives. In other words, control must facilitate the accomplishment of organisational objectives.

Principle of Standards : This principle requires that for ensuring effective control, accurate and objective standards should be established. These standards should be specific and capable of being measured. Good standards will generally be accepted as fair and reasonable by the workers being measured.

Principle of Strategic Point Control : This principle states that for effective control manager's focus should be on strategic or key points of performance. Effective and efficient control requires focus on those crucial activities or operations where variation from standards would cause greatest harm.

Principle of Efficiency of Control : This principle states that control system should be able to detect deviations quickly and to take corrective action immediately with minimum of cost. The results of the control should be worth their cost-both in monetary and human term.

Principle of Control of Responsibility : This principle holds that control should be exercised only by the manager responsible for the execution of the particular plan.

Principle of Future-directed Control : This principle states that effective control system should aim at preventing present as well as future deviations from the standards.

Principle of Direct Control : This principle states that control system should be designed to maintain direct contact between the controller and the controlled. Such a control system will ensure high quality of managerial actions and behaviour.

Principle of Reflection of Plans : This principle requires that control system must be so designed to reflect the character and structure of plans. It will help in implementing the plans effectively.

Principle of Organisational Suitability : This principle states that controls should be tailored to fit the organisation structure. Responsibility for execution of plans and for correction of deviations should clearly point out in the organisation structure. Deviations from plans can best be corrected when they are associated with specific managerial positions having responsibility and accountability for action.

Principle of Individuality of Controls : This principle states that controls must be designed to meet the needs of the individual manager. More specifically, control system should be tailored to suit the personality, quality and authority of the manager.

Principle of Control by Exception : This principle holds that a manager should be concerned with and concentrate only on exceptional deviations *i.e.* significant deviations and ignore others.

Principle of Flexibility of Controls : This principle prescribes that controls should be flexible enough to meet the needs of changing conditions.

Principle of Review : This principle holds that control system should be reviewed periodically.

Principle of Action : This principle states that control should be followed by appropriate action. Any control is justifiable if measures are undertaken to correct the potential or actual deviation from the standards or plans.

Characteristics of Effective Control : An effective control system should meet the following requirements :

Goal-oriented : A control system is effective only when it is goal-oriented. Therefore, before formulating a control system, its goals should be set and properly understood by all concerned. Moreover, everyone should be made known what is his role and expected of him to contribute to the system.

Accurate : A control system should be accurate. It must generate accurate and reliable information. Inaccurate information from a control system may cause the managers to take inappropriate action or no action.

Timeliness : Control system should be able to provide timely information. The best information has little value if it is delayed. Hence, control system should be able to receive and evacuate information quickly and timely for timely corrective action.

Objective : An effective control should be as objective as possible and not biased. It should be fair and reasonable to those about whom information is being received and evaluated.

Understandable : A control system may fail if it cannot be understood by the users *i.e.* employees. A control system that is difficult to understand can cause unnecessary mistakes and confuse or frustrate employees. *[Gray* and *Smetaser]* Difficult system may even be ignored by the employees and very purpose of the system may be defeated. Hence, a control system should be easy to understand.

Flexible and Forward Looking : The modern organisation operates in a dynamic environment where change is inevitable. Hence, control system should be flexible and forward looking. It should be flexible enough to adjust the changing circumstances. It should be able to take advantages of new opportunities and face challenges successfully. It must also keep pace with the ever-changing pattern of dynamic business world. *[Haimann]*

Economical : A control system must be economical to operate. The cost of control system should not exceed the value of its benefits. But the economy need not be exercised at the cost of effectiveness of the system. However, to minimise the cost, management should try to impose the least possible controls. It should be remembered that control should not become the end, rather control should be used as a means to achieve the objective. *[Grayson Jr.]*

Reasonable Standards : A control system should use reasonable and attainable control standards. If they are too high or unrealistic they will not be achieved and hence will not motivate employees. Some employees may even be forced to attain the standards. In such a case, they may resort to unethical or illegal short cuts. Therefore, the control system should enforce the standards that challenge and induce people to reach higher performance levels. They should never be demotivating or encouraging deception . *[Robbins and Coulter]*

Strategic Point Control : Management cannot control everything that happens in an organisation. Hence, managers should focus on those points or factors that are strategic or key ten the organisation's performance. They should focus on those crucial activities and operations where variation from standards would cause the greatest harm. *[Robbins Coulter]*

Consistent to Organisation Structure : A control system should be consistent with the organisation structure. It should be consistent with organisation's activity relationship as well as with the authority relationships. In other words, flow of information for control system should correspond with the organisational relationships. Only such a system can determine who controls what, who provides information, who will control whom and so on.

Emphasis on Exception : A control system should be based on exception principle. This principle states that managers should concentrate on exceptional deviations from the standard. It is due to the fact that managers cannot control all the activities. Hence, managers should concentrate on the exceptional deviations or the significant deviations in performance from the standards.

Multiple Criteria : A control system should contain multiple criteria of control. It means that it should include quantitative as well as qualitative criteria of control. Such criteria are more logical and objective. They are more difficult to manipulate. They promote more accurate evaluation of performance.

Corrective Action : An effective control system not only helps to detect deviation from the standard but also suggests the actions to be taken to correct the deviation. Thus, an effective control should be able to point out the defect and specify the corrective act.

Participation : In order to formulate an effective control system, participation of all concerned should be ensured. In other words, control system should be a joint effort of the manager and his subordinates. Proper participation can greatly influence the success of control system.

Suitability : It is a matter of fact that every organisation is different in its size, operations and needs. Hence, the system and techniques of control will differ from organisation to organisation. Moreover, the system and techniques will also differ from level to level in the organisation. Hence, control system should be designed and tailored to suit the needs of a particular organisation.

Self-control by Sub-systems : A control system should within it have a self-control system for each sub system or department. If a department can have its own control system, much of the detailed controls can be handled within the department. These departments with self-control can then be tied together by the overall control system. *[Joseph L. Massie]*

Direct Control : A control system should be designed to maintain direct contact between the controller and the controlled. Even when there are number of control systems provided by staff specialists, the supervisor at the first level is still important because he has direct knowledge of performance. *[Joseph L. Massie]*

Human Factor : Every control system involves human beings and hence affected by human factors. Hence, a technically well designed control system may fail if human and psychological factors are ignored. Hence, the physiological and psychological factors of human beings (*i.e.* needs of human beings) should be considered while formulating a control system.

It should consider and give allowance to the factors which cannot be controlled.

The system should watch the means used to achieve the ends.

The control factor should be an effective **feedback** mechanism.

Techniques of Control : A plethora of techniques are used in controlling operations of in organisation. A few important techniques are as follows :

Conventional Techniques

1. Personal observation, 2. Setting examples, 3. Plans and policies, 4. Organisation-charts and manuals, 5. Disciplinary system, 6. Written instructions, 7. Statistical data, 8. Special reports and records, 9. Financial statements, 10. Operational audit, 11. Break-even analysis, 12. Standard costing, and 13. Budgets/ Budgetary Control.

Modern Techniques

1. Return on investment, 2. Management audit, 3. Management information system, 4. Zero-base budgeting, and 5. PERT/CPM.

Personal Observation : Personal observation technique is the oldest and most important technique of control. Under this technique, managers occasionally visit personally the subordinates at work place and observes their performance. If they find any deviation, give instructions on the spot. Personal observation is important because it permits first-hand evaluation of work. But control through personal observation is time consuming and busy managers cannot find enough time to inspect personally. However, it should be noted that there is no substitute for direct personal observation and contact. *[Haimann].*

Setting Examples : It is the old saying that "example is better than precepts." Some managers follow this saying and put good examples of performance before subordinates and expect the same from them. Examples set by managers become the norm of behaviour for the subordinates. For instance, if a manager sets the example of punctuality, his subordinates tend to follow the same easily. Thus, behaviour and actions of subordinates can be controlled through exemplary behaviour of the manager.

Plans and Policies : Organisational plans include strategies, policies, procedures, methods, rules, programmes etc. These all are important tools that guide and control the actions of all the organisation members. These prevent deviations in actions and behaviour and ensure uniformity of actions and decisions. Thus, they play crucial role in controlling activities.

Organisation Charts and Manuals : Organisation charts and manuals are the documents that provide a clear picture of relationships, duties and responsibilities of organisation members. These can be used to compare performance of the members. Thus, these can serve as important control techniques.

Disciplinary System : Disciplinary system provides for reprimand, censures, criticism, disciplinary action, punishment etc. Thus, it is a negative technique of control. For minor but regular lapses on the part of an employee, reprimand is issued. Where employee repeatedly makes mistakes or where mistakes are grave, strict disciplinary action is taken. Disciplinary system can ensure control but through negative means. It is through fear and pain. It is demoralising. Hence, it does not create congenial work climate. Managers should, therefore, be judicious in making use of this technique of control.

Written Instructions : Written instructions are issued from time to time to the organisation members. These provide latest information and instructions in the light of changing rules and conditions. These may provide additional knowledge and even remove misconceptions of the members. Instructions may be issued through personal/ individual letters, circular letters, bulletin, notes etc. These are the supplementary control techniques.

Statistical Data : Statistical data are important source of control. Statistical data are collected and presented in the form of tables, charts and graphs. They are analysed in numerous ways such as mean, mode, standard deviations, regression, correlation. These data serve important role in the areas of production control, quality control, inventory control and so on.

Special Reports and Records : Special operational reports and records are also prepared in addition to normal reports and records. These are non-routine reports prepared by experts. They contain much deeper information. They are actually investigative reports. They, therefore, indicate the depth of the problem and suggest the means of correcting/solving the problem.

Financial Statements : Financial statements include the 'profit and loss account' and 'balance sheet'. These show the working and financial position of a business. These are used as techniques of control. For this purpose, financial statements of different time-periods are compared and analysed. Moreover, comparison and analysis of financial statements of different firms are also made. The conclusions drawn from such comparison and analysis are used for controlling financial performance of the firm.

Operational Audit : The audit is an effective tool of control. Operational audit relates to the internal operations of the firm. Statutory audit is more of a nature of financial operations. Some firms use internal audit with the help of special internal staff or external audit team. It provides an overall review of working of the entire organisation. It can reveal to what extent established policies, procedures, rules, work standards and methods have been followed in the day-to-day working of the organisation. These information can be used to control the operations of the organisation.

Break-even Analysis : Break-even analysis is a graphical technique of control. It is a technique of identifying the number of units of a product that must be sold in order to generate enough revenue to cover costs. Thus, it is a technique of finding out a point of break-even where total cost equals to the total revenue. Thus, this technique is useful in controlling production and sales volume in order to avoid loss. [For details and graphical presentation, refer Chapter entitled, 'Planning'.]

Standard Costing : Standard costing is a technique of cost control. Under this technique, standard costs of material, labour, overheads etc. are determined. Then, actual costs are recorded and compared with the standard costs and variances are found out. Then causes of variance are found out. Finally, measures are taken to prevent variances in future.

Budgets/budgetary Control : Budgets are used as a control device by almost all the managers. A budget is a numerical statement showing the allotment of resources to specific activities. Managers prepare various types of budgets for various activities. They include revenue budget, capital budget, expenditure budget, production budget, sales budget, master budget and so on. Budgets are used as a technique to control the concerned activity.

When budgets are used as a technique of control, it is called the budgetary control. It is a process of finding out what is being done and comparing the actual results with the related budget data and finding out the deviations and correcting the deviation. Thus, budgetary control helps managers to control the cost or use of resources as planned.

Modern Techniques : The modern techniques of control are as follows :

1. Return on investment or ROI-Return of investment (ROI) is a technique of control of overall performance. It measures the rate of return on investment *i.e.* capital employed. This technique is based on the assumption that goal of business is not to maximise profits but to optimise return on capital employed. Therefore, in this technique profit of the organisation is not taken in absolute terms but is considered in terms of capital employed. The ROI is calculated as under :

$$\text{ROI}=\frac{\text{Sales}}{\text{Total Investment}}\times\frac{\text{Net-Profit}}{\text{Sales}}$$

Managers compare rate of return between two or more periods of the organisation or of the two or more other organisations and try to reach certain conclusion. On the basis of such conclusion, managers control the activities and operations of their own organisation.

2. Management audit-Management audit is yet another new technique of control. Management audit is a systematic technique of evaluation of the working, and effectiveness of management of an organisation. It is designed to make an assessment for the effectiveness of entire management process. This audit is conducted by an independent team of expert from relevant areas. This audit is a periodic event.

The audit team collects many facts and information from office records, personal interviews with the members of organisation. It also gathers information through questionnaires circulated among the members and clients or customers of the organisation. The audit team then makes certain recommendations for future guidance of management. Management uses these recommendations for controlling the working and performance of the organisation.

3. Management information system or MIS-Management information system (MIS) is a system of collecting, processing and transmitting information needed by managers. More specifically, this system is a centre of facilities and personnel for collecting, processing, storing, transmitting information needed for managing an organisation. Managers use these information for planning, decision-making as well as for controlling the activities of the organisation. In this way MIS is a technique of control.

4. Zero-base budgeting or ZBB-Zero-base budgeting is a new approach to budgeting and used as control technique. It is a budgeting technique which does not consider figures of previous period or year while preparing a budget. It prepares budget afresh without considering the figures of earlier year or period. It takes into account the needs of the activity. Therefore, manager has to justify his entire budget on the basis of facts of the prevailing situations. Such a budget can control the activities in the light of current situations or conditions.

5. PERT/CPM-PERT and CPM are network techniques that are also used in controlling the actions and performance. PERT stands for "Programme Evaluation and Review Technique" and CPM stands for "Critical Path Method". Though these techniques differ slightly, they are based on the same principle.

PERT/CPM is technique of scheduling complex projects involving many activities. In this technique, a network diagram is prepared that displays the sequence of activities needed to complete a project and time and cost associated with each activity. Thus,

PERT not helps in planning the schedule of a project but also helps managers to monitor and control progress of the project, identify possible obstacles, and shift resources as necessary to keep the project on schedule. Thus, with a PERT/CPM a manager can ensure control of complex projects.

Difficulties in Control : Though control is essential for better performance and maintenance of good standards, there are certain limitations also. Some of the limitations are discussed below :

1. Difficulty in setting standards-There are many areas in the context of a business where measurable standards of performance just cannot be set. Importance among such areas are employee morale, customer reaction, and research and development. In the absence of these, control function becomes less effective.
2. Difficulty in qualification-Sometimes standards cannot be fixed in terms of quantity. Hence, control becomes even more difficult.
3. Influence of external factors-There may be an effective control system but external factors which are not in the ambit of management may have adverse effect on the working. These factors may be government policy, technological changes, change in fashion, etc. The influence of these factors cannot be checked by the control system in the organisation.
4. Expensive-The control system involves huge expenditure on its exercise. The performance of each and every person in the organisation will have to be measured and reported to higher authorities. This requires a number of persons to be employed for this purpose. If the performance cannot be quantitatively measured then it will be observed by the superiors. The exercise of control requires both time and effort.
5. Opposition from subordinates-The effectiveness of control process will depend upon its acceptability by subordinates. Since control interferes with the individual actions and thinking of subordinates they will oppose it. It may also increase the pressure of work on subordinates because

their performance is regularly monitored and evaluated. The factors are responsible for the opposition of controls by subordinates.

6. Difficulty in pin-pointing responsibility—Control process is concerned with identifying the factors responsible for deviations. But, in modern times, it is difficult to do so, because a number of persons are concerned with the performance of a single job. To the extent it is so, control is weakened.
7. Time consuming-There are cases when control becomes time consuming exercise. It is due to the nature of techniques used and the work itself.
8. Limits of corrective action-Sometimes deviations are found but no corrective action is possible. Sometimes, corrective action cannot be taken quickly and damages cannot be controlled.

8

Concept of Organisation

Unlike 'management' the term 'organisation' has also been used in a number of ways. Broadly speaking, the term 'organisation' is used in two different senses: as a process and as a structure of relationships.

A Process

Organisation is treated as a dynamic process and a managerial activity which is essential for planning the utilisation of the company's resources plant and equipment materials, money and people to accomplish the various objectives. To coordinate the employee's activities in an orderly and efficient manner is very essential for bringing unity and harmony of their efforts in the pursuit of common objectives. The definitions of organisation provide by Allen, Theo Haimann, Koontz and O'Donnell, Oliver Sheldon and G.E. Milward, etc. can be can be classified under this grouping viz.

According to Allen an organisation may be defined, "as a process of identifying and grouping the work to be performed, defining and delegating responsibility and authority and establishing relationship for the purpose of enabling people to work most effectively together in accomplishing objectives."

According to Harold Koontz and O'Donnell, "Organising involves the grouping of activities necessary to accomplish goals and plans, the assignment of these activities to appropriate departments and the provision for authority delegation and coordination."

According to Prof. Haimann, "Organisation is a process of defining and grouping the activities of the enterprise and establishing the authority relationship among them."

Organisation as a Framework of Relationship : Organisation refers to the structure of relationship and among position jobs which is created to achieve certain objectives. The definitions of Henery, UrDavis, Mooney and Reily, Chester Barnard and Bakke, etc. come under this group, for example:

According to Mooney and Reily, "Organisation is the form of every human association for the attainment of a common purpose."

In the words of Chester Barnard, "A system of cooperative activities of two or more persons is called organisation."

Thus, from the above definitions, it may be concluded that the organisation is the mechanism developed by management to unite the efforts of the people (employees) in order to realise the set objectives.

Basic Elements/Steps/Features of an Organisation : The following are the salient features or steps involved in organising a business enterprise:

Outlining the Objectives : Born with the enterprise is its life-long objectives of profitable manufacturing and selling its products. Other objectives must be established by the administration from time to time to aid and support this main objective. The objectives should be clear, precise and complete because the entire organisation structure is to be built around the firm's objectives clearly. By knowing and defining objectives, it is possible to:

(a) Weigh the necessity of the organisation and the possibility of its success.

(b) Decide if they harmonise with other objectives.

(c) Estimate what financing and personnel are needed.

(d) Break the objectives into functional parts to be assigned to a particular department for accomplishment.

Identifying and Enumerating the Activities: After the objective is selected, management has to identify the total task involved and its break up into closely related component activities that are to be performed by an individual or division or a department. All functions of a similar type are separated and concentrated into four basic functional departments—finance, sales, production and accounting.

Assigning the Duties: When activities have been grouped according to similarities and common purposes they should be assigned to a particular department. Within the department, the functional duties should be allotted to particular individuals.

Defining and Granting the Authority: The authority and responsibility should be well defined and should correspond to each other. A close relationship between authority and responsibility should be established. For establishing a sound and effective organisation structure, the delegation of authority is essential.

Creating Authority Relationship: After assigning the duties and delegation of authority, the establishment of relationship is done. It involves to decide who will act under whom, who will be his subordinates, what will be his span of control and what will be his status in the organisation. Beside this formal relationship, some informal organisation should also be developed. This organisational relationship is very important, Peter F. Drucker aptly opines— "An institution is like a tune, it is not constituted by individual sounds but by the relations between them."

From the above discussion it is clear that the nature of an organisation is two-fold:

(i) First, it is a process of coordination of employees activities in an orderly manner. In this way it is a managerial job. It specifies how work or duties shall be divided among the departments in the company, the policies to be followed while accomplishing the work, who is to do the work, the scope and limits of responsibilities, the relationship of one job to another, etc.

(ii) Secondly, it is a framework of interior relationships. It defines the relationship between person to person, position to position, job to job and so on. It specifies the orderly channels of communications between the various levels of responsibilities in an enterprise. It defines their authority and responsibility in a formal manner.

The Significance

The importance of a sound organisation for any enterprise can hardly be over- emphasised. It is the edifice of managerial success. An organisation is definitely the backbone of management through which operations of an enterprise are run. It sets the relationship between people., work and resources to get productive results. Without good organisation, a one-man enterprise cannot successfully grow beyond the limits of the owner's strength and ability. As a matter of fact, a good organisation can contribute greatly to the continuity and success of an enterprise. A good organisation brings in functions, encourages specialisation, motivates the workers and makes ways through internal friction and lost friction and lost motion; it fails to retain and develop good men and invite into its membership new men of high quality.

Kenneth C. Towe opines, "A sound form of an organisation is the answer to every business problem; that a poor organisation could run a good product into the ground and that a good organisation with a poor product could run a good product to the market."

In the same way, explaining the significance of the organisations, the world famous industrialist of USA, Mr Andrew Carnegie once said, "Take away all our money, our great works, our mines and cock ovens but leave us our organisation and in a few years, I shall have re-established myself." Really, there is no substitute in the whole world for a good organisation.

Significance of the organisation in any institution may be discussed as below:

It Facilitates Administration and Management: An organisation is an important and the only tool to achieve enterprise goals set by administration and explained by management. A sound organisation helps the management in a number of ways. It increases their efficiency, avoids delay and duplication of work, increases managerial efficiency, increases promptness, motivates employees to perform their responsibility. That's why in advanced and modern business units, an Organisation Analysis Unit is established separately in order to improve the organisational structure of the enterprise.

It Helps in the Growth of an Enterprises : Without an organisation, an enterprise is just like a man without a body, leaving head and mind (Management & Administration) only. Good organisation contributes greatly to the continuity and success of the enterprise. It contributes to the growth, expansion and diversification of the enterprise. All such programmes can be successful to the extent the organisation structure permits.

It Ensures Optimum Use of Human Resources: It establishes persons with different interests skills, knowledge and viewpoints. A sound organisation brings harmony in their efforts, places right persons in the right positions, improves the communication network and motivates the employees to contribute their best to the goals of the enterprise.

It Stimulates Creativity: A sound and well conceived organisation structure is the source of creative thinking and initiation of new ideas. Delegation of authority provides sufficient freedom to the supervisors at different levels. It develops a sense of responsibility in them and provides a recognition of their competence and expertise.

Use of Improved Technology: A good organisation provides for optimum use of technological improvements. It accommodates new ideas in respect of organisational relationships while retaining its basic structure. It provides for the use of new automatic techniques of production, control devices and data processing, etc.

Coordination in the Enterprise: In a good organisation, the different departments perform their functions in a closely related manner. Different jobs and positions are welded together by structural relationship of the organisation, the organisational pressures exert their due and balanced emphasis on the coordination of various activities.

Executive Development: The pattern of an organisation structure has strong influence on the development of executives. Managers at different levels are continuously trained, developed and tested for assuming greater responsibilities and meeting new challenges of managerial positions. If an organisation is to survive beyond the life of its existing managers, there is bound to be proper management development programme in the enterprise.

It Ensures Cooperation among Workers: A good organisation promotes mutual goodwill and cooperation among workers also. It disposes of conflict between individuals and the enterprise, enterprise and the economy as a whole. It gives proper recognition to the contribution of each individual, values their cooperation, hence gaining their sincerity and loyalty. Good organisation removes red-tapism and corruption, prevents duplication of work, makes communication easier, provides a sound basis for workers participation in management.

Thus, we see that the organisation helps to improve the operations of the business as a whole. It is not simply an organising function of management, it is more than that. To sum up, it is the only means to carry out the policies and programmes of the enterprise. That is why, it is generally said that the organisation is the machinery of management for its achievement of the ends determined by administration.

Significant Rules

In organising an enterprise, it is necessary to adhere to certain basic principles of organisation, which should serve as guidelines for action. These are as follows:

Principle of Unity of Objective : An enterprise must have a clearly defined objective (or objectives). It must be realised that an enterprise is a means to an end, and not an end in itself.

As a corollary, each unit in the enterprise must have an objective which should logically be related to the overall objective. (Its contribution to the common goal.)

An organisation structure is effective if it facilitates the contribution made by all individuals in the enterprise to the attainment of the objectives of enterprise. All should contribute harmoniously to the achievement of the common goal of the business and also of the good of the individual members of the business. The common goal includes primary objectives such as, producing, selling or profit-making, and secondary objectives like job satisfaction, payment of wages, having good communication, joint consultation, etc.

Principle of Coordination: People working towards a common objective must coordinate their efforts. In a typical organisation, a manager will have:

(i) a boss

(ii) subordinates, often 4 to 6 in number; and

(iii) colleagues, often of his own status.

The structure within a department is often called a chain of command, e.g., *A* is the boss, *B* is his subordinate, C is *B's* subordinate, D is C's subordinate and so on.

Each superior (or boss) in the chain of command is responsible for coordinating the work of those under him and his own efforts. The work of others on his level are in turn coordinated by their common superior.

One of the essentials of coordination is good communication flow, vertically and laterally, e.g., from superior to subordinate and to people of the same level throughout the enterprise.

Coordination committees are usually formed for this purpose (e.g., General Management Committee, Budget Coordination Committee, Planning Committee, etc.).

Principle of Efficiency: The organisation should be planned so that the objective can be attained with the lowest possible cost, which may be either money cost or human costs or both.

Principle of Unity of Direction: There should be one head (or chief person) and one plan of action for each group of activities having a common objective and everyone must work in accordance with the plan towards the objective in one common direction.

Principle of Unity of Command: Each person should receive orders from only one superior and be accountable only to him, i.e., he should have only one boss. If a person receives orders from more than one boss, the orders may conflict, thereby confusing him and often leading to conflicts arising from divided loyalties.

Principle of Specialisation: As far as possible, the work of each person should be confined to a single function. In other words, he should not be a "jack of all trades." Since this is not always possible to achieve, it is generally held that related functions should be grouped together under a common superior.

Scalar Principle: The organisation must have a supreme authority and a clear line of authority should run from that person (or group) down through the hierarchy, e.g., from the Chairman—the Managing Director—Plant Manager—Production Manager—Foreman-rank and file of employees. The more clear the line of authority (from the ultimate authority for management to every subordinate position) the more effective will be the responsible decision-making and organisation communication. This is usually called the scalar principle because the hierarchy is like a scale. The resulting hierarchy is known as the "Chain of Command."

Short Chain of Command: If the chain of command is short, it will enable better communication at various levels within the enterprise and cause fewer delays and bring the top decision-maker to grassroot levels (i.e., the operating personnel).

Authority and Responsibility : Should commensurate with each other, i.e., a man must have sufficient authority to fulfil his responsibilities. Conversely, if a man has the authority, he should be willing to take the responsibility for the results.

Principle of Delegation: Decision should be made at the lowest competent level. For this purpose, authority (or powers for decision-making) should be delegated as far down the line as possible.

Principle of Balance: There are various parts of an enterprise (e.g., Sales, Production, Accounts, Personnel, etc.) which functions in close coordination to meet the objectives of the enterprise. A continuous survey should be made to ensure that there is a reasonable balance, the size of the various parts should be in balance and none of the functions should be given undue emphasis at the expense of others. A continuous survey should be made to ensure that there is a reasonable balance in the size of the various departments, between standardisation of procedures and flexibility, and between centralisation and decentralisation. Imbalances between departments occur as a result of new technology, new products, new marketing plans, etc.

There should also be a balance between the principle of the span of control and the principle of short chain of command.

The application of principles and techniques must be balanced in the light of overall effectiveness of the structure of the enterprise in meeting its objectives.

Principle of Change: Change is one unchanging characteristics of an organisation. In other words, an organisation should be flexible and capable of adjusting to change, it cannot be rigid. It has to be flexible to take care of changing circumstances.

Federal Principle of an Organisation: The enterprise after it has reached a certain position may well be split up into a series of separate semi-autonomous enterprises, to each of which responsibility is delegated.

Types of Organisation

On the basis of relationship, an organisation may be divided into two broad categories: (i) formal and (ii) informal. Both types of relationship are necessary for any group action just as two blades are essential to make a pair of scissors workable.

Formal Organisation : A formal organisation refers to the structure of well defined jobs, each bearing a definite measure of authority, responsibility and accountability. The structure is consciously designed to enable the people of an organisation to work together for accomplishing common objectives. Thus, a formal organisation is created through the coordination of efforts of various individuals. Every member is responsible for the performance of a specified task assigned to him on the basis of authority responsibility relationship in an organisation. According to Edwing O'Stone, "formal organisation is a number of persons who systematically and consciously combine their efforts for the accomplishment of a common task."

Informal Organisation : Informal organisation refers to the relationship between people in an organisation based on personal attitudes, emotion, prejudices, likes and dislikes, etc. These relations are not developed according to procedures and regulations laid down in the formal organisation. Generally, large formal groups give rise to small informal groups. These groups are not pre-planned but they develop automatically within an organisation. In the words of Bernard, "an organisation is informal when the aggregate of interpersonal relationships are without conscious joint purpose."

Informal organisation is very important in all enterprises. It brings cohesiveness to formal organisation. It brings to the members of a formal organisation a feeling of belonging, of status, of self-respect and of gregarious satisfaction. Informal organisations are important means of maintaining the personalities of the individual against certain effects of formal organisation which tend to disintegrate personalities. An informal organisation is created because of limitations of a formal organisation. Sometimes to keep a personnel, who is indispensable for the organisation, the changes are brought in the formal organisation. Sometimes new departments and sections are created for such a personnel.

Positive Aspects

Sense of Belonging: In a formal organisation, there is lack of sense of belongingness and personal satisfaction, but an informal organisation fills this void by constantly emphasising and reinforcing each members individual personality and self-image.

Value for Emotional Problems: In the daily work routine there are many opportunities for tension and frustration. In such situations a worker seeks a sympathetic ear of a friend in the informal group who can share and understands his troubles.

Aid on the Job: In case of accidents or illness, members of an informal group help one another. They may protect one another from authoritative action. They may increase group's efficiency by changing work assignments or by increasing the specialisation of their task beyond what is prescribed in the job description.

Innovation and Originality: By enabling members to modify the job situation more to their liking, the informal organisation creates the necessary environment for individual innovation and originality. The individual can experiment with his ideas.

Important Channel of Communication: News travels quickly via informal groups. They are the clandestine transmitters and receivers of information before it is officially released.

Social Control: Informal groups provide all its members a set of norms or guides to correct behaviour. Members are expected to conform to those norms.

Check on Authority: Informal group forces the manager to plan and act more carefully than he would otherwise. Informal organisation is a check and balance on unlimited use of authority by a manager.

Management

Less Supervision: Informal group is self-policing. This relieves the management of much of the burden of supervision. A manager is encouraged to delegate and decentralise his authority to members of an informal organisation.

An Aid to Management: The information gives the manager much feedback about employees and their work experiences thereby increasing his understanding of what he needs to do. It also helps interpret management to the workers so that they may be more supportive. It makes up for any management failures in communication.

Negative Aspects

Following are the limitations of an informal organisation:

Resistance to Change : An informal organisation is bound by customs, conventions and culture. The organisation resists those management decisions which threaten its culture or existing relationships among the members.

Role Conflict and Sub-optimisation : In an informal organisation, everyone works towards the same objectives. But when informal groups with different interests and needs develop the quest for achieving group goals they may lead members away from the organisation objectives. Members put their own group objectives ahead of organisation's objectives. Hence, the organisation suffers.

Rumour: An informal organisation sometimes functions as a carrier of rumour.

Group Think Philosophy: Workers become loyal to their groups. They believe that what they seek must be good because the group has decided so. Thus, there develops a delusion of righteousness.

An informal organisation develops on its own, management cannot order the informal group out of existence. The logical course therefore is to harmonise it with formal organisation. A number of steps can be taken for this. Firstly, where informal rules are acceptable they should be institutionalised. Secondly, if informal lines of communication exist they should be used by management. Thirdly, informal leaders should be appointed to positions of formal authority.

Area of Influences

The term 'span of control' represents a numerical limit of subordinates to be supervised and controlled by a manager. It is an important principle of a sound organisation. This principle is based on the theory of relationships propounded by V. A. Graicunas, a French management consultant. Graicunas analysed superior-subordinate relationship and developed a mathematical formula based on the geometric increase in complexities of managing as the number of subordinates increases. But he failed to give factors which govern the actual span of control. Thus, his theory is not of much help in the practical life of managers.

Span of control or supervision refers to the number of subordinates, an executive can supervise. The concept is central to the classical theory of an organisation. Proper span of control is considered a necessity for effective coordination. The bias in the traditional theory has been that a small group is better than a large one because an executive must have intimate and direct contact with his subordinates. But in recent years the wide use of delegation and the transformation in the style of decision-making have had an inevitable bearing on questions relating to the number of people an executive can supervise.

Affective Factors : Following are the factors which determine the span of control:

Ability of the Executive: Individuals differ in various qualities like leadership, decision-making and communication. The span may be wider if an executive possesses these skills in greater degree as compared to others.

Time Available for Supervision: It is said that span should be narrow at the higher levels. This is because of the fact that top managers have less time available for supervision. They have to devote the major portion of their time in planning, organising, directing and controlling.

Nature of Work: When the spans are narrowed, the levels in the organisation increase. This involves delegation of authority and responsibility. If the work is of a routine and repetitive nature, it can easily be delegated to the subordinates.

Capacity of Subordinates: If the subordinates are skilled, efficient and knowledgeable, they will require less supervision. In such a case, the superior may go in for a wider span.

Effectiveness of Communication: If there is an effective communication system in the organisation, it favours large number of levels because there will be no difficulty in transmission of information in spite of a large number of intervening layers.

Control Devices: The span of control also depends upon the control practices being followed. Control may be followed either through personal supervision or through reporting. The former favours narrow-span and the latter favours a wide-span of supervision.

Organisational Assistance Available to the Manager: Staff functions such as training, recruiting and quality control free the managers from frustrating routine work and permit them to increase their span. Expert advice and staff assistance enables a manager to carry a greater load and handle more subordinates.

Degree of Supervisory Coordination Needed: The lesser coordination needed, the broader the span. Similarly the lesser the planning required, the larger the span. Activities like launching a new product, surviving in a highly competitive environment demand careful planning whereas activities like filing, indexing, despatching require little planning.

Geographic Proximity: The closer a work group is located physically, the larger the span. It is much easier for a manager to control the affairs of a large group working under the same roof, in one place.

Similarity of Functions: The more similar the functions performed by the work group, the larger the span. The more a subordinate's job involves unpredictability, variety, discretion and responsibility, the smaller the span is likely to be. Office managers generally enjoy a larger span of control.

It can be concluded that every manager should be expected to supervise a reasonable number of subordinates. What is reasonable depends on a variety of factors like individual differences in managers, number and capacity of subordinates, the nature of work, ease of communication, internal checks and controls, and degree of decentralisation in an organisation. If the span of control is narrow there will be more organisational levels, which in turn may impede communication, but if the span of control is widened, the supervisory load may become too heavy. Sound organisation requires a proper balance between supervisory load and organisation levels.

Departmentation means "group of activities and employees into departments." It is, as Allen wrote a means of dividing the large and monolithic functional organisation into smaller, flexible administrative units.

Departmentation, therefore, refers to the organisational device of classifying the activities or operations of an undertaking into functionalised categories. Modern enterprises tend to be larger in size and complex in technological operations. All the activities cannot be managed by a single individual or the Board in a common sweep. Therefore, departments or sections are created for all major activities of the undertaking to bring the administrative and operational functions within compact compass of specialisation and in the range of managerial convenience. The size of an undertaking may be large but departmentation solves the problem of management by compartmentalising the big-sized undertaking into manageable units based on functions, area, product or process. Hence the departmentation enables large firms also to derive the benefits of small functional organisation and at the same time softening the disadvantages that normally arise due to increasing size and diversity. Departmentation, limits the number of persons to be managed by inducting them into different departments. Thus, ensuring suitable span of control. It makes direction and control effective by confining the managerial focus to well-knit and functionally conceived units product-wise, process-wise or area-wise. Costs and revenues can be determined only if the enterprise is parcelled out into departments for administrative convenience. Allocation of duties, selection of specialised staff, fixation of responsibility will have decisive character under departmentalised organisational set-up, sharing of authority and spreading of responsibility are the underlying factors of departmentation subject to coordinating authority of the top management.

The Process : Departmentation is done through the following processes:

(a) Identification of tasks or duties.

(b) Analysis of detail of each task.

(c) Description of the functions.

(d) Entrusting the groups of functions to separate specialist heads and providing them with suitable staff.

(e) Delineation of scope of authority and responsibility of departmental heads.

Various Types : Departments can be made on the basis of:

(a) Functions, e.g., sales, production, personnel, planning, transport, etc.

(b) Products, e.g., air-conditioners, accounting machines, electronic calculators, etc.

(c) Territory, region, or geographical area, e.g., Northern Railway, Western Railway, N.E. Railway, etc.

(d) Customer, e.g., wholesaler, retailer, government.

(e) Process.

(f) Appropriate combination of any of these types.

Functionwise Departmentation : The functional structure is the most common. In most companies, unless they are giant corporations, this is the form of the organisation. The departmental heads will report to the Chief Executive. A typical department, say Production Department, will have the following structure:

Managing Director

Production Manager

- Production Planning Manager
- Production Engineering Manager
- Industrial Engineering Manager
- Maintenance Manager
- Works Superintendent

Under each of these five managers, there will be subordinate managers and under them, the subordinate staff.

The Advantages

(i) It is a logical reflection of functions.

(ii) It follows the principle of specialisation.

(iii) Maintains power and prestige of major functions.

(iv) Inter-departmental coordination is facilitated.

(v) The structure is simple, logical and easy to understand.

(vi) Provides a good means of control at the top.

The Disadvantages

(i) Responsibility for profits tends to be at the top.

(ii) There may be chances of heavy centralisation in decision-making.

(iii) Where geographical centralisation is desirable or required, this form becomes unsuitable.

(iv) This is not very suitable where product lines have to be emphasised.

(v) There is a lower potential for manager development.

Productwise Departmentation : Product wise departmentation is resorted to where specialisation is required in respect of specific products of the company. For example, a company may deal with eight or nine product lines, e.g., chemicals, drugs, foodstuffs, cosmetics, etc. and each under a separate division, e.g., Chemicals Division, Foodstuffs Division, etc.

The Advantages

(i) Places greater effort on individual product line.

(ii) Better customer service arising from greater product knowledge.

(iii) Simplifies departmentation of profitability of each product line. Responsibility for profits is at the Division level.

(iv) Improves coordination of functional activities.

(v) New department may be added without difficulty. Permits growth and diversity of products and services.

(vi) Detailed information on markets for specific products will be generated.

(vii) Extremely suitable where product lines are complex or vary greatly.

(viii) Furnishes measurable training ground for Managers. Some of the disadvantages inherent in such departmentation are:

  (i) A customer has to deal with different salesmen or managers for different products of the same company.

  (ii) Extra costs of maintaining separate sales force for each product.

  (iii) Duplication of costs on travel, etc.

  (iv) Tends to make maintenance of economical central services difficult.

  (v) Results in increased problems of the top management control.

Geographical Departmentation : Such departmentation is especially attractive to large-scale enterprise or others having activities physically or geographically spread out. Such departmentation is proper when its purpose is to encourage local participation in decision-making and to take advantage of certain economies of localised operation.

The Advantages

(i) Regional expertise is generated and managers can tackle customers or competition better. Places responsibility at lower levels.

(ii) Proximity will reduce costs of operation and administration.

(iii) Places emphasis on local markets and problems. Local conditions might warrant different types of selling. This is possible only in territorial departmentation.

(iv) Improves coordination at the regional level.

(v) Better face to face communication with local interests in mind.

Better Manager Development

(i) Involves higher costs of coordination and control from headquarters.

(ii) Results in more managerial levels which increases overhead costs.

(iii) Unsuitable for departments like Finance, where no gains are possible by specialisation on local factors.

(iv) Increases problems of the top management control.

Departmentation by Customers : Departmentation by customers places greater emphasis on the customers and distinguishes one type from the other. For example, the division could be industrial buyers, whole-sellers, government, and public undertakings, agriculturists, etc.

Some advantages of this type of structure are:

(i) Greater specialised customer service.

(ii) Where marketing channels are considerably different for various types of customers, this type of structure is very useful.

Some Disadvantages

(i) May not be enough work for certain types of customers. Hence, under employment of facilities and manpower specialised in terms of customer groups.

(ii) Problems of coordination might pose difficulties.

(iii) Unequal development of customer groups.

Departmentation by Process or Equipment : This structure is used where the machines used need special skills for operating them or have technical facilities which make concentrated location desirable. This type of structure is mainly motivated by cost and economic considerations. For example, a factory might have two processes—electrolytic and the other chemical process.

Some writers use the word 'Divisionalisation' instead of 'Departmentation' and distinguish the two words as follows:

A company has several departments, say Sales, Production, Planning, etc. When it breaks up into Divisions, each Division may have Chemicals Division and Drugs Division which are both autonomous.

The head of a Division is responsible for both production and marketing of a given product or family of products. Just below the chief executive, there is functional structure, i.e., they have functional authority over the staff in the Division—which means, the authority to recommend general policies, which acquire the force or rules if they are approved by the Executive of the Corporation.

Some companies are divided by products, e.g., petroleum, chemicals, etc. The other is geographical divisionalisation. Others may have a combination of both.

The movement towards divisionalisation comes mainly out of an interest in decentralisation of decision-making which becomes necessary because of the increasing size of many companies and the increasing diversification of their activities, both of which increases the burden at the top.

In its extreme form, divisionalisation amounts to this creation of semi-autonomous units.

A basic consideration in divisionalisation is that the output of the division should be able to produce enough revenue to cover the cost of setting it up and running it and produce a substantial contribution to profit.

In product divisionalisation, technological factors are very important.

The location of resources and customers is another important factor in geographical divisionalisation (brings production/ distribution closer to customers).

Some centralisation is necessary because production facilities are labour bound. Some advantages of divisionalisation are:

(i) Greatly reduces the burden of the top management.

(ii) Helps in fixing accountability.

(iii) Brings decision-making close to the scene of action.

(iv) Divisional Manager becomes more of a generalist than a specialist in one function.

(v) More effective performance can lead to greater profitability.

Some of the Disadvantages

(i) Division may become too independent that it may begin to work against the company as a whole.

(ii) Division may maximise short-run gains at the expense of corporate long-run goals.

Key Factors

Management in designing departmentalised organisation should bear the following factors in view for operating the entire undertaking in fulfilling the basic business objectives:

Taking Advantage of Specialisation: Division of labour should permit persons to become specialists in specific types of work. If the specialised skill and knowledge are crucial to success of the enterprise than functional departmentation becomes essential.

Facilitating Control: Departmentation should be thought of in terms of effectively regulating and evaluating the operation of the varied activities of the undertaking. It is said that departmentation makes it easier for management to measure performance and to hold people accountable for results.

Aid to Coordination: Departmentation should not create insoluble problems of coordination. Therefore departments should be created in such a way that mechanism for coordination can be built into the very structure of the organisation. There should be administrative arrangements whereby all departments report to a common authority who can take timely steps to bring in sequential or functional coordination.

Balancing the Costs: Pattern of departmentation should not imply top heavy expenditure on capital equipment, establishment, incidental expenses, etc. Certainly it will require more expenditure to organise multiple departments. But the benefits of specialisation—increased sales, better servicing, etc. expected of departmentation should outweigh the additional costs that needto be incurred.

Preparation or Departmentation: There should be sufficient preparation before departmentation is decided upon. Administrative preparation for departmentation should include a full measure of decentralisation of authority. This will enable vitalisation of the independent administrative units conceived under the departmentalised set-up.

This chapter described the basic concepts regarding organisation such as its meaning, scope, nature and importance. The important elements of an organisation are; (a) Outlining the objectives (b) Identifying and enumerating the activities (c) Assigning the duties (d) Defining and granting the authority and (e) Creating authority relationship. It also concisely described the principles of organisation and concepts such as formal and informal organisation. Formal organisation refers to the structure of well defined jobs, each bearing a definite measure of authority, responsibility and accountability. Whereas, an informal organisation refers to the relationship between people in an organisation based on personal attitudes, emotion, prejudices likes and dislikes, etc. Further it provided glimpses into important concepts of span of control and the process of departmentation. Departments can be made on basis of business functions, products, geographical territories, on customer focus, and process definition.

9

Organisational Setup

In order to make it possible for people to work effectively towards accomplishing goals, an intentional structure of roles must be designed and maintained. This is the purpose of the managerial function of organising. For a meaningful role to exist, it should incorporate verifiable objectives, an understood area of authority or discretion, a clear concept of the major activities or duties involved and a clear understanding of the relationships of that role with others, where coordination is required. To make a role fully operational, these structural requirements must be additionally provided with the required, information, wherever and however it may be obtained.

It is in the sense of a structure of roles, that a formal organisation is conceived. The connotation, implied in organising refers to the grouping of activities necessary to attain objectives, as also, the assigning of each group to a manager with the authority necessary to supervise it, and the provision for coordination, both horizontally and vertically in the enterprise structure. An organisation structure should be designed to clarify the environment so that everyone knows who is to do what and who is responsible for which results, the obstacles to performance caused by confusion and uncertainty of assigning of tasks are removed, and there is a furnished decision making communication network, reflecting and supporting the enterprise's objectives.

Concept of Organisation

According to Haimann, an authority on management, "Organising is the process of defining and grouping the activities of an enterprise and establishing the authority relationships among them. In performing the organising function, the manager defines, departmentalises and assigns activities so that they can be most effectively executed. Organisation is concerned with the building, developing and maintaining of a structure of working relationships in order to accomplish the objectives of the enterprise. Organisation means the determination and assignment of duties to people, and also the establishment and the maintenance of authority relationships among these grouped activities. It is the structural framework within which the venous efforts are coordinated and related to each other."

Characteristics of an Organisation : Organisation means several things to different people. Its meaning or connotation changes with a change of context or application. Generally, the following are considered to be the characteristics of an organisation:

a. An organisation can be construed as consisting of behaviours of a set of participants.

b. It could be equated to a network system of social and cultural relationships.

c. It could be thought of as an enterprise, such as Infosys or Tata Steel.

However, to most practitioners of management, it is a formalised intentional structure of roles or positions. An institutional structure is devised with an intent to optimise the cohesive working of people in a productive group manner. Also, every organisation is a state, a culture, a social, rational and sentient system.

Organisation Culture : The organisations culture is typically defined as the major tenets that help its members to understand what the organisation stands for, how it does things, and what it considers important. Culture can generally be deduced from what members say, do, and think within an organisational setting. Culture also involves the collective learning and transmission of knowledge, beliefs, and patterns of behaviour developed over a period of time. Organisational culture is an important dimension of the organisation's internal environment and sets the tone for managerial behaviour.

Importance of Organisation

Culture : The importance of organisational culture can be succinctly described as follows:

- It sets the tone for conduct of an organisation and establishes implied rules for the way people should behave.
- It is a powerful force in a organisation that shapes its overall effectiveness and long term success.

Determinants of Organisational Culture

- The top leadership of an organisation has a strong influence on developing organisational culture through determination of ideology to permeate everyday decisions.
- A clear vision develops a commitment oriented culture.
- Participative processes of decision making and goal setting create a culture of belongingness.

Various Types : According to Harrison and Handy, organisation culture are of the following types:

a. Power culture

b. Role culture

c. Task culture

d. People culture

Power Culture: Power culture typically has a central hub of power with functional influences emanating as spokes. In such a culture, the powerful hub exercises control through a group of key individuals. The general atmosphere is power oriented and there is a general lack of restraint for risk taking among employees.

Role Culture: Role culture works by logic and rationality. In such culture, roles and rules dominate. This sort of culture is likely to succeed in predictable and subtle operating environments.

Task Culture: Task culture is job or project oriented. This culture is cross functional with project teams made of individuals of different levels of expertise. Organisations with this type of culture often adopt matrix structure.

People Culture: In people culture, the individual is all important. In such an organisational culture, the organisation is subservient to the needs of the individuals in it. Typically, groups of professionals, such as architects, lawyers, doctors, and consultants may associate themselves with this type of culture.

Another classification of culture is provided by Deal and Kennedy. They classify organisation culture as follows:

a. the tough guy, macho culture;

b. the work hard, play hard culture;

c. the Bet-your-company culture;

d. the process culture.

This classification is typically based on the degree of risk and the speed of feedback, as major factors. It can be represented by the following grid:

Degree of Risk

	High	Low
Rapid	Tough guy,	Work hard,
	macho culture	play hard culture
Slow	Bet-your-company culture	Process culture

Organisational Climate : Organisational climate refers to the day-to-day morale of the employees. While one may have a culture stating that, "Our people are the most important part of our business", there may be certain niggles in the environment or management philosophy that can significantly lower the morale.

A research carried out at the Harvard University suggests that 50 to 70% of an organisation's climate can be traced to its leadership or management style. In other words, good managers create good climates.

Generally, most of the organisations conduct organisation climate surveys. At the organisational level, there are three strategies for measuring climate:

- By observing work in progress.
- By carrying out interviews with key members of the workforce.
- By conducting a survey of staff members, using questionnaires.

Difference between Organisation Climate and Culture

- Changing an organisation's climate can provide quick wins and boost productivity dramatically.
- While changing an organisation's culture can often be a long term activity, climate change has a short time span and the payback is immediate.

Consequences of Poor Organisation : The following administrative problems are created by organisational weaknesses:

Failure to Act: This can be caused by a failure to define responsibilities, assigning too much of responsibility, or incompatible duties, or failure to designate an alternative to act in the absence of an employee.

Delay in Acting: This can be caused by overlapping responsibilities or prevalence of committees.

Wrong Actions: This can be caused by overlapping responsibilities, overload of work resulting from inadequate delegation or improper or incomplete job specification.

Lack of Quantity of Effort: This can be caused by poor definition of responsibility, too much supervision, and uncertainty of supervisory responsibility.

Lack of Quality of Effort: This can be caused by overload of work resulting from inadequate delegation or too great a diversity of duties delegated.

Waste of Effort: This can result from failure to define targets and failure to define limits of responsibility.

Excessive Quantity of Effort: This will result from an excessive use of committees or other joint effort, overlapping responsibilities and misunderstandings of the relationships.

Excessive Quality of Effort: This results from an excessive or improper delegation, faulty definitions of responsibilities and assignment of duties, and disproportionate skills.

Ama's Ten Commandments of Good Organisation : The ten commandments of good organisation were formulated by M.C. Rorty, formerly a Vice president of International Telephone and Telegraph Corporation. Shortly after he became the president of the American Management Association (AMA) in 1934. AMA, in 1941, issued these in a commemorative form. They are as follows:

(i) Definite and clear responsibilities should be assigned to each executive, manager, supervisor, and foreman.

(ii) Responsibility should always be coupled with corresponding authority.

(iii) No change should be made in the scope or responsibility of a position, without a definite standing to that effect on the part of all persons concerned.

(iv) No executive or employee occupying a single position in the organisation, should be subject to definite orders from more than one source.

(v) Orders should never be given to subordinates by passing the executive to whom they are responsible. Rather, the officer efforts should be supplemented.

(vi) Criticism of subordinates should not be done in public. In no case should a subordinate be criticised in the presence of executives or employees of equal or lower rank.

(vii) No dispute or difference between the executives or the employees regarding authority or responsibility, should be considered too trivial for prompt and careful adjudication.

(viii) Promotions, wage changes, disciplinary action, should always be approved by the executive immediately superior to the one for against whom these are intended.

(ix) No executive or employee should be assistant to and at the same time a critic of the person he is assistant to.

(x) Any executive whose work is subject to regular inspection should, whenever practicable, be given the assistance and facilities necessary to enable him to maintain an independent check of the quality of his work.

Basic Principles

However, the ten principles of objective as enunciated by Urwick are also very popular and have been extensively quoted in management literature. These are as follows:

Principle of Objective: Every organisation and each part of every organisation, must be an expression of the purpose of the undertaking concerned, or it becomes meaningless and therefore, redundant. One cannot organise in a vaccum, one must organise for something.

Principle of Functionality: The activities of every member of any organised group should be confined, as far as possible, to the performance of a single function.

Principle of Coordination: The purpose of an organisation per se, as distinguished from the purpose of the undertaking, is to facilitate coordination and the unity of efforts.

Principle of Authority: In every organised group, the supreme, authority must rest somewhere. There should be a clear line of authority from the supreme authority to every individual in the group.

Principle of Responsibility: The responsibility of the superior, for the acts of his subordinates, is absolute.

Principle of Definition: The content of each position, both the duties involved, and the authority and responsibility contemplated, and the relationships with other positions should be clearly defined in writing and published for all concerned.

Principle of Correspondence: In every position, the responsibility and authority should correspond with each other.

The Span of Control: No person should supervise more than five, or at the most six, direct subordinates whose duties interlock.

Principle of Balance: It is essential that the various units of an organisation should be kept in balance.

Principle of Continuity: Reorganisation is a continuous process in every undertaking and specific provisions should be made for it.

Organising consist of establishing relationships (responsibility and authority) among the components (personnel, functions and physical factors) for the purpose of structuring (line, line and staff functionalised, project) and directing them towards some common objective. Thus, the elements of the organisation process are:

1. Establishing objectives 2. Determining the functions that need to be accomplished 3. Assessing personnel requirements 4. Determining the physical resources necessary to achieve the objectives (inputs) 5. Grouping the functions, physical resources and the personnel into a coordinated organisation structure 6. Assigning authority and responsibility 7. Determining the levels of accountability of personnel within the established structure 8. Determining the work activities.

Functions of Organisation : Once the objectives have been established, it is then necessary to determine the type of functions that must be performed within the organisation. A function is the work that can be identified and distinguished from other work.

The basic function or activities can be defined in any business, government or educational organisation. For instance, the major functions of a manufacturer would be production, marketing and finance.

Organisational Design : Organisation design refers to the process by which managers create a structure of tasks and authority. It is through the process of decision-making that managers evaluate the relative benefits of alternative tasks and authority structures. This process may be explicit or implicit, it may be one shot or developmental, it may be done by a single manager or by a team of managers. Structure refers to relatively fixed relationships that exist among the jobs in the organisation. This fixed relationship results from the following decision processes:

1. The total task of the unit is broken down successfully into smaller jobs. That is, the task is divided or specialised among the persons in the unit. This is the issue of division of labour.
2. The individual jobs are recombined and grouped together. A common basis for the combined job is defined to rationalise the grouping; this is the issue of departmentalisation.
3. The appropriate size of the group reporting to one superior, must be determined; this is the issue of control.
4. Authority is distributed among the jobs or group of jobs. This is the issue of delegation.

The form and characteristics of an organisation's structure vary depending upon the attributes of each of the four sub problems. Conceptually, each of the four can vary along a continuum as shown:

Specialisation ______________________________

Division of Labour:

High — Low

Basis

Departmentalisation: ______________________________

Homogeneous — Heterogeneous

Number

Span of control: ______________________________

Few — Many

Delegation

Authority : ______________________________

Centralised — Decentralised

Generally speaking, organisational structures will tend towards one extreme or the other, along each continuum. Structures tending to the left are characterised variously by such terms as formalistic, structured, bureaucratic, system and mechanists. Structures tending to the right are termed informalistic, unstructured, non-bureaucratic, system 4 and organic.

Division of Labour or Principle of Specialisation : The issues associated with division of labour are concerned with the extent to which jobs are specialised. All jobs are specialised to a degree and the ability to divide work among many job holders is a key advantage of organisations. Rather than having a book-keeper in a hospital, performing emergency room tasks, the work is divided so that the book-keeper concentrates on preparing bills, and the emergency room clerk concentrates on admitting patients.

A major decision in developing an organisational structure involves determining how much division of labour should exist. Advocates of dividing work into smaller tasks, often cite the advantages of specialisation. Two of the major advantages are:

1. If a job contains few tasks, it is possible to train replacements easily for personnel who are terminated, transferred or absent. The minimum training effort results in a lowering of the training cost.
2. When a job entails only a limited number of tasks, the employees can become proficient in performing these tasks. This high level of proficiency is reflected in better quality of output.

Departmentalisation Structures : Specialisation of labour is normally accomplished by the process of departmentalisation or departmentation. Departmentalisation is defined as the process of grouping related functions or major work activities into manageable units to achieve more effective and efficient overall coordination of organisation resources. The primary means of departmentalisation are by:

1. Function 2. Product 3. Customer 4. Territory 5. Project.

Departmentalisation by Function : Departmentalisation by function is the most common means of grouping related functions.

Departmental lines are drawn on the basis of specialised functions such as production, marketing, engineering, finance, and personnel. This assists management in efficient utilisation of the resources of the organisation. However, departmentalisation by function may create problems for management in the sense that personnel in these specialised functions may become more concerned with their own department, than with the overall company.

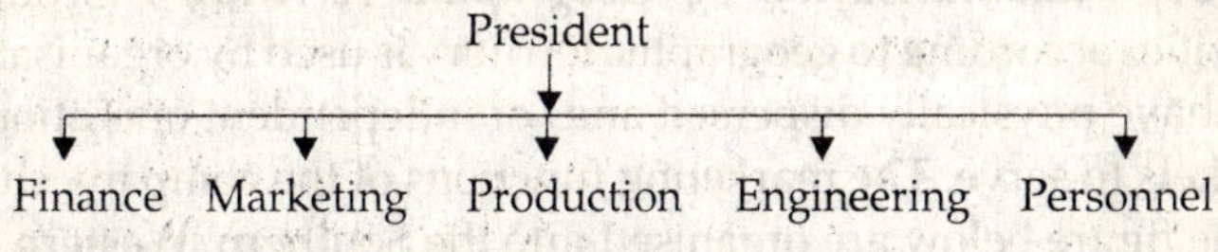

Departmentation by function

Departmentalisation by Product : This form of departmentalisation is concerned with organising, according to the type of product being produced or sold by the firm. It enhances the use of specialised knowledge of particular products or services and is often used by rather large, diversified companies. Shown below is a large electronics firm organised into three product divisions.

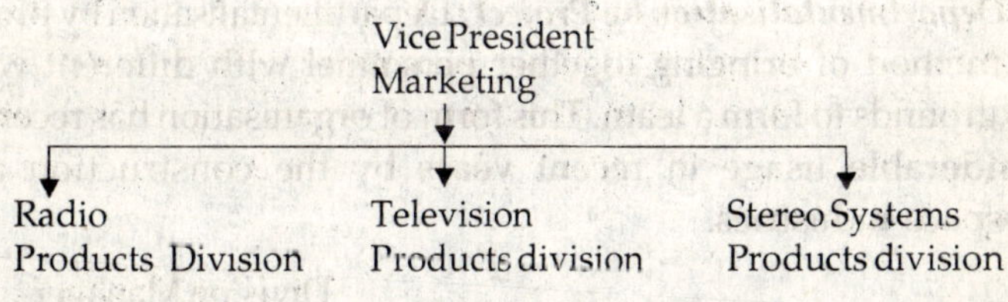

Departmentation by product

Departmentalisation by Customer : Departmentalisation by customers is used by organisations that have a special need to provide better service to different types of customers. As illustrated in the following figure, a diversified manufacturing company has an industrial, government and consumer product divisions. Large retailers and banks use departmentation along customer lines, to provide better service to different customer groups.

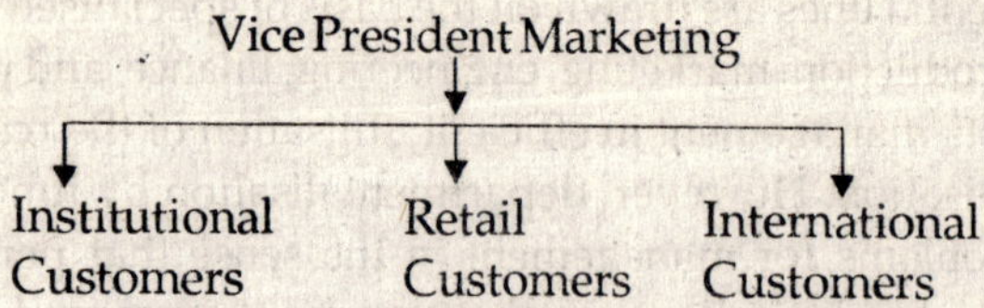

Departmentation by Customer

Departmentalisation by Geographic Territory : Grouping activities according to geographic territory is used by organisations that have physically dispersed and/or independent operations or markets to serve. The marketing functions of the company shown in the figure below are organised into the Southern, Western, and Eastern regional divisions. Geographic departmentation offers the advantages of better service with local or regional personnel, often at lesser cost.

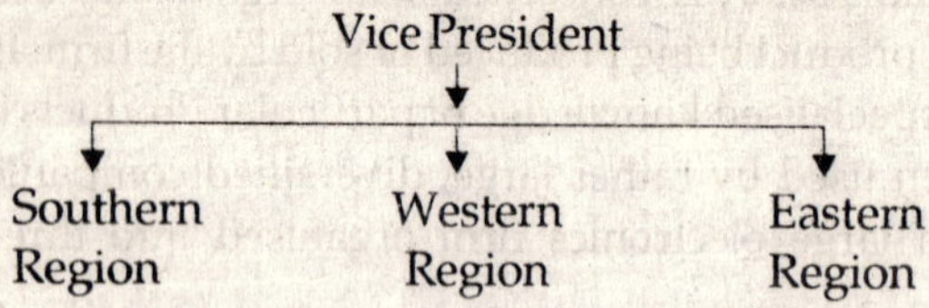

Departmentation by Geographic Territory

Departmentalisation by Project : Departmentalisation by project is a method of bringing together personnel with different work backgrounds to form a team. This form of organisation has received considerable usage in recent years by the construction and aerospace industries.

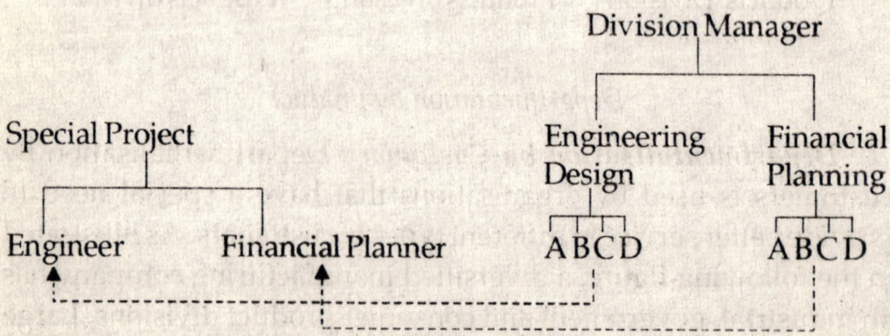

Departmentation by Project

Departmentation: A Combination Approach : Most organisations make use of several different basis for departmentation. In the example of the manufacturing company is departmentalised by type of function performed, i.e., production, engineering, marketing, etc. type of product industrial and consumer and by geographic territory.

Matrix Organisation Design : An emerging organisation design, termed matrix organisation, attempts to maximise the strengths and minimise the weaknesses of both, the functional and product structures.

The matrix organisation form achieves the desired balance by superimposing or overlaying a horizontal structure of authority, influence, and communication.

Matrix structures are found in organisations which require responses to rapid change in two sectors, viz., technology and markets, which face uncertainties, that generate high information processing requirements, and which must deal with financial and human resources constraints.

The matrix organisation arrangement can be described as shown below; personnel assigned in each cell belong not only to the functional department, but also to a particular product or project. For example, manufacturing, marketing, engineering, and finance specialists will be assigned to work on one or more projects or products namely, A, B, C, D, E and F. As a consequence, personnel will report to two managers, one in their functional department and one in the project or product unit. The existence of a dual authority system is a distinguishing characteristic of a matrix organisation. Traditional functional and product based organisations maintain a strict chain of command, wherein, each employee reports to only one superior.

Projects, Products	FUNCTIONS			
A	Manufacturing	Marketing	Engineering	Finance
B				
C				

D

E

F

The Advantages

The following are the major advantages of matrix organisation:

Efficient Use of Resources: Matrix organisation facilitates the utilisation of highly specialised staff and equipment. Each project, or product unit can share the specialised resource with other units, rather than duplicating it to provide independent coverage for each. This advantage is particularly so when projects require less than the full time effort of the specialist. For example, a project may require only half the time of a computer scientist. Rather than having several unutilised computer scientists assigned to each project, the organisations can keep fewer of them, fully utilised by shifting them from project to project.

Flexibility in Conditions of Change and Uncertainty: Timely response to change requires information and communication channels which can efficiently get the information to the right people at the right time. Matrix structures encourage constant interaction among project unit and functional department members. Information is channelled vertically and horizontally, as people exchange technical knowledge. The result is quicker response to competitive conditions, and technological breakthroughs. (and other environmental conditions).

Technical Excellence: Technical specialists interact with other specialists while assigned to a project. These interactions encourage cross fertilisation of ideas such as when a computer scientist discusses the pros and cons of electronic data processing with a financial accounting expert. Each specialist must be able to listen, understand and respond to the views of the other. At the same time, specialists maintain an on going contact with members of their own discipline because they are also members of a functional department.

Freeing Top Management for Long Range Planning: An initial stimulus for the development of matrix organisations is that top management increasingly becomes involved with day to day operations. Matrix organisation makes it possible for top management to delegate on going decision making thus, providing more time for long range planning.

Improving Motivation and Commitment: The opportunity to participate in key decisions fosters high levels of motivation and commitment, particularly for individuals with acknowledged professional orientation.

Providing Opportunities for Personal Development: Members of matrix organisations are provided considerable opportunity to develop their skills and knowledge. They are placed in groups consisting of individuals representing diverse parts of the organisation. They have the opportunities to learn something of other specialities. Engineers develop knowledge of financial issues, accountants will learn about marketing. The experience broadens each specialist's knowledge, not only of the organisation, but also of other scientific and technical disciplines.

Different Forms of Matrix Organisation : Matrix organisation forms can be depicted as existing in the middle of a continuum which has functional organisations at an extreme and product. Organisations at the other as shown in figure below:

Organisations can move from functional to matrix forms or from product to matrix forms. Ordinarily the process of moving to matrix organisation is evolutionary.

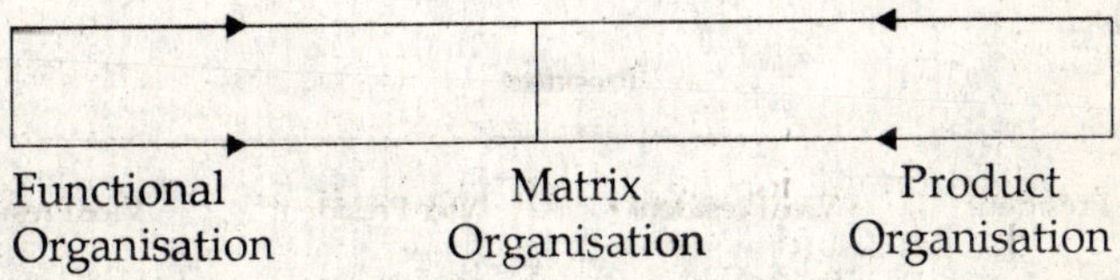

Alternative Matrix Organisation Forms

Galbraith describes the evolutionary process as moving in successive steps from task force to product management departments.

Task Force : When a competition markets a new product that quickly captures the market, a rapid response is necessary. The convenient approach is to create a task force of individuals from each functional department and charge it with the responsibility to expedite the process. The task force achieves its objectives and dissolves, as members return to their primary assignment.

Teams : If the product or technological break through generates a family of products which move through successive stages of new and improved products, the temporary task force concept is ineffective. A typical next step is to create permanent teams which consists of representatives from each functional department the teams meet regularly to resolve inter departmental issues and to achieve coordination. When not involved with issues associated with new product development, the team members work on their regular assignments.

Product Managers : If the technological breakthrough persists such that new product development becomes a way of life, top management will create the roles of product managers. In a sense product managers chair the teams, but they are now permanent positions. Ordinarily they report to top management, but they have no formal authority over the team members.

Product Management Developments : The final step in the evolution to matrix organisation is the creation of product management departments. Figure below depicts the organisation which has a product manager reporting to top management and with sub product managers for each product line.

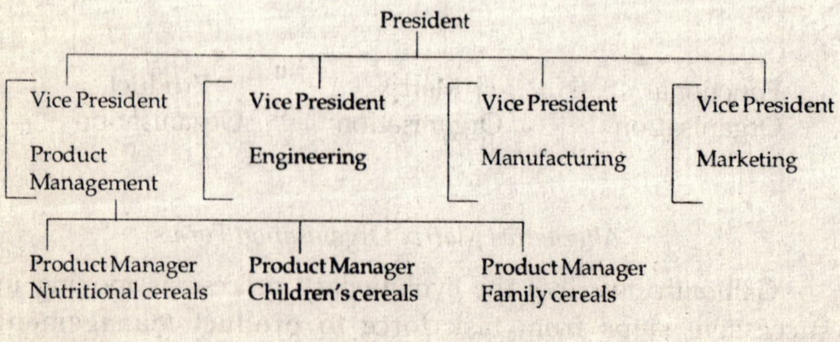

Fully involved matrix organisation

Important Factors

The following factors are to be taken into consideration in departmentation:

Specialisation: Departmentation should be such as to yield the advantages of specialisation which is the most widely recognised characteristics of modern enterprise.

Control: Departmentation should simplify the executives task of control. Departmentation should have a direct bearing on independence of checks, clear-cut accountability, telling comparison of results, or ease of supervision.

Coordination: Quite different activities may be grouped under a single executive because they need to be coordinated.

Securing Attention: An unusually important activity for the success of the enterprise should be given a special recognition in the organisation, for giving it greater attention than other activities, it may be placed in a separate division and also at a higher level in the administrative hierarchy accordingto its importance.

Recognition of Local Conditions: The departmentation should take into consideration local conditions at the places concerned.

Economy: The expense involved in creating separate departments for anyactivity is an important factor and should be kept in mind.

Assignments of Activities : In addition to select alternative methods of grouping activities into departments at the outset as detailed above, the executive is confronted from time to time with the problem of deciding where to fit in a new activity and where to shift an old one. The first need is usually that of recognising a function. A second need is that of combining function so as to realise efficient performance and balanced operation without increasing the number of management levels through creation of splinter departments. Each major department consists of a combination of subsidiary activities narrower in scope. Essential activities of purchasing, inventory control, and production scheduling may well be combining under one individual in a simple organisation. Accounting finance statistics and business economics might all be grouped under a high level controller in a large organisation.

A third need is that of developing principles where by activities may logically be combined.

Two widely recognised principles of underlying departmentation are:

(i) Similarity of function (ii) Closeness of association.

Similarity of function is useful primarily as a basis for classifying activities at the lower levels of organisation structure where duties are not yet highly differentiated. Grouping of typists into a general typing pool is an example. Salesmen, machinists, and of office workers are often grouped into their respective departments by reason of similarity of function.

The principle of similarity has narrow limitations and diversity must be coped within grouping most activities.

Charts and Titles

An organisation chart is prepared to show formal organisational relationships which are intended to prevail. It shows who supervises whom and how the various units are related to each other. It also shows the main line of communication, the downward flow of authority, and the upward flow of responsibility. It enables the top management to assign responsibility by designating different persons entrusted with certain jobs.

The assignment of responsibilities within a sound organisation structure serve several purposes.

(a) It acquaints all members of the enterprise with their own responsibilities and with the responsibilities of others whom they must deal.

(b) It permits greater decisiveness of action by restricting duplication of effort.

(c) It eliminates frictions and playing of politics.

(d) It eliminates unnecessary functions.

(e) It stimulates the execution of activities and the development of individual capacities by providing an understandable framework of authority within which to carry on the activities.

(f) It provides executives with more time for planning and policy formation by assuring them that all operating details are provided for.

(g) It adopts the "principles of organisation" to individual company needs.

To accomplish these purposes it is necessary to define the titles of members and relate them to authority and responsibility. The titles may be such as Production Manager, Works Manager, Factory Manager, Plant Superintendent, General Foreman, Foreman, Supervisor and Department Head, and should be defined and placed in their proper relationship to the whole. The title should not be changed very often. After all, titles are labels which define segment of work. They should be helpful to those out side the organisation and they should build an internal system of procedure.

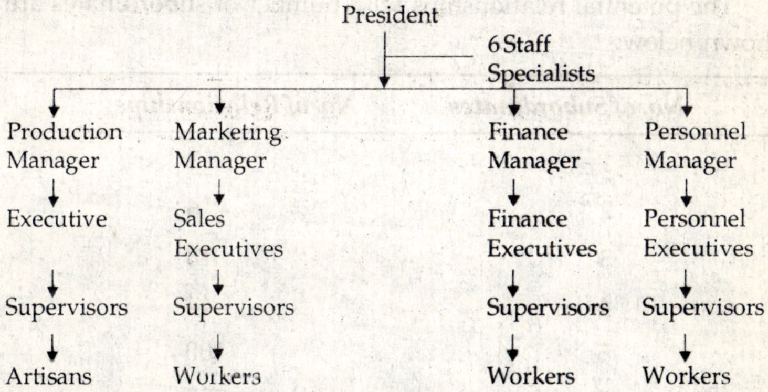

Span of Control : Span of control also called span of management supervision indicates the number of people directed or managed effectively by a single executive or supervisor. Stated differently, it refers to the number of subordinates reporting directly to a single manager who is accountable for their activities. Thus, if a general manager has 5 managers reporting to him directly in a firm employing 10,000 employees, the span of control of the General Manager is 5 not 10,000.

While there is a limit to the number of employees a manager can effectively supervise, the precise span of control varies according to the situation.

Potential Relationships Between Manager and Subordinates : The number of potential relationships between a manager and subordinates can be calculated by the formula:

R = n [2n-1+n - 1]

where, R = the number of relationships; n = number of subordinates.

The calculation assumes that the managers must contend with three types of relationships:

(1) Direct Single (2) Direct Group (3) Cross.

Thus, as shown in figure below a manager with two subordinates has 2 direct relationships, two cross relationships and two group contacts for a total of six possible relationships.

The potential relationships with number of subordinates are shown below:

No. of Subordinates	***No. of Relationships***
1	1
2	6
3	18
4	44
5	100
6	222
7	490
8	1,080
9	2,376
10	5,210
11	11,374
12	24,708

Determining the Optimal Span of Control : The practical solution to the span of control problem is to identify the specific factors which are important in a particular situation. One such solution was undertake at Lockheed Missiles and space company where a model for determining the optimal span was deviced. Following variables must be considered in establishing the span of control:

1. Similarity of functions.
2. Geographical closeness of subordinates.
3. Complexity of functions.
4. Direction and control required by subordinates.
5. Coordination required.
6. Planning importance, complexity and time required.
7. Organisational assistance received by supervisor.

Each of these variables should be assigned weights. The weighting reflect the importance of each of the variables and are summarised in the following table.

The most important variable is direction and control with a maximum weight of 15. The weight values were based on the common sense, experience and experimentation with 150 different situations in Lockheed. Every management position was evaluated, and point values for each of the variables were assigned. The values were summed and the resultant figure was termed the supervisory index. The index reflects the supervisor's burden arising from the type of work of the unit. The higher the index the greater the burden consequently the narrower and appropriate span.

Lockheed Weighting Scales

Span factor

Similarity of functions	Identical	Essentially alike	Similar	Inherently different	Fundamentaly distinct
	1	2	3	4	5
Geographic	All together	All in	Separate	Separate	Dispersed

contiguity		one building	building 1 plant location	locations 1 geographic area	geographic area
	1	2	3	4	5
Complexity of functions	Simple repetitive	Routine	Some complexity	Complex varied varied	Highly complex
	2	4	6	8	10
Direction and control	Minimum Supervision and training	Limited Supervision	Moderate Periodic Supervision	Frequent Continuing Supervision	Constant Close Supervision
	3	6	9	12	15
Coordination	Minimum relation with others courses	Relationships limited to defined controlled	Moderate relationships easily	Considerable close relationships relationships.	Extensive mutual non recurring
	2	4	6 .	8	10
Planning	Minimum Space and complexity complexity	Limited scope and	Moderate scope and complexity	Considerable effort required	Extensive effort requited
	2	4	6	8	10

Middle Management Indexes and Span of Control

Supervisory Index	Suggested Standard Span
40-42	4-5
37-39	4-6
34-36	4-7
31-33	5-8
26-30	6-9
25-27	7-10
22-24	8-11

The Lockheed study revealed that when the span of control was increased, the number of supervisory levels was often reduced.

Span of Management and Organisational Levels : The principle is that wider the span of management, the less direct supervision and the narrower the span, the greater the number of managers necessary and therefore, the higher the cost.

Tall Vs. Flat Organisational Structure : Tall organisations are costly and less effective communication. Narrow spans of management require not only mare supervisors but also the added expense of executive offices, secretaries, and fringe benefits. In all organisation decision and communication process takes longer and is of poorer quality. This results not only in inefficiency but also in demoralisation among the lower level subordinates.

Small organisations generally have a higher level of employee morale and productivity than the large organisations.

Subordinate Relationships

The scaler concept is also known as a chain of direct superior subordinate relationships throughout the entire organisation. In this regard, it seems realistic to consider the scalar concept as a series of steps which establish a clear line of authority from the top of an organisation to the bottom. Adherence to the chain of command is sometimes difficult. A continued violation of scalar relationship, may result in breakdown in coordination, a misunderstanding of managerial positions and general inefficiency. As a general guide all organisational should normally follow prescribed communication channels, however, good judgement should be exercised when time is of the essence. By passing certain managers in the chain of command may be necessary in some instances, but these managers still be kept informed through follow up communication that are initiated as soon as possible.

Unity of Command : The principle of unity of command states that no member of an organisation should report to more than one superior on any single function. The application of this principle is easy in pure line organisation, in which each superior has general authority, however it becomes a complex problem in actual cases in which some form of staff and/or functional organisation is used. In practice, instructions may be received from several sources without loss of productivity. The problem is to avoid conflicts in orders from different people relating to the same subject. The principle of unity of command may be useful in the planning of an organisation if it helps to keep relations between superior and subordinate simple and direct, it is not realistic if it is interpreted as an immutable law that would eliminate useful relationships among a number of managers.

Exception Principle : The exception principle states that recurring decisions should be handled in a routine manner by lower level managers, whereas problems involving unusual matters should be referred to higher levels. This principle emphasises that executives at the top levels of an organisation have limited time and capacity and should refrain from becoming bogged down in routine details that can be handled as well by subordinates.

The exception principle can be very useful to a manager by focussing his attention on those matters that should receive his attention first. It is applicable to all levels, and if kept in mind, can help the inexperienced manager compensate for a human tendency to concentrate on the immediate, concrete, and detailed problems at the expense of more fundamental, difficult and abstract issues.

Types of Organisation Structure : Detailed organisation structure varies widely from company to company, even in the same industry, and within a given company, especially if it is of large size, the relationships of functions and sub-functions usually under go continuing change, to conform to changes in environment, objectives, and needs. Traditionally recognised, however, there are five principal organisation proceedings.

(i) Line, (ii) Line and staff, (iii) Pure functional, (iv) Line and functional staff, (v) Committee.

Line Organisation : A business controlled under the line form of organisation may act more quickly and effectively in changing its direction and policy than any other form of organisation. Authority is passed down from the owners through a board to directors to a general manager, to whom the heads of the various departments respond. Each department in importance is a complete self substaining unit, its head being responsible for the performance of its particular process, product or function. This means that the foreman must (1) Direct its techniques, (2) Formulate the necessary work specifications, (3) Sometimes purchase materials, (4) Plan and schedule the work, (5) the necessary materials handling and (6) Keep the necessary shop cost and production records. The procedure would be repeated in all other departments with complete control centered in each head subject only to the will of the general manager, whatever little research, planning or central record keeping is required fall upon general manager.

Each department has got responsibilities and is working as self supporting unit.

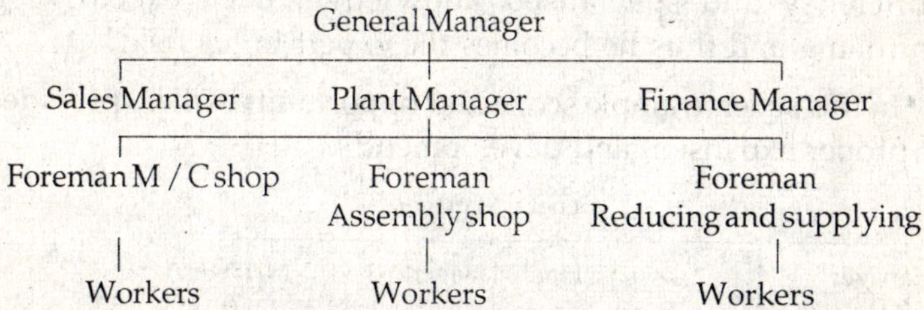

Advantages: (i) It is simple. (ii) There is a clear cut division of authority and responsibility. (iii) It is extremely stable, (iv) It makes for quick action. (v) Discipline is easily maintained.

Disadvantage: (i) The organisation is rigid and inflexible. (ii) Being an autocratic system it may be operated on an arbitrary, opinionated and dictatorial basis. (iii) Department heads carry out orders independently and often in accordance with their own whims and desires. (iv) As division of labour is only incidental crude methods may prevail because of lack of expert advice. (v) There is unique reliance upon the skill and personnel knowledge of operators. (vi) Foreman may offer resistance to much needed changes. (vii) Key men are loaded to breaking point. (viii) The loss of one or two capable men may cripple the entire organisation. (ix) Difficulty of operation occurs in large or complex enterprises.

Functional Organisation : This admits the fact, that today in any industrial enterprise, the functions of directive and controlling any business are so complex, that it is not feasible for any man, may be highly qualified, to handle the situation smoothly. Therefore, overall responsibilities of the enterprise divided according to the functions to be done. This concept was introduced by F.W. Taylor. He was in favour that all the industrial activities should be done and supervised by experts. Taylor contended that a foreman could be specialised in everything, he was expected to do. Therefore instead of having one single superior, as in the line organisation, Taylor arranged for a group of specialists to boss the workers in various aspects of the business. Office work is separated from the shop work. Thus Taylor separated the mental and clerical functions from the production functions. This type of organisation, employing the principle of specialisation is based on individual's proficiency and specialised knowledge. Each executive is controlling and thus he becomes the expert in his field.

In this scheme ample scope and opportunity will be provided for proper expansion and development:

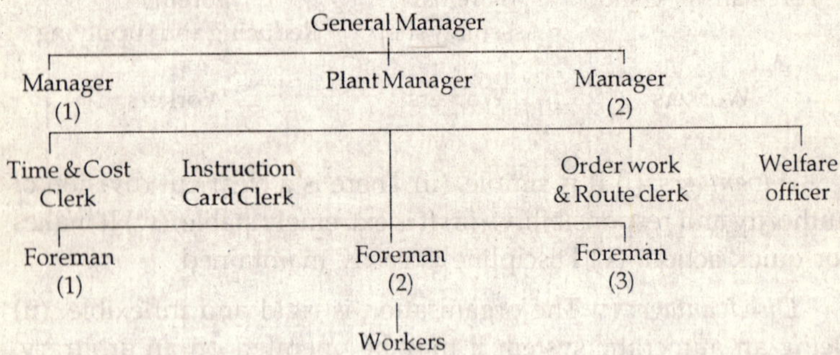

Advantages

(i) Functional organisation is based on expert knowledge.

(ii) Division of labour is planned, not incidental.

(iii) The highest functional efficiency of each person is maintained.

(iv) The manual work is separated from the mental-aspiration initiated by Taylor.

Disadvantages

(i) A relative lack of stability is manifest.

(ii) The coordinating influences needed to insure a smoothly functioning organisation may involve heavy over head expenses.

(iii) The inability to locate and fix responsibility may seriously affect the discipline and morale of the workers through apparent or actual contradiction of orders.

(iv) Overlaping authority may give rise to friction between foreman and supervisor.

(v) The initiative of supervisors may become like a stiffer man may become more automations and routine may become very complicated.

Line and Staff Organisation : The two systems which are discussed above give evaluation of third one, which has got all the good features of both. Today most of the industries in India and abroad are using this form of organisation. Individual industry may bring certain changes in the above said organisation system depending on the size of the industry and the situation.

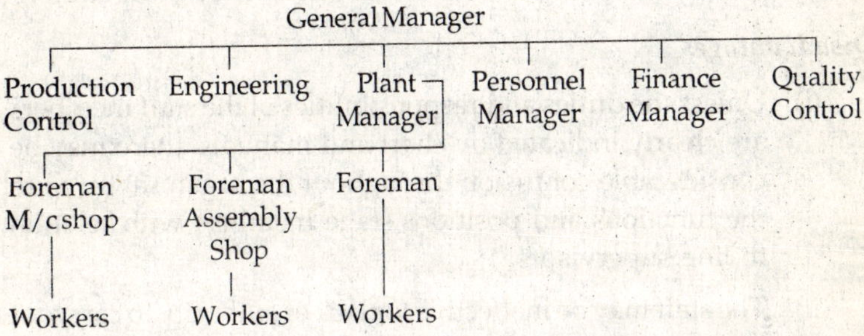

Basically it is the form of line organisation where some experts are introduced at different levels in the line organisation. These experts help in carrying out the work of line executives and thus their work is lightened.

It is very difficult to express the relationship between the line executives and staff executives, but in a very simple way the concept of the duties can be exprcssed. Line executives do while the staff executives advice how it is to be done. In any organisation the staff executives offers four types of services.

(i) Advice (ii) Control (iii) Service (iv) Coordination.

The whole idea of this system is that the specialised work in connection with analysis, research, labour, standardising, costing, material, equipment etc. should be left to experts who can solve the problem of high technical standard and thus the departmental managers are free to organise, control and supervise the productive activities.

Advantages

(i) It is based upon manned specialisation.

(ii) It brings expert knowledge to bear upon management and operating problems.

(iii) It provides more opportunity for advancement for able operators, a great variety of responsible jobs are available.

(iv) It makes possible the principle of undivided responsibility and authority and at the same time permit staff specialisation.

(v) It repays its added costs many times over through the savings resulting from increased efficiency of operation.

Disadvantages

(i) Unless the duties and responsibilities of the staff members are clearly indicated by chart and manuals, there may be considerable confusion throughout the organisation as to the functions and positions stage members with relation to line supervisors.

(ii) The staff may be ineffective for lack of authority to carryout its functions or intelligent backing in the application of its recommendation.

(iii) The inability to see each other viewpoint may cause difficulty and friction between the line supervisors and members.

(iv) Although experts information and advice are available, they reach the operators through line officers and thus run the risk of misunderstanding and misinterpretation.

Line and Functional Staff Organisation : Under the pure line and staff organisation the work of the staff is not regarded as a specific managerial function, but under this plan, however specialists become more than just advisers, they become executives in charge of single techniques which are common under several units of the works. The entire organisation is divided so that no activity is left out and there is no duplication in the allotment of activities to different departments. Under this system the weakness of the pure functional plan is eliminated and no employee is placed under more than one boss. It is really the line and staff type of organisation through functions.

The most important advantage of this system is that it helps mass production by standardisation and specialisation. It makes for organisation growth, because each man grows in his own speciality. If not carried too far, coordinations through cooperation and leadership is easily achieved.

Paramount to Success

The staff system when used with line system corrects to some extent the inefficacies of the pure line system, it also comments the lack of coordination inherent in the pure functional form of organisation. But this is not enough. As every piece of work in any department in any enterprise has some connection with a piece of work in other departments, group participation is essential to ensure coordination and to promote cooperative relationship committees are formed for the performance of special duties, and may be either permanent or temporary, formed to serve a temporary function only. As many problems in an enterprise are plant wide, a high degree of cooperation, which is paramount to success can be achieved through committees, which promote the pooling of knowledge.

A committee is a group of people usually on the same authoritative level specially designated to perform a managerial act and a committee meeting is gathering of these people for the purpose of talking over hinge they have to do. Thus the function of a committee is the assignment of a task to a group rather than to one or more individuals.

Advantages

(i) Under a strong executive chairman, a committee may quickly marshal many valuable points of view, since two heads are better than one.

(ii) In conducting investigations, the several phases of various questions may be quickly assigned to responsible members with a reasonable assurance of speedy action if a time schedule and proper follow up are instituted.

(iii) Decisions are impersonal, leaving the chairman free from the personal criticism so often levelled at an aging executive.

(iv) There is stimulus toward cooperative action.

(v) The members of the committee know better what is going on in the plant so that they can spread the information and team up with other individuals or departments.

Disadvantages

(i) Committee may be too large for constructive action. The number of members should seldom exceed three.

(ii) Committees are expensive in time and usually have to be prodded to prevent delays.

(iii) Important executives may be called too frequently from their work for meetings that the operations of the enterprise slow down.

(iv) The members of the committee offer are unfamiliar with important details of questions at issue and therefore may make wrong or ineffective decision.

(v) Action often be superficial because of lack of time or the disinterestedness of committee members.

(vi) Committee weakens the individual responsibility and makes for compromise instead of clear cut decisions.

(vii) The decisions often are made to conform with what it is assumed some executive wants or to enable the members to avoid direct responsibility for any bad results.

(viii) Aggressive and outspoken members may dominate committee meetings and unduly influence the action often adversely.

Use of Committees : The most common use of the committee in industrial organisations is in policy-making. When so used, it is known as the executive or administrative committee.

Organisation Line-staff Relationships : Line and staff are two terms that are often used in ways that are loose and unclear. Attempts have been made in some organisation to dispense with them, and thus "operating" is frequently substituted for line and "auxiliary" and service are common substitutes for "staff." Clarification will be achieved if we examine the terms in the light of work done and authority exercised.

A line or operating organisation unit is one that is actually doing the work that represents the primary mission of the larger organisation unit of which it is a part. For example, an assembly department in the manufacturing division or a selling branch in the sales division.

A staff or service organisation unit is any unit which is helping to do its work, or making it possible for the line to do its work, but is not actually engaged in the work itself. Examples: a purchasing unit, a time study unit, a payroll preparation unit, in service training unit etc.

When is it Line, and When is it Staff : Misunderstandings arise from failure to realise that whether an activity is "line" (operating) or "staff" (service) depends upon whose shoes you are putting on and when you are looking at the operation. Thus, the total organisation headed up by a controller render service to all of the other organisation units in the entire company. Those other units therefore look upon this organisation unit as staff or service. The controller however, looking at his own operations can consider the various units with in his organising units as far as he is concerned. He may, however, within his own organisation, set up staff units (perhaps an economist to advise him or a special analysis devoted solely to improving procedures in his own department).

Organisational Relations and Lines of Authority : It is frequently said that a member of a staff unit can not tell a manager or a member of line unit to do any thing rather he can only inform or suggest or advise or offer his specific services. This is largely true, but there are exceptions. For example, a safety engineer may shut down a line activity as quality inspector. Similarly it is often said that a line manager can not issue direct orders to staff or service man. This is an over simplification.

Following are seven distinct types of line and staff relationships.

Advisory: Here the staff unit is one that offers advisory help only an operating manager may or may not avail himself of it. He may request it, but the staff unit can not foist itself from him. However, the staff unit may volunteer suggestions on the basis of observations made, even though uninvited.

Services Requested: This relationship is similar to the above, but involves services rather than advise or suggestions. The relationship of the staff personnel is similar to that of an outside contractors personnel—their "boss" is their own staff unit head.

Staff services rendered to an organisation unit as part of fulfilling the units mission supplied on a programmed basis, for example, there may be certain periodic specialised technical services rendered by a head quarters engineering unit to customers served regularly by a customers' service department working out of a branch plant. There should be no question about lines of direct supervision—the direct chain of command of these specialists or technicians is to the head of the central staff unit, and the latter is responsible for the quality of their service and their mode of operating. The head of the customers' service department at the branch can not attempt to supervise the specialists, but he can communicate directly with the head of the central staff unit if he questions the quality of their work, their adherence to schedule etc. At the same time, the head of the central staff unit cannot dictate the degree of utilisation of the services since this is stipulated by an over all programme previously authorised at a higher level.

Auxiliary Services Necessary to Operations, Regularly Supplied: Accounting and procurements are examples. The supplying organisation unit has the right to insist that the operating organisation follow officially specified rules having to do with reporting, requisitions or other information necessary to rendering the service. If established procedures are not complied with, personnel of the service unit after normal courtesies in the form of requests to the operating personnel; have the right to insist to the operating supervisor that corrective action be taken. Personnel of the using organisation unit can communicate directly with the supplying unit to request service or information about service as long as specified initiating or confirming paper work is executed.

Functional relationship between a central staff unit and personnel in a counter part staff unit attached to an operating organisation unit.

Examples are a central quality control department which operates through a quality control department at each plant, and a central personnel department which operates through a personnel department at each plant. On organisation charts a "dotted line relationship" is shown between such central staff units and the counterpart units in the operating organisation. A solid line goes up from the operating organisation is staff unit through the local operating chain of commando, and its ultimate boss is the head of the local operating organisation. However the central staff unit has responsibility for the professional conduct of the work and its personnel can make suggestions for improvement. They do not give direct orders to the counterpart professional people in the local operating organisation's staff unit. If they have strong feelings about the way something is or is not being done, they can make strong suggestions to the head of the operating organisation's staff unit and failing action can only proceed higher in the operating chain of command.

Relationship between a department head and personnel assigned to them by a staff unit—specialised personnel are often assigned to an operating unit by a staff unit which is responsible for their training and for the quality of their professional work. They are considered as being permanently attached to their home staff unit, even though their assignment may be of relatively long duration. But they are under the administrative command of the head of the operating unit and for accounting purposes may be on the operating unit's pay-roll. They are under the "professional command of the head of their staff unit". Professional command means that the staff unit head and not the operating unit head lays down the procedures and sets the standards with respect to their professional work.

Relationship between an operating executive and an advisory or service staff person or unit directly reporting to him and relationship between the staff personnel and other personnel in the organisation units under the operating executives.

The staff man or unit only supplies information and advice and recommends. The operating executive is the one who must make the decisions and take action. The staff unit can act only in the name of that executive-it can not tell other employees what they must do or must not do.

New Designs

Since the early 1980s, organisation designers have been focussing on to effect new structural changes in organisation designs which can enable the organisations to compete effectively. Four of such new organisational designs are : the team structure, the virtual organisation, the boundaryless organisation and the feminine organisation.

The Team Structure : Teams are an important means to organise work activities. When management uses teams as its central coordination device, we have a team structure. The main characteristics of the team structure are that it breaks down departmental barriers and decentralises decision making to the level of the work team. Team structure also requires employees to be generalist as well as specialists. In small companies, the team structure can define the entire organisation. In such companies teams have full responsibility for most operational issues and customer service.

Many large organisations have also made extensive use of team structure, for example companies like Motorola and Xerox improved productivity at the operational level through self managed teams. Such teams are generally composed of 10 to 15 people who take on full responsibility of work related decisions and their outcomes. Members of such teams do their own scheduling, determine work assignments, rotate jobs on their own and even select their own members and evaluate their performance. Also, while designing a new product or to coordinate major projects, organisations can structure activities around cross functional teams. These teams are made up of employees from about the same hierarchical level, but from different work areas to coordinate complex projects, develop new ideas and solve problems.

The Virtual Organisation : The virtual organisation is a small, core organisation that sources out major business functions. It is a highly centralised organisation, with little or no departmentation.

The virtual organisation creates a network of relationships which allows them to contract out manufacturing, distribution marketing or any other business function where management feels others can do it better or cheaper.

In a typical bureaucratic organisation, which has many vertical levels of management, research and development is carried in-house, production occurs in company owned plants, and sales and marketing are performed by the company's own employees. In contrast, the virtual organisation outsources many of these functions and concentrates on what it does best.

One of the major advantage to the virtual organisation is its flexibility. One needs just an innovative idea and little money to successfully compete against large companies. The disadvantage to this structure is that it reduces management's control over key parts of its business.

The Boundaryless Organisation : The Boundaryless Organisation is an organisation that seeks to eliminate the chain of command, have limitless spans of control, and replace departments with empowered teams.

In such organisations, management flattens the hierarchy by removing vertical boundaries and minimises status and rank. Such organisations also emphasise participative decision making and function in cross hierarchical teams which include top executives, middle managers, supervisors and operative employees.

Such organisations also eliminate horizontal boundaries by replacing functional departments with cross functional teams that work in a single process instead of around narrow functional teams that work in a single process instead of around narrow functional tasks.

Some boundaryless organisations also go to the extent of breaking the barriers to external constituencies and barriers created by geography. Globalisation, strategic alliances, customer-organisation linkages and telecommuting are few examples of such organisations.

The Feminine Organisation : In the early 1980s, many organisation theorists studied the relationship between values and structural preference. It was found that women had preferences for those organisations that emphasised relatedness and connecting with others. They argued that since women have been socialised for their role in the family, that teaches the value of supporting and nurturing others, therefore they prefer to work in organisations which value human relationships, and are based on care and trust.

Joyce Rothschild developed a model of the feminine organisation that has the following characteristics :

1. Members are valued as individual human being.
2. Relationships are seen as possessing value in themselves and not just means to achieve organisational goals.
3. Career success is defined in terms of service to others.
4. Create extensive opportunities of personal growth for their members.
5. Members are closely knit and have trust and care for each other.
6. Emphasise on participative decision making.

Organisation design is the process by which managers create a structure of tasks and authority. The form and characteristics of an organisational structure vary depending upon the attributes such as division of labour, departmentalisation, span of control and authority.

Division of labour is the extent to which the organisation's work is separated into different jobs to be done by different people.

Departmentalisation is the process of grouping the related functions or major work activities into manageable units to achieve more effective and efficient overall coordination of organisation can be departmentalised on the basis of function, product, customer, territory and project.

Span of control indicates the number of people directed or managed effectively by a supervisor. However, organisations must give due consideration to similarity of functions, geographical closeness of subordinates, complexity of functions, direction and control required by subordinates etc., in establishing the span of control.

The authority is the legal power to command or extract action from others. Since managers get work done through others, authority constitutes the key to the manager's job authority in this sense is thus shared by the manager with the right to command.

Delegation of authority takes place when organisational power is given to subordinates by a superior. It plays an important role in the organisation as it relieves the manager from performing rest time duties, provides motivation to the subordinates and thus develops the subordinates. However, certain amount of centralised control is essential as it provides a feeling of prestige to the manager, powers cost, tightens control and results in greater uniformity of policy and practices.

The new organisation design developed in the recent years to enable the organisations to compete effectively are the team structure, the virtual organisation, the boundaryless organisation and the feminine organisation.

10

Various Types

One of the important components of the organisation process is the creation of an appropriate organsation structure. The organisation structure represents the hierarchical arrangement of various positions in the enterprise. It helps in allocating authority and responsibility formally. But there is no best structure of the organisational relationship which may be suitable, for enterprise has to evolve its own organisation structure based on the nature of activities and business competence of personnel and the philosophy of management. There are five types of an organisation:

(a) Line Organisation

(b) Line and Staff Organisation,

(c) Functional Organisation

(d) Project of Matrix Organisation,

(e) Committee Organisation.

Line Organisation : Historically, this is the oldest form of an organisation. This is known by different names, i.e., military, vertical, scalar and departmental. All other types of organisation structure have mostly been modifications of the line organisation. The concept of the line organisation holds that in any organisation derived from a scalar process, there must be a single head who commands it. Although an executive can delegate authority, he has ultimate responsibility for results. According to McFarland, "Line structure consists of the direct vertical relationship which connect the positions and tasks of each level with those above and below it." According to Allen, "Organisationally, the line is the chain of command that extends from the board of directors through the various delegations and redelegations of authority and responsibility to the point where the primary activities of the enterprise are performed."

From the above chart, the following special features of the line organisation come up:

(a) There are many levels of management depending upon the scale of business and decision-making ability of managers. Each level of management has equal rights.

(b) There is a vertical flow of authority and responsibility. The lower positions derive authority from the higher positions.

(c) There is a unity of command. Every person is accountable to only one person (his immediate boss) and none else. A person receives orders only from his immediate boss.

(d) There is scalar chain in the line organisation. The flow of orders, communication of suggestions and complaints, etc. are made as it isin the case of a ladder. One cannot defy the claim.

(e) There is limit on subordinates under one manager. A manager has control only over the subordinates of his department.

The Merits : The merits of the line organisation are as follows:

Simplicity: It is the simplest of all types of organisations. It can be easily established and easily understood by the workers.

Clear-cut Division of Authority and Responsibility: The authority and responsibility of every person is clearly defined. Everyone knows as to whom he can issue orders and to whom he is accountable. Further it is easier to fix up the responsibility if there is any lapse anywhere in the performance of activities.

Strong Discipline: Because of direct authority responsibility relationships, discipline can be maintained more effectively. Direct supervision and control also helps in maintaining strong discipline among the workers.

Unified Control: Since the orders are given by one superior, there is no confusion, among the subordinates. This ensures better understanding and quick action.

Prompt Decisions : As the superiors enjoy full authority, quick decisions are taken by them. Such decisions are executed promptly also.

Flexibility: Since each departmental head has sole responsibility for his department, he can easily adjust the organisation according to the changes in business situation.

The Demerits : The demerits of the line organisation are as follows:

Heavy Burden of Work: Since the departmental head has to look after all the activities of his department, he is over burdened with work. He may neglect some of the duties and there may be some inefficiency in management.

Concentration of Authority: It is dictatorial in nature as all important powers are concentrated in the hands of a few top executives. If they are not able the enterprise will not be successful.

Lack of Specialisation: The line organisation suffers from lack of specialised skill of experts. It is extremely difficult for one person to handle activities of diverse nature. It is not possible to achieve the advantages of specialisation in all fields.

Lack of Communication: There is failure to get correct information and to act upon it due to lack of communication. Although there is communication from top to bottom there is usually no communication from the lower ranks to higher ranks and executives. They are not provided with an opportunity to put forward their viewpoint or problems or suggestions to persons at the top level. Thus, they lose their capacity for independent thinking.

Scope for Favouritism: Since the departmental head is almost all-in-all for the activities of his department. There is scope for favouritism. There may be a good deal of nepotism and jobbery and personal prejudices. The executive may appoint and promote his own men in various positions ignoring the claim of efficient persons.

Despite these drawbacks, the line organisation is still considered as very ideal for small enterprises where the work involved is not of a very complex nature and number of people are small. It is also, ideal where automatic machines are in use or where talented and capable executives are at the head of various departments. But it is not very successful in large concerns.

Line and Staff Organisation : The line organisation suffers from three main drawbacks, i.e., heavy burden of work on the line executive, too much concentration of power in the hands of a low line executive and lack of specialisation. In view of these drawbacks, the idea of the line and staff organisation was introduced.

Normally staff means those elements of an organisation that help the line of work most effectively in accomplishing the primary objectives of the enterprise. The staff authority support those executives who hold the line authority. The staff authority consists of experts and specialists in various fields. The main function of the staff is to help the line executives in such activities which require expert and specialised knowledge. The role of the staff is purely advisory and not authoritative. They have to recommend but have no authority to enforce their preference on subordinates or to issue orders to them. In fact, the function of the line executives is to act and that of the staff is to think and suggest.

In short, the line and staff organisation refers to a pattern in which the staff specialists advise the line managers to perform their duties. Thus, in a firm engaged in the manufacture of dyes and chemicals, the works manager, marketing manager and the finance manager are line officials while functions like personnel management, quality control, public relations and accounting are staff functions. Thus, the line and the staff are two types of organisational relationships.

Following are the characteristics of the line and staff organisation:

1. Managers are of two types—Line Managers and Staff Managers.
2. The Line Managers perform the functions of decision-making, issuing orders and controlling while the Staff Managers perform the functions of advising, assisting and providing expert and specialised services.
3. There is a unity of command.
4. There is a scalar chain.

The Merits : This from of organisation came to existence as an improvement over the line organisation. The line and staff organisation has removed serious drawbacks of the line organisation.

Specialisation: It is based on planned specialisation. The line managers get the benefit of specialised knowledge of the staff specialists at various levels.

Encouragement to Research and Development Programmes: The growth of an enterprise depends largely upon various research and development programmes. The staff provides this service to the line departments.

Balanced Decisions: The line managers may not have specialised knowledge in all areas and due to this line managers may sometimes give wrong orders or pass wrong judgement. The suggestions and advice given by staff manager help them in making rational judgement and balanced decisions.

Less Burden on the Line Managers: The staff managers relieve the line managers from the botheration of concentrating on the specialised functions like accounting, selection and training of employees, public relations, etc. Thus, there is less burden on line managers. Many problems that are ignored or poorly handled in the line organisation, can be properly covered. It is more flexible.

Demerits : Demerits of the line and staff organisation are as follows:

Confusion: It is very difficult to clearly establish the authority and responsibility relationship between the line and staff executives. This creates confusion.

Ineffectiveness of the Staff: The role of the staff is purely advisory. Since they do not have the power to get their recommendations implemented, the staff services may prove to be ineffective.

Conflict between the Line and Staff: There is generally a conflict between the line and staff executives. The line authorities feel that staff executives do not always give right type of advice and therefore reject even some very good schemes. Line authorities do not want to give an impression to management that they are in any way inferior to the staff. Thus, there is always a conflict between the line and staff organisations.

The line and staff organisation structure has gained popularity because certain problems of management have become so complex that in order to deal with them, expert knowledge is necessary which can be provided by the staff officers. Whatever drawbacks are there, they are mainly due to its wrong application.

Functional Organisation : In the functional organisation, all activities in the enterprise are grouped together according to certain functions like production, marketing, finance and personnel and are put under the charge of different persons. The person-incharge of a function follows it throughout the organisation and also controls the individuals working in that functional area. This means that if a person performs several functions, he will be under the direct charge of several persons-incharge of these functions. The functional incharge is an expert in his own field. It is rare to find a pure functional organisation. However, many business enterprises follow functional plan to some extent to carry out the primary functions.

Functional organisation may be at different levels. At the top level, it leads to formation of departments each for a common major activity like purchases, sales, production, finance, etc. Each department looks after its function common to all departments. For example, the question of selection, training, promotion, etc. in purchase, sales and other departments will be decided by the personnel department. Taylor recommended functional organisation even at the shop level (lowest level). He expressed the view that a foreman should also be assisted by a number of specialists.

Following chart shows the functional organisation:

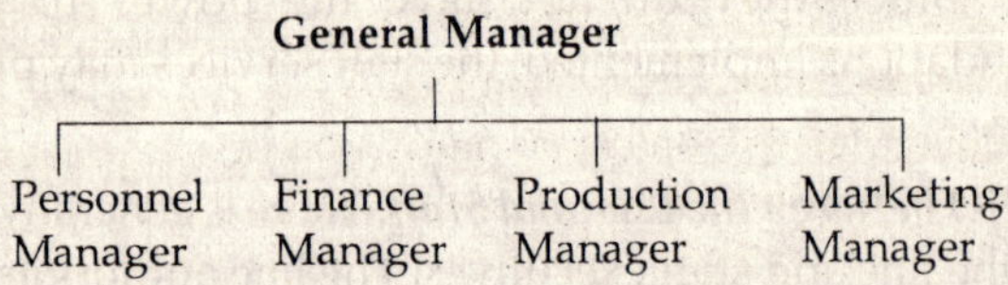

The above discussion brings out the following characteristics of functional organisation:

1. The work is divided into specialised functions.
2. The superior specialist commands an authority and therefore gives orders relating to his specific functions throughout the line.
3. The specialist must be consulted before any decision is taken on matters relating to his specialised area.
4. The responsibilities of functional authority are mainly discharged by other executives.
5. It is flat topped organisation in comparison to the line organisation. A specialist can supervise a large number of employees while in the line organisation, a specialist supervises a limited number of subordinates.

The Merits : The merits of the functional organisation are as follows:

Specialisation: It ensures a greater division of labour and enables the concern to take advantage for specialisation of functions.

More Efficiency: Efficiency of workers is increased as the workers and other have to perform a limited number of operations and they get suggestions and instructions from specialists.

Separation of Mental and Physical Functions : It ensures the separation of mental and physical functions. This ensures better control of the working of the different sections.

Economy: Standardisation and specialisation in various fields facilitates production on a large scale resulting in economy in production.

Expansion: It offers a greater scope for expansion as compared to the line organisation. It does not face the problem of limited capabilities of a few line managers. The expert knowledge of the functional managers facilitates better control and supervision in the organisation.

The Demerits : The demerits of the functional organisation are as follows:

Confusion: The operation of functional organisation is too complicated. Workers are supervised by a number of bosses. This results in overlapping of authority and thus creates confusion in the organisation.

Lack of Coordination: Under this, the work is divided into parts and sub-parts. It poses difficulties in coordinating the functioning of different parts. Thus, it is difficult to take quick decisions.

Difficulty Infixing Responsibility: Because of multiple authority, responsibility for poor performance cannot be fixed easily on a particular person.

Conflict: Supervisory staff of equal rank may not always agree on certain issues. Therefore, there may be frequent conflicts which may lead to non-performance.

This type of organisation is suitable for all kinds of enterprises irrespective of their nature or size. But it can be practised more successfully at the higher levels of the organisation than at the lower levels.

Matrix Organisation : This is one of the latest types of organisational design. It has teen developed to establish flexible structure to achieve series of project objectives. Matrix organisation, also known as grid, is an answer to the growing size and complexity of the undertaking, which require an organisation structure more flexible and technically oriented than the line and staff and functional structures.

The matrix organisation is a combination of the project organisation and the functional organisation. Authority flows vertically within functional departments, while authority of project managers flows horizontally crossing vertical lines. Thus, martix organisation is created, "when project management is superimposed on a stable hierarchical structure, usually of a functional nature. Here the individuals working on a project have a continuing dual assignment; to their project and to their base department."

Significant Elements

The important features of the matrix organisation are as follows:

Built Around Specific Projects: The matrix organisation is built around specific projects. The charge of the project is given to the project manager who has the necessary authority to complete the project in accordance with the time, cost, quality and other conditions communicated to him by the top management.

Personnel from Various Departments: The project manager draws personnel from various functional departments. He assigns the work to the various functional groups. Upon completion of the project, the functional groups return to their functional departments for reassignment to other projects.

Different Roles: The project and the functional manager have different roles. The project manager exerts a general management viewpoint with regard to his project. Each functional manager is responsible for maintaining the integrity of his function. However, both the project and functional managers are dependent on each other as they have to take several joint decisions in order to execute the project. So there is proper coordination between the project and the functional groups.

Management by Objectives : Management by project objectives is paramount to the way of thinking and working in it.

The Advantages : The matrix organisation has many advantages. Many organisations which otherwise face problems of structural and technical complexities should adopt this type of organisation. The functional vertical relationships as well as interdependent horizontal relationships lead to operational flexibility. This makes it more adaptable to crisis and change. It provides focus on projects and retains the benefits of specialised expertise and capabilities of functional departments.

The Limitations : It is of a temporary nature. Further, there may be a conflict between project groups and functional groups. It requires coordination of a number of specialised skills. Project personnel entertain considerable fear that termination of a project may bring discharge rather than reassignment to a new project. Frequent movements from one project to another also create considerable anxiety about career progress.

It is very difficult to say which of the types of organisation is the best. On a careful analysis, we find that the line and staff organisation is quite popular in the business world.

The Distinction : There are many points of similarities between the line organisation and line and staff organisation:

(i) In both forms of the organisation, business activities are divided into many departments and sub-departments.

(ii) In both the organisations, orders and request are in linear form.

(iii) The number of subordinates under every officer is limited.

(a) Difference between the line organisation and the line and staff organisation

In spite of the above similarities, both the organisations can be differentiated on the following basis:

	Basis of Difference	*Line Organisation*	*Line and Staff Organisation*
1.	Services of experts	There is no provision for the services of experts	Services of experts are made available
2.	Principle of specialis-ation is not followed	The principle of specialisation followed	The principle of specialisation is followed
3.	Elasticity	In this form of organisation, the elasticity is less	In this form, the elasticity is more
4.	Investigation	There is no provision for investigation	It encourages investigation

(b) Difference between the functional organisation and the line and staff organisation

In both forms of the organisation the principle of specialisation is followed but the difference between these two may be explained on the following basis:

	Basis of Difference	Function Organisation	Line and Staff Organisation
1.	Direct contact with workers	The workers are in direct contact with experts	The workers are not in direct contact with experts
2.	Order by experts	The experts may give orders to the employees	The experts cannot give orders to the employees
3.	Discipline	The discipline is lethargic	There is very hard discipline

(c) Difference between the line organisation and the functional organisation

	Basis of Difference	Function Organisation	Line and Staff Organisation
1.	Flow of orders	The orders flow from top to bottom	Every worker gets the orders and instructions from many officers at one time.
2.	Responsibility determination	Responsibility of employees can be determined easily	It is not possible to determine the responsibility of employees
3.	Specialisation	It is not based on the principle of specialisation	Based on the principle of specialisation
4.	Role of experts	There is no role of experts	Experts play an important role
5.	Coordination can be	It is very established in the activities of enterprise easily	difficult to coordinate different activities of the enterprise
6.	Discipline	There is very hard discipline	The discipline is lethargic

The Requirement

In this complex business world, each activity taken out by any department, affects the work of other departments. A slight change in production policy will concern the sales department. Similarly, a new sale policy or a change in the sale policy cannot be followed by the sales managers without consulting the finance manager or the production manager. It should be well understood in this reference that such important policy decisions which concern other departments also, should not be taken by the incharge of the department concern alone but they should be referred to a committee consisting of the managers of the affecting departments. It will ensure cooperation and better coordination. Thus, committee organisation is extensively used to solve the multifaceted problems of large and complex business units.

The Definition

Committee is a group of individuals especially designated to take decision in matters referred to it through free exchange of ideas among its members. Louis A. Allen states that "A committee is a body of persons appointed or elected to meet on an organised basis for the consideration of matters brought before it." W. H. Newman defines it as "A group of people specifically designated to perform some administrative act. It functions only as a group and requires the free interchange of ideas among its members." On the basis of the above definitions, the following broad characteristics may be spelled out:

Characteristics of Committee Organisation: A committee is a group of two or more persons appointed or elected.

Scope: It deals with specific problems referred to it. There are strictly defined jurisdictions within which committee is expected to justify its existence.

Deliberation: The members can go into details of the problems and can discuss each and every aspect of the problem concerned.

Authority: A committee may have the authority either to take final decisions or to recommend the action in the matter.

Types of Committees : Committees may be classified in various forms. The most common are:

Standing or Ad hoc Committees: A committee may be permanent (standing) or *ad hoc* (temporary) in character. A standing committee has permanent existence while *ad hoc* committee is constituted for a specific purpose.

Decision-making or other Committees: A committee may be delegated authority to make a final decision while others may merely deliberate on the problems. Some committees are authorised only to make recommendations to the line executives.

Line or Staff Committees: The line committee is charged with the authority of decision-making affecting subordinates responsible to it.

Formal and Informal Committees: Formal committees are those which have been established under organisational rules, regulations and with specific authority spelling out its duties and authority. Most committees in business are formal ones. An informal committee, on the other hand, is organised without specific delegation of authority. It does not form a part of the organisation.

Principles of the Committee Organisation : Main principles of the committee organisation are as under:

Principle of Minimum number of Members: The number of members of the committee should not be very large. There must be maximum 5 or 6 members in the committee so that it may be managed properly.

Principle of Inclusion of Concerned Experts: Only those persons must be included in the committee organisation who are concerned with the particular works.

Principle of Regular Meeting of Committee: The meetings of the committee must be called in proper manner and every member of the committee must be duly informed of the meetings of committee.

Principle of Rights and Duties of Members: The rights and duties of all the members of the committee must be clearly defined.

Principle of Liabilities of Members: The liabilities of all the members of committee must be in accordance with the rights delegated to them.

Principle of Agenda of the Committee: The meetings must be conducted in accordance with the programme which must be pre-determined.

Principle of Mutual Trust: There must be mutual trust and feeling of cooperation among all the members of the committee.

Principle of Membership Retirement: Members of committee must be liable to retire by rotation.

If the committee is set up and managed according to the above principle, it may be expected that the committee will be successful in obtaining its objects.

Merits of the Committee Organisation : The committee organisation is becoming more and more popular day by day. Important merits or advantages of the committee organisation are as under:

Collective Decisions: All the important decisions are taken collectively in the committee organisation. Such decisions are more logical and sound and are affected by the skill, intelligence and experience of all the members of the committee.

Communication of Information: The committee organisation provides a suitable stage for effective communication.

Increase in Mutual Cooperation: The committee organisation depends on the feeling of mutual cooperation and coordination. Thus, the committee organisation is helpful in developing the feeling of mutual trust and mutual cooperation among the members.

Decentralisation of Power: The committee organisation is based on decentralisation of power because in this system, the rights to take the important decisions are not centralised with any individual officer. All the members of the committee take collectively decisions.

Encouragement to Democracy: It encourages democracy because all the decisions of committee are taken by majority.

Indiscriminate Decisions: All the decisions of the committee organisation are taken collectively by all the members of the committee. Therefore, such decisions are also not effected by personal thinking and personal opinion of any officer.

Advantage of Ability of Members: All the members of the committee organisation participate in all the functions of the committee. They make their whole-hearted contribution in the functions of the committee. In this manner, the business enterprise gets the advantage of abilities of all the members.

Coordination: This is based on mutual cooperation and mutual trust. Therefore, the activities of all the members are coordinated.

Easy to Control: The process of control becomes quite easy in this organisation because all the members take active participation in the decision-making process and they contribute their whole-hearted efforts in implementing the decision.

Other Advantages: There are some other advantages also in addition to the above advantages. These are common directions, increased knowledge of members, etc.

Demerits of the Committee Organisation : In spite of the above merits, the committee organisation is considered to be defective and impractical. According to Koontz & O'Donnell, "It is an association made of the unit selected by the unwilling to do the unnecessary." Demerits of the committee organisation can be briefly discussed as follows:

Delay in Decisions: A great disadvantage of the committee organisation is that the decisions become a project and thus delayed because all the decisions are to be taken by majority. Sometimes, the decisions are so late that they become meaningless.

Delay in Action: As the decisions are late, their implementation is late and the action gets late.

Lack of Motivation: As no individual officer is authorised to take an important decision, it creates lack of motivation.

Lack of Responsibility: As all the decisions are taken collectively, it creates the problem of assigning responsibility to any individual officer.

Leadership of Aggressive Nature: A great disadvantage of the committee organisation is that the leadership of such committee is of aggressive nature because the person who speaks more and loudly dominates the committee.

Lack of Secrecy: As all the important decisions are taken collectively by the heads of all the departments, there is a lack of secrecy.

Against Minority Members: As the decisions are taken by the rule of majority, there are some persons against these decisions. This way, the decisions of the committee remain against such minority members.

Useless Functions: Sometimes the committee performs some functions which are of no use to the enterprise.

Slackness in the Activities of Enterprise: As the members of the committee are the heads of their departments and these members frequently call their meetings, it causes slackness in the activities of enterprise.

Other Disadvantages: In addition to the above-mentioned disadvantages, there are some more disadvantages also, as difficulty in the discharge of duties by officers, etc.

Thus, we see that the committee organisation is meaningless and useless because of the above disadvantages. Koontz & O'Donnell has stated in this regard as, "You go to purchase a horse and you come back with a camel in your hands."

Misuses of the Committee Organisation : The committee organisations are generally found only in big business enterprises because the organisation of a big business and industrial enterprise is possible only through the committee organisation. Some examples of misuse of the committee organisation may be as under:

Decisions by Compromise: Decisions by compromise is a very common misuse of the powers of officers of the committee. The opinions of members of committee are also different so that it becomes almost impossible to take the unanimous decisions. In this case, almost all the decisions are taken by compromise. These decisions are not very sound and effective. Sometimes these decisions are against the interests of enterprise.

Expensive: A committee organisation is a very big organisation. Therefore, it is an expensive organisation. The members of the committee make many unnecessary expenses in the name of the organisation.

Injustice with the Members of Minority: All the decisions of the committee are taken by the rule of majority. It means that there are some members against the decisions taken by committee. Thus, the decisions of committee are imposed upon these members which is against the interests of enterprise itself.

Documentation of Few Persons: Theoretically all the decisions of the committee are taken by majority. All the members have right to express their opinions on all the subjects discussed at the committee. But practically the committee is dominated by a few persons who can speak loudly and fluently. Such members of committee influence the decisions of committee in undesirable manner.

Time is Less and Problems are More: The committee organisation is a big organisation. It has to perform a large number of functions, and the time is limited. There is always a shortage of time in relation to the works to be performed. Therefore, the members do not take due interest in the functions of committee and they waste their time on meaningless and fruitless discussions.

No Responsibility of any Member for a Wrong Decision: As all the decisions of the committee are taken collectively by all the members of committee, it becomes very difficult to determine the responsibilities of an individual member, if any of the decisions of committee is wrong and against the interests of enterprise.

Suggestions for making Committee Organisation more Effective : The committee organisation may be made effective by the following suggestions:

Suitability of the Committee Organisation: The committee organisation must be set up only when it is felt that the advantages of committee will be more than its expenses. If, it is felt that the expenses of such committee will be more than its advantages, it should not be set up.

Appropriate Size of the Committee Organisation: The size of committee must be appropriate in accordance with the size of enterprise. It is necessary so that the opinions of members of committee may be easily and conveniently exchanged.

Selection of Capable Members: Its success depends upon the capability of the members. Therefore, only those members must be selected as the members of committee who are capable enough to discharge their duties properly and which may represent their departments properly. The members must be capable enough to understand, analyse and decide the problems.

Capacity of the Chairman: Success of the committee organisation depends to a large extent upon the capability of the chairman. Therefore, it becomes necessary that the chairman of the committee must be selected very carefully, the person must be an experienced person who may conduct the committee meetings properly. Chairman must be a person who can move, direct and control other members of the committee.

Clarification of Scope: An important suggestion for the success of the committee organisation is that its scope must be clearly defined and properly communicated so that there may be no dispute of opinion about the functions to be performed by the committee.

Rights and Duties of Members must be Specified: Mutual trust and mutual cooperation for the members of committees is necessary for the success of committee. For developing the feeling of mutual trust and mutual cooperation, it becomes necessary that the rights and duties of all the members of committee must be clearly defined.

Suitability of the Subjects under Consideration: The committee should consider only the proper subjects. Only those matters must be assigned to the committee which are of great importance to the enterprise. If the matter is not so important, it should not be delivered to the committee otherwise it will be wastage of time, energy and money.

Meetings of Committee should be According to Pre-determined Programme: A programme must be determined well in advance for the meetings of committee and programmes must be properly communicated to all the members of committee so that the members can prepare themselves for the discussion and decision. It will save time and make the decisions more sound and effective.

In this chapter various types of organisation were described. These include, line and staff, functional, matrix and committee form of organisation. The concept of the line organisation holds that in any organisation derived from a scalar process, there must be a single head who commands it. In the functional organisation, all activities in the enterprise are grouped together according to certain functions like production, marketing, finance and personnel are put to under change of different persons. The matrix in organisation has been developed to establish flexible structures to organisation has been developed to establish flexible structures to cope up with growing size and complexity of an enterprise. The distinctions between various types of organisation were also highlighted. The committee form and its need were described at great length.

11

Significance of Leadership

Leadership is one of the essential functions that must be performed by all the managers. The success of all the managers largely depends on the capacity to lead their subordinates. However, it is not easier to master the art of leadership.

The Concept

Leadership has different meanings to different persons. But in terms of managing, leadership is the art of leading others towards a goal. More specifically, leadership is the process of influencing others to work enthusiastically to achieve predetermined goals.

According to Keith Davis, "Leadership is the ability to persuade others to seek defined objectives enthusiastically. It is the human factor which binds a group together and motivates it towards goals."

According to Stoner *et al.*, "Managerial leadership is the process of directing and influencing the task-related activities of group of members."

In the words of Keys and Case, "Leadership is the process of influencing and supporting others to work enthusiastically towards achieving objectives."

In the opinion of Weihrich and Koontz, "Leadership is the art or process of influencing people so that they will strive willingly and enthusiastically towards the achievement of group goals."

Thus, leadership is the process and the art influencing the behaviour, attitudes, activities of people to work willingly and enthusiastically towards the accomplishment of group goals.

The Characteristics : Following characteristics highlight the nature of leadership :

Personal Quality : Leadership is a personal quality of a person. It is a behavioural quality and ability to influence others towards accomplishing a goal. Barnard has very rightly stated that "Leadership is the quality of behaviour of individuals whereby they guide people or their activities."

Leadership Depends on Doing : Leadership is a kind of personal quality. But effectiveness of leadership depends on its application or on performance. Peter Drucker has very aptly remarked, "Leadership has little to do with leadership qualities and even less to do with 'charisma'. It is mundane, unromantic and boring. It is work. Its essence is performance."

Followers : Leadership presupposes existence of followers. There cannot be leadership without followers. In the words of Koontz and O'Donnell, "The essence of aleadership is followership. It is the willingness of people to follow that makes a person a leader." Thus, effective leader makes his followers to act willingly to achieve the goal.

Influencing and Inspiring Process : Leadership is a process of influencing and inspiring others to work towards objectives. Influencing means regulating and changing behaviour, attitudes and feelings of others. The means of influencing others include reward, coercion, expertise, reference and tradition. Leaders can also influence with rational faith, participation and persuation.

Continuous Process : Leadership is a continuous process. A leader continuously makes efforts to influence behaviour of his group members. He carries on this process by maintaining free flow of two-way communication with the entire group of his followers.

Interpersonal Relations : Leadership involves interpersonal relations between the leader and his group members. A leader influences his group members and at the same time group members also influence the leader. Thus, a leader does not dominate the will of others but tries to relate the wills of many people to get them work as a team.

Common Goals : Leadership is the ability of influencing behaviour of people to work willingly to achieve some common goal. Terry and Franklin state that "It is the activity of influencing people to strive willingly for mutual objectives." Thus, leadership involves of community of interests between the leader and his followers.

Shared Function : Leadership is a shared function. A good leader shares everything with his followers. He shares ideas, opinions, experience, credits, blames and so on with his followers.

Pervasive Function : Leading is the function that pervades all the levels and functions of management. Planning, organising, motivating and controlling cannot be performed effectively without effective leadership.

Dynamic Art : Leadership is a dynamic art. No particular style of leadership is effective in all situations. The effectiveness of leadership depends heavily on the situational variables. Therefore, art of leadership is exercised and applied in accordance with the demands of the situations.

Power : Leadership is based on power. A person holding power over others is a leader. By virtue of power, a person is in a position to influence the behaviour of his group members. A leader may derive power from (i) superior knowledge, information experience or performance, (ii) formal authority, (iii) charisma, and (iv) distinct personality characteristics.

Leadership may be formal and informal.

Managing and leadership are not one an the same. But it is not always possible to distinguish between them in practice.

Leadership may be positive or negative.

Relation with Management

Although some people treat leadership and management as synonymous but the two should be distinguished. The major points of distinction between the two are outlined as follows :

Basis of Distinction	Leadership	Management
Meaning	Leadership is the process or art of influencing people to work willingly for achieving a goal.	Management is the process of getting things done through others.
Formal and informal organisation	Leadership exists in both formal and informal organisations.	Management operates only in formal organisations.
Power and Authority	Leadership is based on power. The power may be derived from formal authority or from any other source.	Management is based on authority which is delegated to a managerial position by a person in superior position.
Scope	The scope of leadership is narrower than that of the management. It is only a function of management.	The scope of management is wider than leadership. Management is the process of certain functions including the leading or leadership.
Relationship	There need not be a formal relationship between the leader and his followers.	There is a formal relationship between a manager and his subordinates.
Structures	Leadership structures are more flexible, open, informal and dynamic than management.	Management is bound by organised formal structures.
Achievement of goal	Leaders achieve goals by influencing and inspiring others.	Managers achieve goals by directing and controlling activities of others.
Guidance	A leader guides his followers through a special kind of behaviour.	Manager guides his subordinates through policies, plans, rules, procedures etc.
Education and	There is almost neglibile	There are many programmes

Training	arrangement for formal education and training for leadership.	for formal education and training of management.
Dependence	Leadership does not depend on managership. Hence, all leaders need not be good managers.	Managership includes leadership. Hence, all managers need to be good leaders.
Accountable	Leaders are not accountable for the actions and behaviour of their followers.	Managers are accountable for the actions and behaviour of their subordinates as well as for their own behaviour.
Following	People follow the leader willingly.	Subordinates follow the manager by the force of authority, rules and regulations.
Organisational environment	Leaders try to influence and change the organisational environment.	Managers try to adapt itself according to the organisational
Existence of position	Existence of a leader's position depends on the pleasure of his followers.,	Existence of manager's position is independent of the will of his subordinates. It depends on the terms and conditions of his service.

The Functioning

Leadership is a dynamic and constructive force in any organisation. It plays a crucial role in the success and survival of an organisation. It is the crucial factor that helps individuals to identify their goals. Newstorm and Keith Davis have very rightly stated, "Without leadership, an organisation would be only a confusion of people and machines, just as an orchestra without a conductor would be only musicians and instruments. The orchestra and all other organisations require leaders to develop their precious assets to the fullest." Briefly the importance and functions of leadership are as follows:

Determination of Goal : A leader plays a crucial role in laying down goals and policies of his group or the institution. He acts as a guide in setting organisational goals and policies.

Guides and Inspires or Motivates : According to Terry and Franklin, "leaders trigger a person's 'will to do', show the way and guide group members towards group accomplishment." Thus, an effective leader guides and inspires or motivates his group members to work willingly for achieving the goals. He makes every effort to direct and channelise all energies of his followers to the goal-oriented behaviour. He creates enthusiasm for higher performance among his followers.

Boosts Morale : Morale refers to the attitude of employees towards organisation and management and will to offer voluntary cooperation to the organisation. Morale is an internal feeling of a person. A good leader can arouse will to cooperate among the employees. According to Terry, "Leadership triggers a person's 'will to do' and transforms lukewarm desires for achievements into burning passions for successful accomplishments."

Creates Confidence and Enthusiasm : A good leader creates confidence among his group members. He does so by providing guidance, help and support in their day-to day work. He even provides psychological support and infuse the spirit of enthusiasm among them.

Develops Team-spirit : A good leader constantly tries to develop team-spirit among his group members/followers. He inculcates a sense of community of interests. He provides a satisfying work climate by harmonising individual and group goals. Thus, a leader reconciles conflicting goals and creates team-spirit among his followers.

Creates Vision and Initiative : It has been rightly said, where there is no vision, people perish. Leader give vision to their followers which, in turn, create initiative and enthusiasm among them. The followers use this vision and initiative to take up challenging tasks.

Transforms Potential into Reality : According to Newstorm and Keith Davis, "Leadership is the catalyst that transforms potential into reality." In fact, effective leadership can transform potential or dream into reality. Leaders can identify, develop, channelise and enrich the potentials existing in an organisation and its people.

Representation : A leader represents his group members. He is the connecting link between his group members and the top-management. He carries the views and problems of his group members to the concerned authorities and tries to convince them. Thus, he is in real sense an ambassador and guardian of his group feelings and interests. He also protects the interests of his group members against any outside challenge and threat.

Development and Use of Human Resource : An effective leader can develop and utilise human resource in a most effective way. A leader can influence the activities and behaviour of his followers to contribute their best. In fact, leadership can lift man's vision to higher sights, raise man's standard to higher performance and build man's personality beyond his normal limitations. *[Peter F. Drucker]*

Facilitates Change : According to Gordon, "In a world of change and uncertainty, business leader becomes a vital element in the very process of change itself." Thus, leaders can induce and introduce change. They are the instrumental in conceiving and managing change. They introduce change by convincing their followers about the positive effects of the change.

Ensures Survival and Success of the Enterprise : According to McFarland, "Administrative leadership is vital to the survival and effectiveness of organisation." No doubt that leadership plays a vital role in the survival and success of an enterprise. The quality of leadership goes a long way in the success and survival of an enterprise. Without effective leadership, many well established enterprises have miserably failed. Glover has also stated that "most failure of business concerns are attributable to poor leadership than to any other cause."

Contributes to Effective Management : Leadership is an essential and integral part of management. Effectiveness and efficiency of management largely depends on its leadership qualities. A strong leader can transform a lack lustre organisation into a successful one. Without leadership an organisation is but a muddle of men or machines .... Management activities such as planning, organising etc. are dormant cocoons until leader triggers the power of motivation in people and guides them towards goals. *[Keith Davis]*

Create Work Environment : Effective leadership can create work environment in which group members can work with pleasure. For this, the leader creates and maintains interpersonal relations of trust and confidence among the group members. Albanese has stated that "leadership is necessary in organisations in order to create work environments that are productive and satisfying for human beings."

Maintains Order and Discipline : An effective leader has qualities to maintain order and discipline in the organisation. He lays down standards of behaviour and sees that his followers follow the same in their behaviour. He shows exemplary behaviour and maintains self-disciple in order to maintain discipline among his followers.

Resolves Conflicts : Leaders play crucial role in resolving the conflicts arising in the group. He does it by harmonising the diverse intense interests of group members and the organisation.

The Traits : It has been widely accepted that a leader should have certain special qualities or traits. A large number of experts have opined about the qualities of an effective leader.

According to Ordway Tead, a leader should have the following qualities : (i) physical and nervous energy, (ii) enthusiasm, (iii) sense of purpose and direction, (iv) technical mastery, (v) integrity, (vi) technical skills, (vii) friendliness and affection, (viii) decisiveness, (ix) intelligence, and (x) faith. Terry and Franklin have identified the following qualities necessary for a leader : (i) energy, (ii) emotional stability, (iii) knowledge of human relations, (iv) personal motivation, (v) communication skills, (vi) teaching ability, (vii) social skills, and (viii) technical competence.

Prof. Robert L. Katz has found that managerial leaders need three kinds of skills : (i) technical skills, (ii) human skills, and (iii) conceptual skills.

Prof. Ivancevich *et al.* have suggested the following skills as important for managerial leader : (i) technical skills, (ii) analytical skills, (iii) decision-making skills, (iv) computer skills, (v) human relations skills.

The skills or qualities of a managerial leader suggested by Katz and Ivancevich *et al.* have already been discussed. A general description of qualities of successful leader is given under the following sub-heads :

Personality and Stamina : It is rightly said that sound mind resides in sound body. Hence, a leader should have sound health and good stamina to work hard. He should be handsome with charming personality. Such a leader has a lasting impact on the minds of his followers.

Intelligence : A leader should be intelligent. He should have above average level of intelligence. He should be capable of thinking scientifically.

Self-confidence : A leader should have self-confidence. He should be fully confident of his actions and decisions.

Vision and Foresight : A leader is,required to have sharp vision and foresight. He should be able to foresee the future trend of events. This quality prepares him for future challenges.

Ability to Inspire : An effective leader is one who has ability to inspire. Hence, he should be capable of influencing people by his ideas, actions and behaviour.

Ability to Communicate : A leader should have ability to communicate effectively. He should be efficient in verbal, written, gestural communication skills.

Sincerity and Honesty : A leader should be sincere and honest. His integrity should be above doubts. Sincerity and integrity makes a man truthful, high minded and gives him aspirations and high ideals. [*F. W. Taylor]*

Courage and will Power : It has been rightly said "without courage there are no virtues." No faith, hope, aspiration etc. can be transformed into realities without courage and will power. Hence, a leader should be courageous.

Flexible and Dynamic : A leader should be with flexible and dynamic mind-set. He should be capable of adapting ideas and views in accordance with the needs of the changing situations.

Emotional Stability i.e. Maturity : A leader should be capable of keeping his emotions under control. Emotional stability and cool temperament are necessary for a matured leader. Hence, he should remain cool, patient and undisturbed by the happening of unusual and unanticipated events.

Sound Judgement : A leader should have sound judgement power. He should be a shrewd judge of behaviour, actions and events. He should be able to judge the things judiciously.

Tact and Humour : A leader should be tactful in dealing with people and situations. He should have a sense of humour. These qualities help a leader to get the things done pleasantly without stress and strain.

Education and Knowledge : A leader should have proper education and knowledge. Particularly, the business leaders should have education at least in the field of accountancy, management, economics. It would be better if he has specialised knowledge in the field of management. Moreover, he should have up to-date knowledge of economic laws, policies and events.

Conceptual Skills : A leader should have and acquire conceptual skills. Conceptual skill is the ability to see the organisation as a whole and the relationships among its sub-units. It also includes the ability to visualise how the organisation fits into its external environment. Such ability helps a leader to understand problems and identify opportunities of the organisation and plan accordingly.

Administrative Skills : A manager-leader essentially needs to have administrative skills. He should be able to implement the plans and policies, to organise and to mobilise resources of the organisation in a pragmatic manner.

Analytical Skills : A leader should possess and develop analytical skills. These include the abilities to understand the things, situations, and problems in a systematic manner. Such skills are needed in evaluating performance, making decisions and handling complex situations.

Human Relations Skills : A leader should have human relations skills. Human relations skills refer to the ability to work well with others. It includes the ability to understand people and their problems and feelings.

Technical Skills : A leader should also possess technical skills. Technical skills relate to job knowledge and expertise. These include the ability to apply methods and techniques in performing the job and the ability to provide guidance and instructions to the followers.

Various Types

Leadership style is the general way or pattern of behaviour of a leader towards his followers in order to influence their behaviour to attain a goal. Every leader usually develops his own style of leadership. Hence, style of every leader differs from the other. However, a particular leadership style is affected by the degree of delegation of authority, types of power employed, degree of concern for human relations etc. Thus, there exists different leadership styles. The main styles of leadership are as follows :

1. Autocratic or authoritarian style, 2. Participative or democratic style, 3. Free-rein or *laissez-faire* style, 4. Patternalistic style.

Autocratic or Authoritarian Leadership : An autocratic leader is one who centralises power and makes all the decisions himself. He tells his followers what to do and expects to be obeyed without question. Thus, such a leader imposes his will on his followers. This style is typically of a person who accepts McGregor's Theory X assumptions. The characteristics features of such a leader are as follows:

(i) He centralises power.

(ii) He makes all the decisions himself.

(iii) He structures the work of his group members, as far as possible.

(iv) He exercises close supervision and control over his group members.

(v) He expects to be obeyed by his subordinates without question.

(vi) He gets the things done through fear or threats of punishment, penalties and so on.

(vii) He motivates his subordinates by satisfying their basic needs, through threats of punishment and penalties.

(viii) He believes in maintaining one-way communication *i.e.* from him to the subordinates.

Autocratic leaders may be of two types :

(i) Pure autocrat or negative leader-He is a dictator and makes all decisions himself. He superimposes his decisions on his subordinates. He carries out his decision by coercive or negative power. He uses fear of punishment or penalty to carry out his decisions. Thus, it is a negative leadership.

(ii) Benevolent autocrat or positive leader-When an autocrat leader avoids negative coercive power and uses reward power to influence his subordinates, he is called a benevolent autocrat leader. Such a leader shows active concern for the feelings and welfare of his subordinates. He may even encourage their participation in planning but he retains his power to make and execute decisions.

Autocratic leadership has the following advantages :

(i) It provides strong motivation and reward for the leader.

(ii) It permits quick decisions.

(iii) It provides structured work for employees.

(iv) It allows managers to hire less competent subordinates because their principal job is to carry out orders.

(v) It ensures compliance and execution of orders with certainty.

(vi) It permits close supervision and control of subordinates.

(vii) It helps manages to get things done with certainty.

But this style of leadership suffers from the following drawbacks/disadvantages :

(i) It overburdens managers because of centralisation of authority.

(ii) It creates fear and frustration among subordinates.

(iii) It hampers creativity of subordinates.

(iv) It blocks the free flow of two-way communication.

(v) In the absence of consultation and feedback from subordinates, decisions may cost heavily.

(vi) It is disliked by the subordinates specially when it is negative.

In spite of these limitations, autocratic leadership is suitable in the following situations :

(i) Where subordinates are not educated or untrained or incompetent.

(ii) Where subordinates are submissive and do not want to take responsibility.

(iii) Where leaders do not want *to* delegate authority.

(iv) When the organisation endorses fear and punishment as accepted disciplinary techniques.

(v) When achievement of target of performance is urgently required in time.

Participative/democratise Leadership : It is just opposite to autocratic leadership. Participative leaders decentralise authority. Such leaders involve subordinates in decision-making process. Thus, decisions are not unilateral. The leaders and their group members work at a social unit. They freely exchange their views and express opinions and suggestions. Such leaders exercise control through forces within the group. The main features of democratic leadership are as follows :

(i) Leader decentralises authority.

(ii) He involves subordinates in decision-making process. Hence, decisions are not unilateral.

(iii) He believes in free-flow of two-way communication.

(iv) He leads by mutual consent.

(v) He explains the reasons for his actions.

(vi) He and his, group members work as a social unit.

(vii) He motivates his subordinates through positive means *i.e.* rewards.

Participative leadership offers the following advantages :

(i) It helps avoid hasty decisions. Hence, it improves quality of decisions.

(ii) It encourages cooperation between the leader and his subordinates.

(iii) It motivates subordinates to perform better.

(iv) It contributes to higher productivity of resources.

(v) It tends to reduce employee grievances, dissatisfaction and turnover.

(vi) It facilitates introduction of change.

(vii) It helps create congenial work environment.

(viii) It helps develop future leaders and, thus, promotes organisational stability.

Participative leadership also suffers from the following disadvantages/limitations :

(i) It tends to slow the decision-making process.

(ii) It tends to dilute responsibility for decisions. It may develop a tendency of buck-passing.

(iii) It tends to reduce the role of the leader at the top.

In spite of these limitations/disadvantages, this leadership style is suitable in the following cases:

(i) Where the organisational goals are well set and understood by the subordinates.

(ii) Where leaders really intend to consider the views and opinions of the subordinates.

(iii) Where the workers are reasonably well educated and trained.

(iv) Where the leaders really desire active involvement of subordinates in decision-making process,.

(v) Where sufficient time is available for attaining the objectives.

Free-rein or Laissez-faire Leadership Style **:** Free-rein leadership style is one under which leader uses his power very little. The leader gives high degree of freedom to his subordinates in their operations. He depends largely on his subordinates to set their own goals and make their decision regarding their jobs. Thus, such a leader completely delegates his authority to his subordinates and allows them to make their own plans, procedures and decisions. He simply aids his subordinates in performing their job. He exists as a Contact person with the subordinates' external environment.

Free-rein leadership style is permissive and leader least intervenes his subordinates. The leader remains passive observer but intervenes only during the crisis.

Free-rein leadership is suitable where subordinates are highly competent and duty-conscious. It is successful where subordinates are able to train and motivate themselves. However, chaotic conditions may prevail all over the organisation under such leadership.

Free-rein leadership helps subordinates train and develop themselves independently.

Paternalistic Leadership : A paternalistic leadership is authoritarian by nature. It is heavily work-centred but has consideration for subordinates. Such a leader tends to look after his subordinates the way farther looks after his children. Such a leader helps, guides and encourages his subordinates to work together as members of a family.

This is a personalised leadership. The leader exercises his authority personally. He maintains direct personal contacts with his subordinates. He treats affectionately them like elderly member of a family. The subordinates, in turn, tend to remain submissive and faithful.

Under paternalistic leadership style, subordinates feel force to meet their leader. They also feel job security. Their problems and grievances are sympathetically considered and solved. The issues affecting subordinates' interests are sympathetically addressed. But this leadership style is usually resented and resisted in modern times.

Style Selection

These are the four basic leadership styles identified by the experts. But, in practice, no particular leader's style strictly falls under any of these categories. Moreover, no expert can suggest one best leadership style because leadership style is influenced by several forces/factors. A leader should, therefore, consider the following factors/ forces while choosing a leadership style :

Forces in the Leader : The forces operating in leader include the (leader's personality) characteristics, qualities and job skills, value system, interaction skills, self- confidence, confidence in subordinates, feeling of security 'and so on.

Forces in the Group : There are the forces that operate in the group which affect leadership. These include perceptions and attitude of group members towards the leader, toward their tasks and towards organisational goals, characteristics, skills, knowledge, needs and expectations of group members, size and nature of the group and so on.

Situational Forces : These are the other impersonal forces in the work environment of leader and his group members. Nature of the job and its technology, organisation structure and authority-relationships, organisational goals, policies, control system, trade unions and their influence, political, economic, cultural and ethical conditions of society.

Tannenbaum and Schmid's Situational Leadership Continuum : One leadership theory was developed by Robert Tannenbaum and Warren H. Schmidt in 1958. They modified and refined it in 1973.

Tannenbaum and Schmidt developed a leadership continuum. This continuum depicts a range of leader behaviours. It can be seen from the continuum that they identified, variety of leadership styles (seven styles shown) ranging from highly boss centred to highly subordinate centred.

On the extreme left of the continuum, leader behaviour is characterised by exercise of high degree of authority over subordinates. Such leadership style is regarded as boss-centred or authoritarian style. On the extreme right side of the continuum, leadership is subordinate-centred or democratic style. There are many other styles in between these two extremes. These styles vary with the degree of freedom a leader grants to his subordiantes.

Tannenbaum and Schmidt instead of suggesting a choice between the authoritarian and democratic styles of leadership offered a range of styles. They emphasised that no one particular style is always right or no other is always wrong.

The two extreme ends of the continuum have been referred as manager power influence and non-manager power influence. In moving from left to right, less and less authority is used by the leader (manager) and more and more freedom is allowed to subordinates in decision-making. In between the two extremes, five more leadership styles have been shown. All the seven styles of leader behaviour are as follows :

Manager makes Decision and Announce it : It is the extreme form of autocratic leadership where by the leader/manager is able to take decisions and subordinates are bound to accept and implement the decisions without any modification.

Manager Sells the Decision : In this kind of leadership, the leader (manager) takes decisions and persuades the subordinates to accept them.

Manager Presents Ideas and Invites Questions : Under this style, the leader/manager arrives at the decision and asks his subordinates to express their views on it. The leader responds to the questions of his subordinates.

Manager Presents Tentative Decision Subject to Change : In this case leader (manager) takes a tentative decision and review it in the light of the suggestions/views expressed by subordinates.

Manager Presents Problems, Gets Suggestions and takes Decision : In this kind of leadership, leader (manager) presents problems and takes decision after hearing the views/suggestions from the subordinates.

Manager Defines the Limits and Asks the Groups to make Decisions : Under this style, the decision is taken by the group subject to the limits set by the boss.

Managers and Subordinates Jointly make Decisions : In this kind of leadership, leader/manager and subordinates jointly make decisions within the limits defined by superior.

Tannenbaum and Schmidt believed that there is one best style of leadership for all situations. Hence, selection of leadership style depends on the demands or forces of the situation. These forces include the following :

(i) The forces operating in the Leader's/Manager's personality, such as his education, knowledge, experience, value system, confidence in subordinates etc.

(ii) The forces in subordinates such as their background, education, experience, values, willingness to assume responsibility.

(iii) The forces in the situation such as size, complexity, goals, structure, climate, values, traditions of the organisation, nature of work, technology used.

Tannenbaum and Schmidt revised the model in 1973 and emphasised that organisational environment and societal environment greatly influence the leadership style. According to them trade union movement, consumer civil rights movement etc. are the important organisational and societal forces which influence leadership style. These forces challenge the rights of managers/leaders to make decisions or deal with their subordinates. They cannot make effective decisions without considering the interests of the groups outside the organisation.

Four Systems

Prof. Rensis Likert and his associates at the University of Michigan have studied the patterns or styles of leaders. In the course of this research, Likert has developed four systems/styles of leadership that exemplify different behavioural aspects of leaders. They are as follows : System 1 : Exploitative-authoritative leadership System 2 : Benevolent- authoritative leadership System 3 : Consultative leadership System 4 : Participative group leadership.

System 1 : Exploitative-authoritative-System leadership is described as "exploitative-autocratic or authoritative." In this kind of leadership system, leaders/ managers are highly autocratic. They have little confidence and trust in subordinates. They motivate subordinates mainly through fear and punishment. They rarely or occasionally reward them. They make all decisions. They mostly use downward communication and have little interaction with subordinates. Likert found that productivity under this system is modiocre.

System 2 : Benevolent-authoritative-Under this system style of leadership, leaders have patronising confidence and trust in subordinates. Leaders take a very paternalistic attitude. Managers make decisions but subordinates have some degree of freedom in doing their job. Leaders motivate subordinates with rewards and also through some fear and punishment. They permit some upward communication and solicit some suggestions and ideas from subordinates. Under this system, productivity ranges from fair to good.

System 3 : Consultative leadership-In this style of leadership, leaders/managers have substantial but not complete confidence and trust in subordinates. Leaders consult their subordinate managers before setting goals and making policy decisions. However, operating decisions are made at lower levels in the organisation. Subordinates have considerable degree of freedom in making decisions about their job. Leaders usually try to make use of subordinates ideas and suggestions. They tend to use rewards for motivation with occasional punishments. Leaders usually tend to rely on two-way communication.

System 4 : Participative group leadership-Participative group leadership style is the Likert's recommended style of leadership/management. Likert considered it as the optimal style of leadership in our educated and dynamic society.

In this style of leadership, leaders/managers have complete trust and confidence in subordinates. They extensively interact with subordinates. They always try to get and use ideas and suggestions from subordinates.

Thus under this leadership style, the whole group participates in the process of establishing goals and making job related decisions. Leaders tend to give economic rewards on the basis of group participation in goal-setting and decision-making and evaluation of performance on jobs. They tend to engage in free flow of down-ward, up-ward and horizontal communication. They encourage decision-making across the organisation. Likert's 4 system management leadership is shown in the table given here.

Likert found that managers who applied the system 4 style to their operations had the greatest success as leaders. Likert, therefore, stressed that all leaders should strive towards a system 4 style if they want to maximise the quantity and quality of performance from subordinates.

Various Theories

Several theories of leadership have been developed by management theoreticians. These theories may be classified into three categories :

I. Personality theories

II. Behavioural theories

III. Situational or contingency theories

Personality Theories of Leadership : Personality theories are theories that focus on the personal qualities or traits of leaders. Such theories include the following : (A) Great man theory, and (B) Trait theory

(A) Great man theory of leadership-Great man theory of leadership claims that "leaders are born, not made". This theory asserts that great leaders are born with necessary qualities. Leadership qualities are inherited or carried in genes. Leadership qualities cannot be acquired or developed through formal education and training. Supports of this theory usually prove its validity by drawing examples from the great leader such as

Mahatma Gandhi, Pt. Nehru, Abraham Lincoln, Napoleon and others. They were born as leaders, it is asserted. Thus, the great man theory emphasises and implies the following things :

(i) Leaders are born and not made. Leaders are gifts of God to mankind.

(ii) Hence, every person cannot aspire to become a leader.

(iii) Qualities of leadership are inherited or carried in genes from generation to generation.

(iv) The inborn leadership qualities alone are necessary and sufficient for an effective leader.

(v) Leadership qualities cannot be acquired or developed through formal education and training.

(vi) Leadership qualities and effectiveness are independent factors. Hence, situational factors like the nature of followers, demands of the job, and the environmental factors have little or no effect on leaders effectiveness.

The theory has some credibility to the extent that leaders have certain mystic and their followers can realise them. Hence, qualities and actions of such leaders influence and inspire their followers at least to a limited extent. But this theory has been criticized and rejected by many experts for the following reasons :

(i) This theory does not have scientific basis and has no empirical validity. It does not provide a logical explanation of why, how and when an effective leader is born. It is more of a matter of chance that some great leaders were born with leadership qualities.

(ii) This theory does not prescribe the set of essential qualities of a great leader.

(iii) There is nothing inborn leadership qualities. Inborn leaders are imaginary characters.

(iv) This theory is also based on absurd belief that leadership is not affected by the situational/ environmental variables.

(v) Leadership qualities can now be acquired and developed through education and training.

(vi) Leadership qualities alone are not necessary to become a successful leader. Competence to deal with situational variables is considered a most essential leadership quality.

It is a matter of fact that Great man theory is totally rejected by most of the modern theorists.

(B) Trait theory of leadership-Trait theory of leadership is a modified version of the Great man theory. According to this theory leadership is largely a function of certain traits or qualities. This theory states that there are certain unique traits or qualities essentials for a successful leader. Any person who wants to be a successful leader must possess those traits. This theory also emphasises that these traits need not necessarily be inborn but may be acquired through education, training and practice.

The trait theorists have identified a long list of traits related to leadership qualities. Stogdill found the following traits :

1. Five physical traits such as energy appearance and height.
2. Four intelligent and ability traits.
3. Sixteen personality traits such as adaptability, aggressiveness, enthusiasm and self-confidence.
4. Six task related traits such as achievement drive and initiative.
5. Nine social traits such as cooperativeness, interpersonal skills and administrative ability.

Edwin Ghiselli has identified thirteen traits which included eight personality traits and five motivational traits. The personality traits include : (i) intelligence, (ii) initiative (iii) supervisory ability, (iv) self-assurance, (v) affinity for working class, (vi) decisiveness, (vii) masculinity-feminity, and (viii) maturity. The motivational traits include : (i) need for occupational achievement, (ii) self-actualisation, (iii) power, (iv) high financial reward, and (v) job security.

Of these 13 traits, Ghiselli found the following six to be very important leadership traits : (i) supervisory ability, (ii) need for occupational achievement, (iii) intelligent, (iv) decisiveness, (v) self-assurance, and (vi) initiative.

Thus, trait theory is a simple theory. It simply describes the qualities which a person must possess in order to become a successful leader. It, therefore, helps persons to develop such leadership qualities. It is also useful for those who train and develop leaders. But this theory is criticised for its following limitations :

(i) Trait theory is not based on scientific or systematic research. It is only a descriptive theory which states how some persons emerge as leaders. It does not offer any explanation why leaders emerge.

(ii) It offers a painfully long list of traits. Moreover, there is no universally acceptable list of traits for a successful leader.

(iii) It fails to state which set of traits are more important for leaders than others.

(iv) It does not highlight the traits which are necessary for acquiring leadership and which are necessary for nurturing and maintaining leadership.

(v) It fails to highlight the traits which may clearly distinguish leaders from followers.

(vi) This theory does not provide a method of measuring traits in a person.

(vii) It does not consider the whole leadership environment which determines the success of a leader. In other words, it fails to consider situational and environmental factors which determine the success of a leader.

(viii) It does not consider the fact that different roles and positions require different traits. Leaders at higher level more require conceptual skills where as the leaders at lower level more require technical skills. Similarly, leaders at middle level more require human relations skills.

Theory of Leadership : The personality theories focus on who the leaders are (Great man theory) or what the leaders are (Trait theory). Behavioural theory, on the other hand, focuses on what the leaders do *i.e.* on the actual behaviour of the leader.

Thus, behavioural approach of leadership attempts to emphasise actual behaviour or dimensions of behaviour in order to identify leadership. It is based on the premise that effective leadership is the result of effective behaviour of the leader. Hence, success of leadership depends on the behaviour of the leader and not on his traits.

A particular behaviour pattern of a leader (functional behaviour) makes him a successful leader and its opposite (dysfunctional) would reject him as a leader. The functional dimension of leader's behaviour include setting goals, motivating employees towards achievement of goals, making effective communication and interaction, building team-spirit etc. The dysfunctional dimensions of leader's behaviour include inability to accept subordinates' ideas, poor communication and ineffective interaction with employees, poor human relations and so on.

This approach asserts that favoural or functional dimensions of behaviour of leader provides greater satisfaction to his subordinates and hence, they recognise him as their leader. However, this approach recognises the fact that a particular behaviour of a leader may be effective only at a particular point of time and may be ineffective at other times.

Behavioural approach to leadership assumes that a leader uses conceptual, human and technical skills to influence and lead his subordinates.

Several attempts have been made to identify the basic dimensions of leadership behaviour. The most systematic and comprehensive research studies include the studies by Lickert, Blake and Mouton, and studies at Ohio State University and University of Michigan.

Behavioural approach to leadership is an improvement over the personality approach. It identifies the behavioural dimensions of leadership that may contribute to the success of a leader. But this approach does not use scientific tests. It uses questionnaire, observation and interviews to identify dimensions of behaviour. Hence, behaviour dimensions cannot be measured objectively.

Situational/Contingency Approaches/Theories : Personality theories hold that a leader can be successful if he has certain traits. Behavioural theories, on the other hand, hold that a leader can be successful if he behaves in a particular manner. Thus, both the personality and behaviour theories ignore the effects of situational factors on leadership. The situational approach of leadership emphasises that emergence and success of a leader is largely determined by situational factors apart from the traits and behaviour of the leader himself.

The focus of the situational approach is on the behaviour of a leader in a particular situation and not on the traits or qualities of the leader. This approach stresses that a leadership behaviour which is effective under one particular situation may be ineffective under the other. If a leader behaves in the same manner under all situations, he may fail.

Thus, situational leadership approach states that leadership is strongly affected by the situations under which a leader works. These situations are created by the following forces :

(i) Forces in the leader.

(ii) Forces in the subordinates.

(iii) Forces in the situation.

There are several different situational models of leadership have been developed. Fildler's contingency model, Path-goal model, Blanchard's model etc. are some of the well-known situational leadership models.

12

Significance of Motivation

William F. Glueck has rightly stated that "motivation is concerned with why people work hard and well or poorly." In fact, motivation is said to be the cause of behaviour. It is the cause what makes people to do things. It is the main spring of action in people. A manager has to find out and understand the cause of particular type of behaviour of his subordinates in order to get the things in the best possible manner.

The Concept

The term motivation is derived from 'motive'. The term 'motive', implies action to satisfy a need. The need, desire, drive, want, motive are often used interchangeably by the psychologists. Any motive, need, drive, desire or want prompts a person to do something. It is, therefore, said to be the mainspring of action in people. Thus, motivation simply means the need or reason that makes people to do some work or to take some work. For instance, a person needs respect from others. It makes him to do outstanding work. Consequently, he gets praise, recognition, higher pay, promotion and so on. Ultimately he gets respect from others in the family as well as in society.

According to Dale S. Beach, "Motivation can be defined as a willingness to expend energy to achieve a goal or a reward."

In the words of William G. Scott, "Motivation means a process of stimulating people to action to accomplish desired goals."

In the opinion of M.J. Jucius, "Motivation is the act of stimulating some one or oneself to get a desired course of action."

According to McFarland, "Motivation refers to the way in which urges; drives, desires, aspirations, strivings, needs direct control or explain the behaviour of human beings."

According to Terry and Franklin, "Motivation is the need or drive within an individual that drives him or her towards goal-oriented action."

In the words of Mondy *et al.*, "Motivation may be defined as the willingness to put forth effort in the pursuit of organisational goals."

In the words of Mescon *et al.*, "Motivating is the process of moving oneself and others to work towards attainment of individual and organisational objectives."

According to Kreitner, "The term motivation refers to the psychological process that gives behaviour, purpose and direction."

In the words of Robbins and Coulter, "Motivation is the willingness to exert high levels of effort to reach organisational goals, conditioned by the effort's ability to satisfy some individual needs."

In the words of Fred Luthans, "Motivation is a process that starts with a physiological or psychological deficiency or need that activates behaviour or a drive that is aimed at a goal or an incentive."

Thus, motivation is the need or reason that makes people to work or to take action. It includes the processes and forces in an individual that influence or encourage him to act or not to act in particular ways. It arouses or energises the willingness to put in effort in a particular direction.

The Characteristics/Nature : Following characteristics of motivation highlight the nature of motivation :

Motivation is Internal Feeling : Motivation is internal feeling of an individual. It points out the energising forces within an individual that direct or influence him to behave in a particular way.

Continuous Process : Motivation is a continuous or never ending process. It is so because human needs, desires, wants or wishes are endless. All of them can never be satisfied simultaneously. Satisfaction of one need gives size to another need. Therefore, motivation process goes on forever.

Dynamic Process : Motivation is a dynamic and complex process. It is so because it relates to human behaviour which is never static but dynamic. It keeps on changing continuously.

A Psychological Concept : The concept of motivation is mainly psychological. It relates to those forces operating within the individual employee which impel him to act or not to act in certain ways. *[McFarland]*

A way to Direct and Explain Behaviour : Motivation refers to the way in which urges, drives, desires, inspirations or needs direct, and explain the behaviour of human beings. *[McFarland].* It is the psychological process that gives behaviour, purpose and direction.

It is the Willingness to Exert Effort : Motivation is the willingness of an individual to exert effort in the pursuit of organisational goals and to satisfy some individual needs.

System-oriented : Motivation is system-oriented. It is the system that contains three main factors : (a) factors operating within an individual *i.e.* his needs, aspirations, wants, wishes, values etc.; (b) factors operating within the organisation such as organisation structure, technology, physical facilities, work environment etc.; (c) factors operating in the external environment such as customs, norms of society, culture etc. Motivation is the result of interaction among these factors.

Need-satisfying Process : Motivation is a need-satisfying process. An unsatisfied need creates tension that stimulates drives within an individual. These drives, generate a search behaviour to find particular goals that (if attained) will satisfy the need and reduce tension. *[Robbins and Coulter]*

Energising Force : Motivation is the process that energises or encourages individuals to put in effort to achieve organisational goals and to satisfy their needs.

Positive or Negative : Motivation can be positive or negative. Positive-motivation implies use of incentives such as increase in pay, reward, promotion, and so on for better work. Negative motivation, on the other hand, means punishment and penalties such as reprimands, threats of demotion, fear of loss of job etc.

Whole Individual is Motivated : Every individual is an integrated whole in himself. Therefore, whole individual can and should be motivated. A part of the individual cannot be motivated. It is so because motivation is a psychological concept that is concerned with the whole individual.

Frustrated Individual cannot be Motivated : A frustrated individual cannot be satisfied and motivated. In other words, an individual who is unable to satisfy his basic needs becomes frustrated. Such an individual cannot be motivated until his such needs are satisfied.

Motivation is Different from Morale : It is true that both motivation and morale relate to individual and group psychology. But distinction is made between the two terms. Firstly, motivation is the reason what makes an individual to do work. It consists of forces and procedures that direct or influence an individual's behaviour. On the other hand, morale is individual's or group's attitude and feelings about his work and work situation. It is a resultant state encompassing the willingness to cooperate. Secondly, motivation is an individualistic concept whereas morale is a group concept. Thirdly, motivation is the result of satisfaction of needs, desires, aspirations etc. whereas morale is the result of good motivation.

Motivation and Job Satisfaction are not Synonymous : Motivation is different from job satisfaction. Job satisfaction is the positive emotional attitude of an individual towards his job resulting from his job performance and job situation. It is a psychological contentment which an individual experiences from the factors associated with the job. Motivation, on the other hand, is the result of job satisfaction as well as individual's needs satisfaction.

The Requirement

Motivation is regarded as one of the most important functions of management. Importance of motivation can hardly be over-emphasised. Highly motivated people can make things happen in organisations. On the other hand, poorly motivated people can nullify the sounded organisations. *[Allen]* The importance of motivation is summarised in the following points :

Inspires Employees to Work : In the words of Clarence Francis, "You can buy a man's time and physical presence but you cannot buy enthusiasm, initiative and loyalty. You have to earn these things." These can be earned through the process of motivation. Effective motivation system inspires employees to do work or to take action. It prepares them to do their work with full devotion. It creates willingness among the employees to perform their work with great enthusiasm, zeal and loyalty.

Higher Performance : Highly motivated employees perform better and higher as compared to the employees with low level of motivation. Motivation is the mainspring of performance. Without motivation, the other contributors to performance become rather irrelevant. *[Gray and Smeltzer]*

Higher Productivity : Motivated employees can use their skills and organisational resources more efficiently and effectively. This ultimately results in higher productivity of all the resources of the organisation. David Holt has rightly remarked that "productivity is achieved through excellence and excellence is achieved by having an organisation of highly motivated individuals."

Effectiveness of Managerial Functions : A proper motivation system is key to the effectiveness of all managerial functions. Effectiveness of all managerial functions will go for naught if employees cannot be motivated to fulfill their responsibilities. Planning and organising cannot be successful if the employees are not properly motivated.

Helps Achieve Organisational Objectives : Motivation is core of management. Through motivation, managers encourage employees to direct their energies for achieving organisational goals. Thus, motivation helps achieve organisational objectives. Brech has rightly stated that "the problem of motivation is the key to management in action; and in its executive form, it is among the chief tasks of the general manager. We may safely lay it down that the tone of an organisation is a reflection of the motivation from the top."

Human Resource Development : Motivation help develop human:resource *in* an organisation. Through motivation, employees can be directed to enlarge their job skills. In order to maintain a continual reservoir of well trained and highly motivated employees, a sound motivation system should be in place.

Satisfied Human Resource : A sound motivation system ensures proper supply of motivated human resource. Such a system in an organisation can also ensure the satisfaction of needs and aspirations of individuals. Thus, it can attract and retain satisfied human resource in the organisation.

Boosts Morale : Morale refers to the attitude and feelings of employees about their work and work situation. Through motivation, employee attitudes and feelings towards work can be improved. This in turn boosts employee morale.

Sense of Belongingness : A proper motivation system promotes close ties between the enterprise and its employees. Employees begin to feel that enterprise belongs to them. Hence, employees become more concerned about the well being of the enterprise.

Reduced Employee Turnover and Absenteeism : Satisfied employees tend to stay longer and remain regular in the organisation. This, in turn, reduces employee turnover and absenteeism.

Facilitates Change : It is a research based fact that properly motivated employees are more receptive to new things and ready to accept change. This attitude facilitates introduce change and keep the organisation on the path of progress.

Effective Utilisation of Resources : Motivated employees concentrate on finding new and more effective ways of doing a job and utilising resources. Poorly motivated employees usually avoid work and misuse resources. Thus, effective utilisation of resources largely depends on the level of employee motivation.

Better Industrial Relations : A good motivation system creates congenial work environment and job satisfaction. Employees tend to work with cooperative spirit and in a disciplined manner. Management also offers them better wages and incentives. Hence, chances of conflict are greatly reduced. All this leads to better industrial relations.

Enhances Corporate Image: An organisation with motivated staff commands reputation in the business world and the society. Such organisations can easily obtain talented persons whenever the need arises.

Innovation and Development of Technology : Motivated employees can innovate and develop new technology and products for the organisation. There are many organisations where talented employees carry on research regularly and innovate. They develop new technology and products which are essential for the wellbeing of the organisation and the society as a whole.

Theories of Motivation : There are several theories of motivation. A few important theories are as follows :

I. Maslow's need hierarchy theory.

II. McGregor's theory X and theory Y.

III. Herzberg's two-factor theory.

IV. William Ouchi's theory Z

V. McClelland's achievement theory

VI. Vroom's expectancy theory

VII. Adam's equity theory

First four theories have been described in this chapter.

Maslow's need Hierarchy Theory : A.H. Maslow, a noted psychologist, propounded the need hierarchy theory of motivation. It is one of the best known theories of human motivation. According to Maslow, within every human being there is a hierarchy of five needs which are as follows :

1. Physiological needs
2. Safety needs
3. Social needs
4. Esteem needs
5. Self-actualisation needs

Physiological Needs : Physiological needs are concerned with the basic biological functions of the human body. These needs relate to the essentials for survival. These include the needs for food, water, clothing, shelter, rest, sexual satisfaction, recreation etc. These needs are inherent in the nature of a human body.

Physiological needs are the most powerful motivators as no human being can survive without them. These needs are at the lowest level in the hierarchy of needs. Hence, these needs have to be satisfied before higher level needs can be pursued. Therefore, an extremely hungry person can never think for things other than food. He dreams food, remembers food, perceives only about food and wants only food. Freedom, love, and respect are useless since they fail to fill his stomach. *[A.H. Maslow]*

Safety Needs : Safety needs are concerned with protecting the person from physical and psychological harm as well as the assurance that physiological needs will continue to be met. These include the needs of job security, economic and social security, *e.g.* pension, insurance etc. There needs can be satisfied by making provisions for pension, group insurance, provident fund, gratuity, safe working conditions, job security and so on. Safety needs begin to dormate when the physiological needs of a person are fairly met.

Social or Belonging or Love Needs : Social needs relate to the desire to have social interaction, friendship, affiliation belongingness with groups, acceptance, affection, support from others and so on. Such needs become motivators when physiological and safety needs have been fairly satisfied.

Self-esteem or Egoistic Needs : Self-esteem needs constitute the fourth level in the hierarchy of needs. These needs arise when physiological, safety and social needs have been fairly satisfied.

According to Maslow these needs are of two types :

(i) Need of self-respect or self-esteem, and

(ii) Needs for esteem from others or public esteem.

Self-respect means the respect in the eyes of oneself. Self respect needs include the needs for self-confidence for competence, for independence and freedom, for achievement, and personal strength. Esteem from other means the respect or image in the eyes of others. The needs of esteem from others includes the needs for prestige, recognition, acceptance, attention status, reputation and appreciation from others.

Self-actualisation Needs : The four needs described above motivate people by their absence. In other words, when people feel lack of food, clothing, shelter, security, social relationships, self-respect and respect from others, they are motivated to do something or take action. But self- actualisation needs are the needs and aspirations for growth. Such needs motivate people by their presence.

Self-actualisation needs concern the needs for maximising the use one's skills, abilities, potential to become everything that one is capable of becoming. Such needs relate to realisation of one's full potential for development growth arid fulfilment. This category of needs is placed at the apex of the 'need hierarchy' and hence are the highest level of needs.

It is pertinent to note that self-actualisation need is a distinct one. Each person's journey towards self-actualisation is distinct and unique. Therefore, every person finds his own ways for satisfying such needs.

Assumptions : Maslow's need hierarchy theory is based on the following propositions or assumptions :

1. A man is perpetually wanting animal. As soon as one of his wants or needs is satisfied, another appears in its place. This process goes on in every one's life.
2. An unsatisfied or fresh need motivates influences behaviour. Satisfied needs are.........................
3. Needs can be arranged in an order or a hierarchy.

In this hierarchy, physiological needs are at the lowest and most basic. These needs are followed in ascending order by the safety needs, social needs, esteem needs and self-actualisation needs.

4. There is always a sequence of emergence of needs. Higher level needs do not emerge or motivate unless all lower level needs have been fairly or minimally satisfied.
5. Higher level needs can be satisfied in more than one ways. But the ways to satisfy lower level needs are very limited.
6. Maslow separated the five needs into higher-level needs and lower-level needs. According to him physiological and safely needs are lower-level or lower-order needs whereas social, esteem and self- actualisation needs are higher level needs. Maslow believed that lower-level needs are mainly satisfied externally whereas the higher-level needs are satisfied internally.
7. The first four needs (physiological, safety, social and esteem needs) motivate people by their absence. In other words, when people feel a lack of food, clothing, sex, security, social relationships, respect etc., they are motivated to work. But self-actualisation needs motivate people by their presence.
8. Maslow believed that no need is ever fully satisfied. Needs can be largely or substantially satisfied.

For motivating someone, a manager should understand that person's level of need in the hierarchy and focus on satisfying needs at or above that level. It is the job of the manager to lift employees from lower-level needs to higher level needs.

The Merits : Maslow's need-hierarchy theory is best-known theory of motivation. It has received a wide recognition. It has been highly appreciated on the following grounds :

1. It is a logical theory because it recognises that an individual do something to fulfil his diverse needs.
2. It clearly states that satisfied needs are not motivators.

Therefore, managers can easily concentrate on unsatisfied needs of their subordinates.

3. It clearly states that a person advances *to* the next level of the need hierarchy only when the lower level need is minimally or fairly satisfied.
4. It offers useful ideas for understanding human needs and ways for satisfying them.
5. It helps to find out the reasons that influence behaviour of a person. Thus, it explains the reasons why people behave differently even in the similar situations.
6. It is a dynamic model because it presents motivation as a constantly changing force. It considers that every individual strives for fulfilment of fresh and higher-level needs.
7. It is a positive theory. It assumes that man is a healthy, good and creative being, capable of working out his own destiny.
8. It is a simple and humanistic theory.
9. It is based on reasonable assumption and has been substantiated by several research studies.

Limitations/Demerits : Maslow's theory suffers from the following limitations :

1. It is a simplistic theory and cannot be tested and validated in practice. It lacks empirical testing. It is difficult to interpret and analyse its concepts.
2. Maslow's theory is based on a small sample of subjects. It is a clinically derived theory which may not be accurate in real life.
3. Some criticise on the ground that hierarchy of needs does not exist. Individuals unlikely to behave in such a neat, step-by-step manner while perceiving and satisfying their needs. Moreover, all the needs are present at a given time. For instance, an individual motivated by self- actualisation needs also has the physiological needs. Hence, the need hierarchy is artificial and arbitrary.

4. Need hierarchy may not be the same among all the employees. Generally, socially, culturally and economically advantaged employees have higher-level needs whereas the socially and economically disadvantaged employees have lower-level needs.
5. There are some who argue that there is no evidence that a satisfied need is not a motivator.
6. Similarly, there is no evidence that satisfaction of one need automatically activates the next need in the hierarchy.
7. Human beings are not motivated by their needs alone but also by many other things. Therefore, it is doubtful weather deprivation of a need motivate an individual.

In spite of these limitations, the need hierarchy theory of motivation is important because of its rich and comprehensive view of the needs. The theory is relevant because need hierarchy helps managers to understand the behaviour of people. In the words of Fred Luthans, "The theory does make a significant contribution in terms of making management aware of the diverse needs of humans at work. The number or names of the levels are not important, nor is the hierarchical concept. What is important, is the fact that humans in the work-place have diverse motives."

Two Factor Theory

During the late 1950s Fredrick Herzberg, a US behavioural scientist (psychologist), and his associates developed two factor theory of motivation. This is also known as the 'Motivation-Hygiene theory'. This theory is based an empirical research on job attitudes of 200 engineers and accountants of a company. The researchers asked two questions from those two hundred employees:

(i) "Can you describe, in detail, when you felt exceptionally good about your job ?"

(ii) "Can you describe, in detail, when you felt exceptionally bad about your job ?"

They were all asked to describe the conditions that had led to those feelings.

Herzberg analysed the responses and revealed that factors which made respondents feel good were totally different from those which made them feel bad. Herzberg grouped those responses in two categories : (i) Hygiene factors or maintenance factors, (ii) Motivators or satisfiers. These are described in the table given below :

Herzberg's Hygiene Factor and Motivators

Hygiene Factors	Motivators
* Company policy and administration	* Achievement * Recognition
* Working conditions	* Advancement
* Job security	* Responsibility
* Salary	* Personal growth
* Quality of supervision	* Opportunities
* Interpersonal relations with superiors, co-workers and subordinates.	* Work itself

Hygiene factors or maintenance factors are related to the job environment. There are eight factors : working conditions, job security, salary, quality of supervision, company policy and administration, interpersonal relation and fringe benefits. Presence of these factors in job environment is essential if a reasonable level of satisfaction in employees is to be maintained. The absence or deficiency in these factors can cause dissatisfaction. The presence of these factors is necessary to avoid dissatisfaction and pain in the work environment. These factors do not motivate employees.

Motivators Motivate Employees : According to Herzberg, there are six motivators or motivation factors : achievement, recognition, responsibility, advancement, personal growth and the nature of the job itself. Adequacy of these factors make employees satisfied with their job and consequently motivate them. Their absence, however, rarely dissatisfies or demotivate the employees.

According to Herzbergs job satisfaction and job dissatisfaction are not opposites of each other. Absence of job dissatisfaction does not mean presence of job satisfaction. Satisfaction is achieved through motivators and dissatisfaction results from absence of adequate hygiene factors.

Therefore, managers should maintain adequate amount of hygiene factors in order to avoid dissatisfaction among employees. On the other hand, managers must ensure adequacy of motivating factors in order to motivate employees. However, presence of hygiene factors is essential for creating favourable frame of mind for motivation.

The Merits or Contribution : The merits or contributions of Herzberg's theory are summarised as follows :

1. It clearly distinguishes between the factors that motivate employees on the job and the factors that maintain employees on the job. In other words, it clearly states that the presence of hygiene factors is necessary in order to avoid dissatisfaction in employees. On the other hand, the presence of motivation factors is essential to motivate employees. Thus, both the groups of factors have different roles to play.
2. It recommends specific measures (*i.e.* motivators) to improve motivation levels.
3. It helps in understanding the effect of job content on motivation of employees.
4. It explains the significance of job enrichment on the job redesign and motivation.
5. It is a rational approach to motivation.

It clearly explains that the factors which cause job dissatisfaction are different from the factors which cause job satisfaction. In other words, absence of job dissatisfaction is not the presence of job satisfaction. Hence, presence of maintenance of hygiene factors avoid dissatisfaction in employees but does not cause satisfaction. Similarly, presence of motivators cause satisfaction and motivation.

The Limitations or Weaknesses : Though Herzberg's theory of motivation has gained wide-spread popularity among managers and management educators, it suffers from the following limitations :

1. It is alleged that research base was very narrow and was not representative enough to make justified generalisations.
2. It is difficult to distinguish job-context factors from the job-content factors. In many cases, job context factors have elements of job-content factors. Moreover, for some individual job content factors, *i.e.,* motivators have no significance because their job-related aspirations are very limited.
3. Sometimes in real life situations, there is no direct cause and effect relationship between satisfaction and performance. Many employees are satisfied with their job but their performance is not high.
4. The methodology used by Herzberg is sometimes questioned. Since raters have to make interpretations, different raters may have interpreted the responses in different ways.
5. It explains the reasons of job satisfaction and dissatisfaction. Thus it is, in fact, not a theory of motivation.
6. Not all the measures of satisfaction have been explored and utilised.
7. It ignores the impact of situational variables on motivation.
8. Herzberg assumes that there is a relationship between satisfaction and high performance. But in his research work he looked only at satisfaction and not at performance or productivity, *[Robbins]*
9. As a matter of fact, two factors are not distinct. Both hygiene factors and motivators may cause satisfactionand dissatisfaction.
10. The theory lays much emphasis on motivators and ignores the impact of hygiene factors on motivation.

Despite these limitations/criticism Herzberg's theory has made significant contribution to the manager's understanding of employee motivation. This is a valuable insight into employee motivation.

The Similarities : A careful study and analysis of these two models would suggest that they are not very much different from each other. Rather there are marked similarities between the two. The similarities between the two are as follows :

1. Both the models are content model. They focus on identifying needs that motivate people to do something.
2. Both the models assume that needs are the driving force that cause a person to do something.
3. Both the models fail to explain individual differences in motivation.
4. Both the models consider the similar needs. Herzberg's hygiene factors correspond to the Maslow's lower-level needs *i.e.* physiological safety and security needs.
5. Both tend to over simplify the motivation process.
6. Both emphasize the same set of relationships.
7. Both deal with the same problem.

Distinction Between Maslow's And Herzberg's Models

In spite of many similarities, the two models differ on the following counts :

Basis of Distinction	Maslow's Model	Herzberg's Model
1	2	3
1. Basis based on hierarchy of needs.	Maslow's model is is based on factors that avoid dissatisfaction and pain and the factors that satisfy and motivate employees.	Herzberg's theory
2. Order of needs needs in the order they emerge.	Maslow arranged the of needs in this model.	There is no such order
3. Nature of model	It is descriptive model.	It is prescriptive model.
4. Essence of theory model is that the unsatisfied needs	The essence of this gratified or satisfied needs motivate individuals for	The essence of model is that the

motivate individual to work.	higher performance.	
5. Effect of factors hygiene factors as motivators of behaviour. If a man ager offers opportunity to satisfy one of them, employee would exert increased effort.	This model considers factors come into play only when employee perceives them as inadequate.	This model considers that hygiene
6. Motivators or drive serve as motivator.	Any unsatisfied need serve as motivators.	Only higher order needs
7. Applicability the human beings working anywhere in the society irrespective of their need level.	It is applicable to all people whose lower-level needs have been satisfied.	It is more applicable to those
8. Division of needs are divided into primary (lower-level) and secondary (higher-level) and arranged in a hierarchy of five levels.	In this model, needs into hygiene factors and motivators.	In this model needs are divided
9. Motivators lowest unsatisfied need on the hierarchy motivates employees.	According to this model, correspond roughly to Maslow's higher-level needs, motivate employees or influence their behaviour.	Only motivators, which
10. Effect of satisfaction of needs	According to this model, once a need is satisfied, it no longer motivates.	According to this model, managers must concern themselves with the satisfaction of employees in order to motivate them.

McGregor's theory x and theory y : Prof. Douglas McGregor was a psychologist, management consultant and author. He wrote a book entitled *Human Side of Enterprise.* In this book he described two distinct set of assumptions about people at work. McGregor labelled these set of assumptions as Theory X and Theory Y. He believed that these assumptions influence the thinking and attitude of most managers about the people at work.

Theory X presents a pessimistic or negative view of human nature whereas Theory Y reflects an optimistic or positive view of human behaviour. Both the theories and their assumptions are described in the ensuing paragraphs.

Theory X : Theory X lists a set of assumptions which presents a pessimistic view of human nature. The assumptions of Theory X are as follows :

1. The average human being inherently dislike work and will avoid work, if possible.
2. Since human beings dislike work, they must be coerced, controlled or threatened with punishment to make efforts to achieve objectives.
3. The average human being prefers *to* be directed.
4. The average human being wishes to avoid responsibility.
5. The average human being has relatively little ambition.
6. The average human being wants security above all other factors associated with the work.
7. The average human being is inherently self-centred and indifferent to organisational objectives.
8. The average human being by nature, resists change.
9. The average human being is gullible, not very bright. He may be duped by charlatans.

Theory Y : Theory Y views human beings in optimistic or positive terms. The assumptions of this theory are as follows :

1. The average human being does not inherently dislike work. Employees find that work is as natural as play or rest if organisational conditions are appropriate.
2. Employees will exercise self-direction and self-control if they are committed to objectives. External control and the threat of punishment are not the only means to make employees to work towards objectives.
3. Commitment to objectives, is a function of the rewards associated with their achievement.
4. The average human being can be motivated by higher-level needs *i.e.* esteem and self-actualisation needs.
5. The average human being learns not only to accept but to seek responsibility. Avoidance of responsibility, lack of

ambition and emphasis on security are generally not inherent human characteristics.

6. The average human being seeks responsibility because it allows him to satisfy higher-level needs.
7. The capacity to exercise imagination and creativity in the solution of problems is widely spreaded throughout the population. It is not the sole province of the managers.
8. Under the conditions of modern industrial life, the intellectual potentialities of the average human being are only partially utilised.

Contribution : Theory Y suggests or contributes the following thoughts :

(i) Management is responsible for organising the resources of the enterprise for achieving organisational objectives.

(ii) Employees are not lazy or passive or resistant to organisational objectives.

(iii) Work is natural to employees if managers can release and channelise the employees' potential.

(iv) Employees can exercise self-direction and self-control if they are committed to objectives.

(v) Employees commitment to objectives can be ensured if the rewards are associated with the achievement of objectives.

McGregor believed that a manager's view about the employees affect the behaviour or motivation of the employees. If a manager treats employees lazy and irresponsible, the employees will behave accordingly. Conversely, if a manager treats his employees as mature and responsible, they would respond accordingly. Thus, if employees are treated in a Theory X manner, they will become lazy. If they are treated in accordance with Theory Y, they will be motivated and committed to the organisational objectives.

Theory X assumes that lower-order needs dominate individuals. Theory Y assumes that higher-order needs dominate individuals. McGregor believed that Theory Y assumptions were more valid than Theory X. Therefore, he proposed such ideas as participation in decision-making, responsible and challenging jobs and good group relations for maximising employee job motivation.

Criticism : Though McGregor's motivation theory has its significance, but it is criticised on the following grounds :

1. It tends to over-generalise or over-simplify behaviour of human beings. It is not easy and possible to classify people in two extreme categories.
2. Almost all the employees do not become good or bad because of the views that a manager has about them.
3. McGregor suggests that the job itself is a motivator but it is not so in all the cases. Jobs alone cannot motivate equally to all the persons.

The Distinction : The distinctions between Theory X and Theory Y are as follows :

Basis of Distinction	Theory X	Theory Y
1	2	3
1. Views about the human behaviour	It represents a negative or pessimistic view of human behaviour.	It represents a positive or optimistic view of human behaviour.
2. Liking for work	This theory assumes that people dislike work and will try to avoid work, if possible.	This theory assumes that people regard work as natural as play or rest.
3. Direction	It also assumes that people seek direction from superior.	It assumes that people will exercise self-direction and self-control if they are committed to the objectives.
4. Responsibility	It assumes that people avoid responsibility.	It assumes that people seek and accept responsibility.
5. Creativity and change	It assumes that people lack creativity and resist change.	It assumes that people are creative by nature and ready to accept change.
6. Focus on needs	It focusses on lower-level needs *i.e.* physiological and safety needs.	It focusses on higher-level needs *i.e.* social esteem and self-actualisation needs.
7. Style of leadership	It represents autocratic leadership.	It represents democratic leadership.
8. Role of incentives	It emphasises the role of financial incentive in motivation.	It emphasises the role of non-financial incentives in motivation.

9. Role of job factors or job	It assumes key role of job factors in motivation.	It assumes key role of job itself in motivation.
10. Nature	It is a traditional theory of motivation.	It is a modern theory of motivation.
11. Applicability	It is more applicable to illiterate or unskilled and lower-level employees.	It is more applicable to skilled employees occupying higher positions.

William Ouchi's Theory Z : William Ouchi wrote a book entitled, *"Theory Z : How American Business can Meet the Japanese Challenge"*. In this book, he described management practices in a number of U.S. Companies that are similar to those that successful Japanese companies have been utilising for years. Ouchi identified IBM, Hewlett-Packard, Intel, P & G, Eastman Kodak as Theory Z organisations.

According to Mondy *et al*, "Theory Z is the belief that a high degree of mutual responsibility, loyalty and consideration between companies and their employees will result in higher productivity and improved employee welfare."

According to Weihrich and Koontz, "Theory Z refers to selected Japanese managerial practices adapted to the environment of the United States as suggested by William Ouchi. For example, one of the characteristics of Type Z organisations is the emphasis on interpersonal skills needed for group decision-making."

Features of Theory Z : Theory Z is a hybrid management system which incorporates the strengths of Japanese and American. management. It describes characteristics common to certain successful Japanese and American Companies. The distinguishing features of Theory Z are as follows :

Strong Bond between Organisation and the Employees : Theory Z suggests strong bond between organisation and its employees. Ouchi has suggested certain ways for this, including the life-time employment and avoiding retrenchment and lay-off. Moreover, financial and non-financial incentives should be offered to motivate employees. Theory Z also emphasises that as against vertical promotions of employees, more emphasis should be placed on horizontal promotions. Such promotions/movements will reduce stagnation. A career plan for each employee should be prepared so that every one reaches to the right position in the organisation.

Employee Participation : Theory Z suggests that employee participation should be ensured in decision-making. Employees should be consulted and their suggestions should be considered while making decisions. However, the decisions affecting employees' interest directly should be made jointly. This will increase their commitment to the implementation of the decisions.

Informal or Integrated Structure : Theory Z suggests no formal organisation structure. There should not be charts, divisions, or any visible structure. It emphasises on perfect team-work with cooperation along with sharing of information, resources and plans. Members of organisation should work as a team and solve all the problems with no formal reporting relationships. There should be minimum of specialisation of positions and of tasks.

Human Resource Development : Theory Z recommends that managers should develop new skills among the employees. Managers should, therefore, recognise the potentials of their subordinates. They develop their potentials through proper career planning, training and incentives. Managers can also use job enrichment and job enlargement techniques for developing their subordinates.

Informal Control : Theory Z also suggests that managers should pay more attention to informal control procedures. Managers should lay more emphasis on mutual trust and cooperation rather than on formal authority in ensuring control. In other words, managers should control through informal mechanisms.

Mutual Trust : Theory Z requires that there must be climate of mutual trust and confidence between the employees, the managers and the unions. According to Ouchi, trust, integrity and openness are closely related. All these are the prerequisites of a sound organisation. Trust grows where the openness of minds and relationships exists.

Evaluation and Training are Important : Theory Z suggests that more emphasis should be given to evaluation and training than to promotion. The employees should be evaluated over a fairly long period using both quantitative and qualitative measures. This will increase commitment of employees to the organisation.

Responsibility : Theory Z requires that responsibility should be assigned on an individual basis. Individuals should assume responsibility for decisions. However, employees should be allowed to share or participate in decision-making.

Career Paths : Theory Z suggests that there should be non-specialised career paths. The career paths should involve multiple function experience. For this emphasis should be laid on job rotation and broad-based training. This, in turn, gives an employee a better feel for the entire organisation.

Concern for the People : Theory Z suggests that there should be holistic concern for people. Such holistic concern should extend beyond the work-place and reflect genuine concern for the total employee personality including the employee's family, hobbies, personal ambition and so on.

Thus, theory Z provides a new dimension of motivation of employees. It is not merely a motivational technique but it provides a complete theory of management. It calls for mutual trust and cooperation between managers and workers.

Theory Z has been successfully employed by the Japanese companies operating in U.S.A. The process of implementing Theory Z in India has already been started.

Maruti Udyog Ltd., a company with Japanese collaboration, is one such company where theory Z is being applied. For this purpose, work-place has been designed on the Japanese pattern. A common canteen has been provided for all the employees irrespective of their position in the company. Similar uniform has been introduced for all. All this has been done to avoid class or group feelings among the employees and to remove status difference among the employees.

Appraisal of Theory Z : Theory Z is considered a comprehensive theory or philosophy of management. It involves a complex amalgamation of management principles and practices for obtaining cooperation of the employees. It provides a complete transformation of motivational aspect of employees. But it suffers from the following limitations of drawbacks.

Difficulty in Life-time Employment : The provision for life-time employment seems to be difficult for *two* reasons :

(i) No employer would like to retain an employee who is less productive.

(ii) No employee will hesitate to an organisation if there is a better chance of employment.

Common Culture Difficult : Theory Z emphasises on common culture in organisations which is very difficult. People come from different backgrounds and environments and with different religion, habits, languages etc. All these create barriers in developing common culture.

Difficulty in Participation : Participation in decision-making process is also very difficult. Some managers dislike the idea because it hurts their ego and freedom. In some cases, employees are also reluctant to participate actively in decision-making process because of the fear of criticism. Sometimes, employees are not capable to participate in decision-making. Consequently, participation of employees in decision-making becomes difficult.

Operational Problems : There may be operational problems to managers in implementing theory Z. For instance, theory Z emphasises organisation without formal structure. But it is difficult to run an organisation without a formal structure. In the absence of formal structure, there may chaos in the organisation because no one knows who is accountable to whom.

Cultural Difference : Theory Z is based on the Japanese management practices which are influenced by the Japanese culture. But each country differs in its culture. Therefore, the same management practices cannot be applied to each country.

No Complete Solution to Motivational Problems : This theory does not suggest the total solution to motivational problems. It provides a complete philosophy of management.

In spite of all these criticisms, theory Z is becoming popular among many managers and organisations.

Classification of Motivation : Motivation may be classified in the following categories :

Positive and Negative Motivation : Positive motivation is the process of influencing others to do work or to behave in accordance with the desire of the leader through the use of reward. Thus, positive motivation is based on reward or gain either monetary or non-mortetary.' The methods of positive motivation include pay, fringe benefits, praise, responsibility, participation in decision-making, social recognition and so on. Positive motivation creates congenial and optimistic work environment in the organisation. It inculcates sense of belongingness among the employees.

Negative motivation is the process of controlling negative behaviour/efforts of employees through fear and punishment. Thus, negative motivation is based on fear of force or threats. When employees fail to perform desired work or fail to behave in the desired manner, they are threatened or forced not to do so. Such threats or forces include wage cuts, retrenchment, demotion, transfer, reprimands and so on. Experts are of the opinion that as far as possible, negative motivation techniques should not be used. It is due to the reason that in the long-run, negative motivation may result in lower productivity. It creates frustration and hostility among the employees.

Extrinsic and Intrinsic Motivation : Extrinsic or external motivation is one which arises from external factors. It is related to job environment. It is the incentive or reward that a person receives after finishing his work. It includes higher wages, profit-sharing, fringe benefits and so on.

Intrinsic or internal motivation is that which comes from the satisfaction that arises while performing a job. It is an internal reward *i.e.* satisfaction that comes while a person is performing his job. Thus, it is a motivation that arises out of a job itself. It is an internal stimulus resulting from job content and not from job environment.

Herzberg suggested for job enrichment in order to provide intrinsic motivation. Higher responsibility, opportunity for achievement and individual growth, praise social recognition, are the basic sources of intrinsic motivation.

Intrinsic motivators motivate some people more than extrinsic motivators. But in reality both are necessary. If wages, job security, fringe benefits are inadequate, it would be difficult to recruit and retain good personnel. Turnover, absenteeism and grievances will tend to be higher where management ignores extrinsic motivators. Therefore, a sound motivation system should provide both extrinsic and intrinsic; motivators.

Financial and Non-financial Motivations : Financial motivation is the pecuniary motivation and occurs from direct or indirect monetary benefits. Wages, fringe benefits etc. are the direct monetary benefits. Bonus, profit-sharing plans, pension plans, health insurance plans etc. are the indirect financial benefits.

Non-financial motivation is one which is not associated with monetary rewards. In fact, non-financial motivation is psychic in nature. It comes from the satisfaction of higher-level needs *i.e.* social, esteem and self-actualisation needs. Work environment, praise, recognition, promotions, more authority and responsibility etc. are the non-financial motivators. Financial and non-financial incentives are being discussed in detail in the ensuing paragraphs.

Techniques of Motivation : Managers use variety of techniques for motivating employees. Such techniques may be broadly classified under the following two heads :

I. Financial or monetary techniques.

II. Non-financial or non-monetary techniques.

Financial Techniques/Incentives : Financial techniques of motivation are those which involve financial expenditure for an organisation and increase money income of its employees.. These include (a) pay, (b) dearness and other allowances, (c) bonus, (d) profit-sharing, and (e) fringe benefits and so on.

Fringe benefits are the benefits over and above regular pay and variable payment related to performance. Fringe benefits is, thus, a wider term includes housing, transport, recreation facilities, lunch, clothing and washing allowance or facilities, payment for holidays and leave-travel benefits, free medical services or mediclaim insurance, disability benefits, retirement benefits including pension and gratuity and so on. Thus, financial techniques are the financial incentives that provide pecuniary or monetary benefits or rewards to employees.

Monetary techniques are, thus, pecuniary benefits or rewards to the employees. These are tangible and visible incentives. These incentives can satisfy the physiological and safety and security needs of employees. These also play crucial role in satisfying the social and esteem needs of the employees. Money recognised a symbol of social status and source of power in the modern times. William F. Whyte has, therefore, very candidly stated that "man has not born loving money. He has *to* learn to love it. This learning takes place in varying degrees in various parts of the world." Thus, financial techniques beyond doubt serve most powerful role in motivating employees.

Non-financial Techniques/Incentives : Non-financial techniques of motivation are those which are not associated with financial rewards. Such techniques are mainly psychic in nature. These are associated with the work and work environment. Such techniques contribute to the satisfaction of higher-level needs such as social, esteem and self-actualisation needs. Some of the non-financial techniques of motivation are as follows:

Job Enlargement : Job enlargement is one of the modern techniques of motivation. Job enlargement means enlarging or adding more and different but simple tasks to a specialised job. Thus, it increases the number and variety of tasks a worker should do. Consequently, employees are encouraged to learn new skills or take new responsibility. This presumably reduces monotony and boredom and increases satisfaction and motivation of employees. This technique is also called the horizontal job loading.

Job Enrichment : Job enrichment is another technique of motivation. It is a technique of vertical job loading. It is a technique which focusses on job depth. Job enrichment refers to the basic changes in the content and level of authority and responsibility of a job so as to provide greater challenge to the employees. It is the process of adding several positive inducement and attractions in a job with a view to make the job more interesting, meaningful and challenging. The job-holder is vested with more authority and autonomy for making decisions on operational matters of his job.

Thus, it permits self-direction and self-control which, in turn, motivates employees.

According to Herzberg job enrichment is a process of building motivators into jobs. He believed that motivators lead to job satisfaction which, in turn, leads to higher performance. Therefore, Herzberg strongly advocated job enrichment as the most important technique to improve motivation and performance of employees.

It may be pointed out that both job enlargement and job enrichment are the job redesign techniques. But job enlargement is the horizontal job-loading whereas job enrichment is vertical job-loading. Former technique assigns new and more tasks to employees whereas latter grants additional authority, autonomy and control to the employees.

Job Rotation : Job rotation is also regarded as a motivation technique. It is a technique in which employees are provided an opportunity to perform different jobs or functions by rotation. The purpose of job rotation is to broaden the scope of job and to increase the knowledge and skill of the employees about the job. This, in turn, relieves employees from boredom and monotony and improves their motivation level.

Praise and Recognition : Praise appreciation and recognition are the most effective and direct means of motivation. These techniques acknowledge the performances of employees to the society. These satisfy the social and esteem needs of the employees. For instance, a pat on the back of an efficient employee brings more happiness to him than the increase in the pay. Managers, therefore, give away prizes, certificates, plaques, letter of appreciation, etc. to the employees performing the best.

Participation : Employee participation in management is yet another technique of motivation. Employee participation means involvement of non- managerial personnel in the organisational and managerial activities, such a practice can ensure commitment of employees towards accomplishment of organisational goals. Consequently, employees feel involved in the organisation and their level of motivation improves. Employee participation may brought about by information sharing, suggestion system, consultation, representation on committees, board of directors and so on.

Competition or Contests : Competition or contests are means of motivation among employees. People usually like to compete with others and win over them. Therefore, managers may arrange competitions or contests for the employees. Managers fix certain goals or standards of performance for employees and challenge them to achieve them ahead of others. The winners are awarded prizes, given certificates of performance or appreciation letters with or without financial rewards. The winner gains recognition for his performance and social status and prestige. This all satisfies his social and esteem needs.

Promotion/Status : Promotion to a higher post or increase in the status of a person improves his motivation level. Promotion may not always result in more pay or financial rewards but increases social status of the employees. This satisfies his social and esteem or ego needs. Therefore, managers take various measures to increase status of their subordinates. These include, bigger air conditioned chamber with superior furniture and fixtures, personal assistant, cellular phone, computer, lap-top computer, air travel facility and so on.

Delegation of Authority : Delegation of authority to execute a given task often proves to be a strong motivating force. This enables subordinates to have effective control over the work and its environment. Job enrichment also involves delegation of authority.

Feeling of Accomplishment : Employees are motivated to work better if they have a feeling of accomplishment. This feeling can be inculcated by providing more authority, autonomy, applying the MBO technique, better career planning and development and so on.

Security of job-In the modern age, there are threats of loss of job from technological change. By providing security of job, employees may be motivated to work hard.

Congenial Social Environment : Employees may also be motivated by creating congenial social environment. For this, managers can carefully plan and execute induction programmes, provide means to socialise employees through rest pauses and recreation programmes, promote the informal relations among the employees. These measures can go a long way in satisfying social and ego needs of employees.

Opportunity for Advancement : Opportunity for advancement can serve as a strong motivating force. This helps to develop their personality and talent. Such opportunity satisfies social ego and self-actualisation needs.

Quality Circles : A quality circle is a group of employees of a work unit who meet frequently with their superior to identify and solve work related problems of their unit. This circle provides an opportunity to express opinions or suggestions in a frank, free and informal setting about the matters relating to product quality, cost and productivity of resources. Such circles, therefore, serve as a means to satisfy employees needs for interaction and self-expression. Hence, such circles are regarded as a means of motivation to employees.

Sound Work Climate : Work climate refers to the physical environment of the work-place. It is the basis of employee motivation. Creation and maintenance of sound work climate is a prerequisite for sound motivation system. Therefore, the factory layout, surroundings, facilities such toilets, canteen, rest-rooms etc. should be properly planned and maintained in order to motivate employees.

There is not exhaustive list of non-financial techniques of motivation. There are many more techniques. A manager should use any or all the techniques keeping in view the needs of the employees and the prevailing circumstances.

Essentials of a Sound Motivation System : According to Koontz and O'Donnel, "A sound motivation system must be productive, competitive, comprehensive and flexible." In fact, a sound motivation system should have the following essentials:

Purposive : A motivation system should be purposive. Therefore, motivation system should clearly state its objectives. It must reflect the objectives and philosophy of the organisation.

Productive : A motivation system should aim at increasing productivity of the organisational resources. It should be able to increase efficiency and effectiveness of all employees and other resources as well.

Positive : As far as possible, a motivation system should be positive- It should adopt a positive approach towards employees. It must aim influencing behaviour and actions of employees through rewards and satisfaction of needs.

Simple : Motivation system should be simple to understand by employees. Moreover, it should be simple to implement for the managers. A complex system can never produce the desired results.

Challenging : A motivation system should be challenging. It should set challenging but attainable goals before the employees.

Competitive : A motivation system should be competitive for the employees as well as for the organisation. It should be able to create competitive spirit among the employees. Moreover, it must be able to compete with other organisations. In other words, it should be better and more attractive to the employees than that of the competitive organisations. It must be capable of attracting employees of competitive organisations.

Comprehensive : A motivation system should consider all the needs of all the employees in the organisation. It should recognise and consider individual nature, perceptions, values, needs and abilities. It should be capable of motivating efficient as well as inefficient employees.

Flexible and Dynamic : A motivation system should be flexible and dynamic. It should be capable of being adapted to changing needs of the employees and environmental situations as well.

Stable and Permanent : Motivation system should be reasonably stable and permanent. It should be a permanent feature of an organisation. *Ad hoc* motivation system cannot motivate employees on a continuing basis.

Equitable : A motivation system should be equitable to all the employees. It Should be free from biases to any individual or group of individuals.

Linkages between Performance and Reward : There should be direct and positive linkages between performance and reward in the motivation system. The linkages between the two should be clearly made known to the employees.

Integration of Organisational Individual Goals : A motivation system should always integrate organisational goals with individual goals. It should contribute to the achievement of organisational goals along with the individual goals.

Blending Financial and Non-financial Incentives : There should be a perfect blending or combination of financial and non-financial incentives. This will help in satisfying the lower-level as well as higher-level needs of the employees.

Provision for Punishment : A sound motivation system should be positive but it must contain a provision for punishment too. It must provide for penalty for persistent unacceptable performance and behaviour of the employees.

Feedback : There should be adequate and effective mechanism for feedback on the application of motivation system. Employees should be periodically informed about their performance and rewards.

13

Planning Procedure

Planning, like organising is a fundamental managerial function. In simple words, planning is deciding in advance what is to be done, when, where, how and by whom it is to be done. Thus, a plan is a determined course of action. It is an attempt on the part of a manager to anticipate the future in order to achieve better performance. In the management literature, the word 'planning' has been defined like this:

A careful analysis of above definitions reveal that planning is in essence all about choosing an optimum alternative from managerial point of view. It is also concerned with the setting of organisational goals or objectives and determining the approach by which the goals and objectives are to be accomplished. Thus, planning coordinates the activities of the organisation towards defined and agreed upon objectives. The following are the important elements to planning:

1. The essence of planning is looking ahead. It is always concerned with future.
2. It involves a pre-determined course of action.
3. This action course is determined after a careful study of alternative courses.

4. It is a continuous and integrated process.
5. It has always a dimension of time.
6. Its main object is to achieve better results.

The Significance

The importance of planning lies in the fact that it is like a navigator of business circumstances. A business organisation has to work in an environment which is uncertain and ever changing. It is proper planning only that enables a manager to carve out the future course of action. Terry has very rightly said that, "Planning is the foundation of most successful action of an enterprise." It brings orderliness, efficiency and stability in managerial actions and decisions. It provides rational approach to managerial activities. The following are some important benefits of planning.

Planning Offsets Future Uncertainty and Change: Future is uncertain and full of changes. Both these elements make planning a necessity. Planning brings a higher degree of certainty, rationality and order into the organisation. Without planning a manager is forced to react to situations or problems. Planning permits a manager to act with initiative and to create situations to the organisation's advantage. It helps a manager in shaping the future of his organisation rather than let him be caught in an endless trap of reacting only to current crises.

Planning Helps in Management by Objectives: The first element of planning is setting the goals and objectives for the organisation as a whole and all its components. This gives a sense of direction to the working of the organisation and saves it from going astray or drafting about aimlessly. As efforts are directed towards desired and well defined objectives, haphazard approaches are minimized, efforts are coordinated and duplications are avoided.

It Helps in Coordination: Planning helps the management in the coordination process also. As Koontz and O'Donnell say, "Plans are selected courses along which the management desires to coordinate group action." The well defined objectives, well published policies, well developed programmes and procedures—these all things help in coordination. It avoids duplication of work and interdepartmental conflicts also.

Economy in Operation: Planning is the way to realise the business objectives in the cheapest and the best way. It paves the way for proper utilisation of company resources. Planning involves the development of one best way of doing things which is economical in also.

Helps in Control: Planning is always a prerequisite for controlling. No control can be exercised without planning. Planning distributes the responsibilities to different persons and jobs, develops the standards for comparison of actual performance, estimates the time and cost of the operations through forecasts and budgeting process, etc. It brings effectiveness and smoothness in the process of control. It is planning only that enables a manager to check the performance of his subordinates.

Helps in Executive Development: Planning helps in executive development also. The formal planning leads to disciplined thinking, because executives have to put their approach to improve their thinking and imagination in their minds.

Various Steps

After having discussed the meaning and importance of planning let us discuss the various steps involved in the planning process. The following are the important steps in the process of planning:

Determination of Objectives: The first step in planning work is to determine the objectives of the enterprise. These objectives set the pattern of the proposed course of action and shape the future policies. The objectives should be for the organisation as a whole and then it must be broken down into departmental, sectional and individual objectives. Objectives indicate the end-points of what is to be done, where the emphasis is to be placed and what is to be accomplished by the network of policies procedures, rules, budgets and strategies. Objectives must be specific, clear and informative.

Establishment of Planning Premises: The second step in planning is to establish planning premises. Premises are planning assumptions, the future setting in which planning takes place. Thus, it is a forecast of those business conditions under which a plan is to operate, for example, population trends, production costs, government policies and availability of material, power of labour, etc. Forecasts and trends analyses provide most of the information required in planning.

Determination of Alternative Courses: The third step in planning is to search for and examine alternative courses of action. There is hardly a plan for which a number of alternatives cannot be found. In business, there exist a number of Management Planning Processes, achieving the desired objectives. All possible alternatives should be found out for their comparative and analytical evaluation.

Evaluation of Alternatives and Sof courses of Action: The next step is the evaluation of alternative courses of action and selecting a suitable and the best course of action. All the possible alternatives should be compared and evaluated in the light of premises and goals, with reference to considerations like cost, speed and quality. The selection of a satisfactory course of action is the point at which the plan is adopted.

Preparation of Derivative Plans: The next step in the planning process is to formulate the derivative plans in support of the basic plan. There are sub-plans or departmental plans. The basic plan prepared for the whole enterprise cannot be effectively operated in the absence of such plans. So within the framework of a primary or basic plan, derivated plans are developed in each area of the business to integrate objectives with a network of policies, programmes, procedures, etc.

Timing and Sequence of Operation: Timing is an essential consideration in planning. After developing the plans and sub-plans, the starting and finishing times should be fixed for each plan. Scheduling is very useful not only in sales and production areas but in other functional areas also.

Securing Participation of Employees : The execution of a successful plan depends to a large extent upon the loyalty and sincerity of the subordinates. It can be secured only when planning their proper participation is secured. Plans must be communicated, explained and consulted with them thoroughly. Such participation improves the quality of planning and involvement of subordinates in it.

Considering the Strategy: Strategy has a significant contribution towards the execution of a plan. So, consideration of different strategies becomes an integral part of the planning process. A suitable strategy should be planned and followed for the successful implementation of the planned course.

Providing Follow-up to the Proposed Course of Action : Lastly a provision for follow-up measures should be made for the time when a plan is put into action. In the context of current problems and situations, necessary adjustment in plans becomes imperative, so necessary provision should be made before hand.

Various Types

Planning consists of several individual plans or component parts. From its objectives an organisation develops standing plans and single-use plans. Standing Plans lead to the development of policies, procedure and rules, etc. Single-use plans produce programmes, budgets and strategy, etc.

Standing Plans: These are permanent plans. They are used again and again and include procedures, methods and rules, etc.

Objectives: Objectives provide the basic foundation upon which the structure of plans are built. To guide and unite the efforts of employees in a desired direction, the management must set its objectives. The objectives must be defined in clear terms. It is only clearly defined objectives that will enable a management to effectively plan policies, procedures, methods and strategies and so on. Objectives may be general or specific, short-term or long-term, tangible or intangible. As effective management nowadays implies management by objectives, all planning work must spell out the objectives to be realised from the proposed plan.

Policies: General statements that guide decision-making are called policies. They define the boundaries within which decisions can be made by the subordinates. They direct decisions toward the accomplishment of objectives. The basic purpose of policies is to secure a consistency of purpose and avoid decisions which are based on expediency. Policies may be either written statements or oral understanding in general terms governing actions in repetitive situations. Policies help in realisation of business objectives.

Procedures: Procedures indicate the specific manner in which a certain activity is to be performed. Where policies lay down the broad area of action, the procedures determine the sequence of definite acts. Thus, they are a guide to action and not a guide to thinking. They are developed to avoid the chaos of random activities and mark a fixed path through the defined area of policy. Thus, they show the way to implement policies.

Methods: Methods deal with the best way in which a particular task is to be performed. Thus, a method is more detailed than a procedure. A procedure shows us a series of steps to be taken, a method is only concerned with a single operation. It tells us how a particular step is to be performed. Use of uniform and standard methods brings in various advantages.

Rules: Rules are specific statements of what may or may not be done. The only discretion left to the managers is whether or not to apply the rule. The development and communication of rules provides way for informing the organisational members exactly what the boundaries of acceptable behaviour are. Thus, a rule is different from a procedure or method.

Single-use plans: Single-use or single-purpose plans are designed to accomplish specific objectives—usually within a relatively short period. Budgets, Programmes and Projects are example of such plans. They are as follow:

Budgets: A budget is a plan which carves the course for business activities for a future period to achieve the prescribed objective and to provide the desired profits for operation. It may be stated in time, materials, money or in any other unit. Money budgets are very common. Budgets serve two purposes-planning as well as control. In budget formulation, a company estimates the general trend of economic conditions within its industry. The budgeting process includes sales budget, production budget, overheads budget, personnel budget, cost budget, each budget and master budget, etc.

Programmes: A programme is a sequence of activities designed to implement policies and accomplish objectives. They are developed under the umbrella of organisational goals. Programmes may be major or minor. Expansion programmes training programme, management development programmes are some examples of major programmes. Replacement of a particular machine, training a few operators can be made for both repetitive and non-repetitive course of action.

Projects: A project may be called a specific programme. So it has some characteristics of programming and some characteristics of strategy. Construction of a new plant and marketing a new product are some examples of projects.

Strategies: A strategy is also a special kind of plan formulated basically to meet the challenge of special circumstances. They are actually counter plans. For example, strategy can be planned to face the excessive competition in marketing field. Choice of a strategy depends on a number of factors like available resources, urgency of achieving an objective, external atmosphere temperament of the concerned executive, etc.

Nature of Planning : The planning has the following inherent characteristics:

Planning is an Intellectual Process: Koontz and O'Donnell have defined planning as an intellectual process, the conscious determination of courses of action. Thus, it is an intellectual stimulation. It possesses an element of day-dreaming. In the initial stage it may involve what might be called vision. It involves foreseeing future development, making forecasts or predictions and then taking decisions. Thus, it becomes an important mental exercise.

Planning Contributes to the Objective: A plan starts with the setting of objectives and in order to realise it develops policies, procedures, and strategies, etc. Obvioulsy, without setting the goals to be reached and lines of action to be followed, there is a continuous and never-ending activity of a manager to keep the enterprise going.

Planning is a Selective Process: Planning is a selective process. It involves the study and a careful analysis of various alternatives and then selecting the best one. It not only pertains to defining a problem which immediately confronts the manager, but often it mentally searches the possibilities for problems that might appear in the future.

Planning forms the Premises for the Decision of the Future: Plans become premises, for the decisions of the future. Detailed planning may include several plans which are mutually exclusive. It provides series or sets of decisions that can be made under various possible circumstances. Thus, planning aids in making specific decisions, since it includes all of the important alternatives which should be considered and their consequences.

Planning Pervades all Managerial Activities: Planning is a pervasive activity covering the entire enterprise with all its segments and its every level of management. It is not the exclusive responsibility of top management but it extends to middle and lower management as well. It is a primary function of the management and its level and extent, etc. will depend upon the level of management.

Planning is Directed Towards Efficiency: The main purpose of planning is to increase the efficiency of the enterprise. It is an attempt on the part of a manager to anticipate the future in order to achieve better performance. It has become an important function due to uncertain and ever changing environment of business. Terry has very aptly stated that, "Planning is the foundation of most successful action of an enterprise."

Planning is a Continuous and Flexible Process: Because of uncertainties of the future the planner must be ever alert and should form his plans in such a way as to adopt them to changing circumstances without inconvenience and undue costs. Koontz and O'Donnell emphasize, "effective planning requires continuous checking of events and forecasts and the redrawing of plants to maintain a course towards a desired goal."

Scope of Planning : Planning provides a future course of action. Such course of action may involve either repetitive or non-repetitive operation as well as short-range or long-range operation.

According to the nature and use of planning, the scope of planning can be extended to every field of business-whether it is finance area, personnel area or marketing area. Financial Planning, Personnel Planning, Marketing Plans are some common expressions. Another way to look at the scope of planning in its division into three groups—objectives setting, standing plans and master plans. Objectives are basic plans and they are necessary for all types of planning and operation. They are really the starting point of planning process. Standing plans provide a ready guide to action in solving recurring problems. On the other hand, master plans are programmes which indicate the short-term or single-use plans. They include budgeting, programming and deciding upon strategy for a particular project. Thus, we see that the scope of planning is very wide. It is extended to all types of activities—whether short-term or long-term, repetitive or non-repetitive and so on. It is the basis of all other managerial functions.

Essentials of a Good Plan : L.F. Urwick has summarized the characteristics of a good plan as follows:

(i) It should be based on clearly defined objectives.

(ii) It must be simple.

(iii) It should be rational, appropriate and comprehensive.

(iv) It should provide for a proper analysis and classification of actions.

(v) It must be flexible.

(vi) It must be balanced.

(vii) It must use all available resources and opportunities before creating new authorities and new resources.

(viii) There should be a proper coordination among short-term and long-term plans.

(ix) It should be free from social and psychological biasis of the planners as well as subordinates.

The Limitations : Planning is very advantageous for any enterprise. It leads to effective and faster achievements in any organisation. It brings orderliness, stability and continuity in the operation of a business. But against these benefits, it has following limitations also:

Limitations of Forecasts : Forecasting is the very basis of planning. The success of plans depends upon the accuracy and reliability of facts and figures. If reliable information and dependable data are not available planning is sure to loose much of its value. The longer the period of forecasts, the lesser will be the accuracy of planning. So a manager must keep in mind that planning will not enable him to predict the future with absolute accuracy nor will it prevent him absolutely from making mistakes.

Rigidity and Inflexibility in Administration: Planning directs, the management and subordinates to work on a predetermined course of action. It may lead to internal inflexibility and procedural rigidities, planning restricts individual's freedom, initiative and desire for creativity. This difficulty can be overcome by making flexible plans so that subordinates may be directed according to circumstances.

Time Consuming and Expensive Process: Planning is said to be a time consuming and an expensive process. But this is not to put blame on plans. The main fault lies with the planners. It is true that it is an expensive process but its economics can be availed by making intensive use of these plans.

Other Limitations: Enterprises with rapidly changing situations present a serious difficulty to the task of planning. It is claimed that working on a day-to-day basis proves more economical in such cases rather than on a planned basis. But it is not a controversy between planning and no planning, it suggests the choice between planning techniques and calls for the use of short-range plans.

Thus, we see that various limitations to planning arise on account of the unpredictability of human nature and conduct, uncertainty of political and economic factors, conflicts in organisation, insufficiency of information, inbuilt resistance to change, insufficiency of time and lastly unpredictability of future. So, a manager will have to face many limitations to planning while exercising upon plans. If planning is to be useful and purposive it is highly imperative that a manager understands these limitations of planning. It should always be kept in mind though it is not a hundred per cent check on mistakes. If planning is used with due respects and adjustments to its limitations, it can certainly help the management in minimizing uncertainties, risks and hazards.

Fundamental Functions

Planning is a fundamental managerial function. In simple words, planning is deciding in advance what is to be done, when, where, how and by whom it is to be done. Thus, a plan is a determind course of action. It is an attempt on the part of a manager to anticipate the future in order to achieve better results. But effective planning is largely dependent upon the knowledge and accurate choice of plannig premises. Hence, the definition, description and analysis of such planning premises become imperative.

Planning premises are those basic assumptions upon which the process of planning proceeds. The established background environment or framework within which a firm operates is called planning premises. Thus, planning premises provide the bedrock upon which the plans are based. There are enumerable forces and factors which have a bearing on the business of a firm. The management cannot successfully plan without their knowledge. It is neither possible nor practical for a manager to research for and analyse all these factors. The manager tries to forecast only those factors which are strategically important and which have material bearing on his business. There basic planning premises are called building stones as they will form the foundation on which the managers can do their own planning.

The Classification : Planning premises can be classified in several ways:

External and Internal Premises: Internal planning premises are those factors which exist within the firm or which belong to the firm's own climate. Important internal premises include the resources and abilities of the firm in form of men, money and methods. The ability and competence of management as well as subordinates determine the size, quality and extent of sales forecasts, capital budgeting decisions and preparation of other plans and policies. They are definite, known and fully controllable factors.

Tangible and Intangible Premises : The second classification of premises is tangible and intangible. Tangible premises are those premises which are quantifiable in some unit. On the other hand, intangible premises are those factors which cannot be quantified. Thus, they are qualitative in character, for example, firm's reputation. Tangible and intangible premises are both considerably important and play an important role in the firm's decision-making process.

Controllable, Semi-controllable and Uncontrollable Premises : The factors which are entirely within the approach and control of management are said to be controllable. Managerial, policies, programmes and rules, etc. are examples of such premises, strikes, wars, natural calamities, new inventions, imposition of emergency etc. are some uncontrollable premises. They are neither predictable nor controllable. Due to the impact of such factors the management has to revise its plans and adjust them according to the current situations. Semi-controllable premises are those over which management has partial control. Worker's attitude and efficiency, firm's pricing policy, marketing programme, etc. are examples of such premises.

Thus, we see that effective planning depends to a large extent upon knowledge and accurate choice of planning premises. As fully controllable factors are within the control of management, there is no need to predict their impact. But in respect of external and uncontrollable premises, the management will have to forecast their future trends and variations. No successful and sound planning can be done without discussing all possible planning premises. The various planning premises provide the bedrock upon which the planning is projected. The knowledge of strategic factors (or key factors) guides the management to select the proper and adequate premises upon which he can raise the superstructure of planning. In the absence of their reorganisation, any exercise in planning will be a sheer waste of energy, time and resources.

External planning premises pertain to the outside environment of the firm for example—product market, material market, capital market or labour market, etc. In the same way the political philosophy of national and state government's fiscal and monetary policies, control and distribution policies, trends in population growth, education and national income are also external factors with exercise their deep impact on managerial planning and discussions.

The Objectives : Objectives are an integral part of the planning process. They are the end-points towards which all business activities are directed. They are needed in every area where performance and result directly and vitally affect the survival and prosperity of the business. They decide the direction, nature and quantum of efforts. It is only the objective of the organisation which justify its existence.

Rober C. Appley defines 'objectives' as follows: "Objectives are goals, they are aims which management and administration wish the organisation to achieve." Thus, the words goals, aims and purposes are also used to denote objectives. Though, they have different meanings but from a wider prospective point of view, the word 'objectives' cover all these. As Newman and Summer say "For managerial purposes, it is useful to think of objectives as the results we want to achieve, objectives cover long-range company aims more, specific departmental goals and in very short-run the individual assignments also." In military circles, the word 'mission' is used instead of 'objectives.' It also denotes the end-point of the activities which a doer wants to fulfil. In the same manner the business firms have their objectives. The major objectives of a business can be classified as profit objectives and social objectives Newman and Summer have explained them as the objectives of survival and growth.

Characteristics : Business objectives have the following characteristics:

They are Multiple in Nature : Business enterprises can never have only one objective. To manage a business is to balance a variety of goals. Though the major objectives of a business can be classified as profit earning and social service, Peter Drucker, also classifies the following as objectives: market standing, innovation, productivity, physical and financial resources, profitability, performance and development, worker's performance and attitude and finally fulfilling public responsibility.

Objectives have Hierarchy: Objectives are laid down for each position in an organisation structure. At the top the objective may be to earn a certain rate of return on investment. This objective in turn may generate other objectives of manufacturing and selling a certain product. Objectives from a hierarchy from the top level to the lowest position in the organisational structure.

Objectives form a Network : Objectives are interdependent and mutually supportive and the realisation of one objective does not mean the automatic realisation of other objectives. At the same time, it cannot be assumed that one objective shall be realised irrespective of the fact whether other objectives are realised or not. That is why the coordination between enterprise activities is emphasised both at planning as well as at implementation stage. Objectives, must support one another so that they may be realised simultaneously.

Ojectives may be Long-range or Short-range: Business objectives arc of two types: long-range and short-range. For example, survival and growth are long-term objectives; while maximisation sale, increase in profits or market standing may be short-term objectives. Obviously long-range objectives are bound to be vague while short-range objectives are specific and definite.

Business Objectives are Verifiable: In business, objectives are expressed in numerical terms so that they may be verifiable. Verifiability is the key to success in business. Verifiable objectives provide standards against which to measure actual performance. Although in some cases such objectives in personnel department cannot be expressed in numerical terms, yet in such circumstances attempts can be made to make objectives verifiable directly.

Other Characteristics: The business objectives may be general or specific also. They all are significant. Specific objectives give a sense of purpose to the activities of individuals while general objectives bring coordination in an organisation.

Multiplicity of Objectives : A business organisation works for the attainment of certain objectives. The establishment of objectives is the prerogative of the administration or the top management. Objectives are generally referred to as purposes, missions, goals or targets. In very simple terms, the term 'objective' means any ultimate thing to be achieved as profitable growth of business enterprise. The identification of objectives is the first step in the process of planning because objectives determine the shape of future actions and events in the business. Objectives provide the spotlight over the routes along which activities are to be organised and efforts are to be directed.

While discussing the nature of business objectives, Peter Drucker states that they are multiple in nature. To quote him, "To manage a business is to balance a variety of needs and goals. This requires judgement. The search for one objective is essentially a search for a magic formula that will make judgement unnecessary. But the attempt to replace judgement by formula is always irrational." It proves the existence of various objectives. Professor Newman and Summer also says that business objectives are plural objectives. It proves that objectives are needed in every area where performance and results directly and vitally effect the survival and prosperity of the business. Thus, a business enterprise requires a number of objectives. Though, the major objectives of a business can be classified as profit objective and social service objectives. But apart from these two major objectives, a business enterprise has a number of other objectives such as market standing, innovation and product development, productivity, effective utilisation of physical and financial resources, etc. These subsidiary objectives help the business in ensuring its long-term growth and survival, etc.

The Advantages : The following are the important benefits accruing from the objects:

1. They bring unity of planning.
2. Objectives are the effective means to decentralisation of authority.
3. Objectives facilitate the coordination of workers, efforts and resource of the enterprise.
4. They motivate the individuals. Objectives specify the purpose of each job and fit the individual purposes and goals into the overall company goals. By making the job meaningful and worthwhile, they stimulate human motivation.
5. Objectives provide the basic standards for control by way of clarifying the expected results.

Setting the Objectives : The process of setting objectives is not a simple procedure. The main problem encountered in practice is to establish realistic targets which are capable of being attained and yet represent a high level of efficiency. If the set objective are too high for workers and managers, they may become frustrated at never being able to achieve them; if too low they are meaningless and serve no useful purpose. Hence, the process of setting the objectives is quite complicated. Theoretically, in establishing the objectives, the aim should be to establish targets for all levels of personnel representing a high level of attainment. A faulty specification of objectives will vitiate planning, waste time and cost and result in frustration. In the words of L. Gullick, "A clear statement of purpose universally understood is the outstanding guarantee of effective administration." The process of setting the objectives can be broken in the following steps:

Classifying Objectives : First of all, objectives should be classified in major and derivative goals, and long-range and short-range objectives. Major objective are broad in scope, wide in character and are applicable throughout an organisation. Then objectives should be broken down into departmental, sectional and individual objectives. Major objectives should be translated step by step down to the lowest level of the organisation so as to indicate the contribution of each segment and individual towards the enterprise objectives.

Reasonableness and Consistency: The selected objectives must represent hopes or whishes but must be responsible and attainable. Most enterprise have multiple goals at a time. So each must be established in the light of the others. They must be consistent.

Areas of Objectives: According to Peter Drucker, there are eight areas in which objectives of performance and results have to be set—market standing, innovation, productivity, physical and financial resources, profitability, manager performance and development, workers' performance and attitudes, and public responsibility. Specific planning objectives must be deducted from broader enterprise objectives.

Realistic and Practical: Objective should be set in realistic terms rather than in idealistic terms. Realistic objectives based on measured expectations provide incentive, job satisfaction for high performance.

Balancing of Short-range and Long-range Objectives : Short-range objectives should be recognised as a distinct step in the realisation of long-range objectives, otherwise the achievement of long-range objectives becomes difficult if not impossible. There is a necessity of balancing the various objectives for removing their conflicts. Pressing and dominant objectives should be given more care than long-range and distant objectives.

Change of Adjustments : Dynamic business environment makes the company objectives dynamic in nature and objectives call for changes along with changing time and situations. Although objectives are more stable than other plans, periodic adjustment of objectives becomes necessary to keep pace with the progress in time and to cope with the expanding size of the business.

Environment Factors : The objectives of a particular enterprise depend upon many factors. The socio-economic-political set up of the country within which an enterprise functions has a very dominant effect on the business enterprise. Thus, in USSR a factory has output as its main objectives, each factory aims at producing certain stipulated quantity of goods of required quality from a given set of resources. Profit as an objective has a minor role for firms working in a socialistic economies like that of formulas soviet union (FSU). This is because the prices of goods as well as their marketing and distribution systems are controlled by the State and an increase in the profits is important only to the extent it represents the effectiveness of cost control and efficiency in the use of resources. On the other hand, business enterprises in USA have profits is their main objective, since the political and economic thinking in that country recognises profit as the main spring of human activity in a free enterprise economy. Business enterprises in India have also to set their objectives keeping in view the dominant stream of our political and economic thinking. Thus, firms in India have to keep social objectives in view while working for profits as an objective. Working in a mixed economy with a dominant public sector, a firm may not find profit maximisation as a feasible long-term objective since the government is bound to enforce controls on to profitable companies sooner or later. Each business enterprise has therefore, to set its objectives keeping in view the overall political and economic structure of the society in which it functions.

Concept of Policy

Policies are guides to thinking and action of subordinates for the successful achievement of business objectives. According to George R. Ferry, "Policy is a verbal, written or implied overall guide setting up boundaries that supply the general limits and directions in which managerial action will take place." Thus, policies are specific guidelines and constraints for managerial thinking on decision-making and action. They provide the framework within which the decision-makers are expected to operate while making organisational decisions. As such, they are the basis of executive operations. They are the planned expression of the company's official attitudes towards the range of behaviour within which it will permit or desire its employees to act. But they provide scope for interpretation. They are guides to thinking and lead to consistent decisions at some future point of time. The purpose of policy formulation is as under:

(i) To ensure that there will be no deviation from planned course of action.

(ii) To ensure consistency of action.

(iii) To provide a guide for thinking in future planning.

(iv) To leave scope for interpretation.

The Classification : Policies may be of different types:

Policies

- On the basis of sources
  - Originated Policies
  - Appealed Policies
  - External Policies
- On the basis of functions
  - Production Policy
  - Financial Policy
  - Credit Policy
  - Marketing Policy
  - Personnel Policy
- On the basis of level
  - Basic Policies
  - General Policy
  - Departmental Policies

Originated Policy: These policies are formulated by the top managers. Such policies tell subordinates how to act in a given situation. These policies have the support of organisation authorities and subordinates can be asked to follow them strictly. Thus, they are basic policies.

Appealed Policy: When a subordinate is doubtful whether he has sufficient authority to handle a situation, he may seek the verdict of a superior. Superior's verdict generates what is known as appealed policy which becomes wide to subordinates's action in future. Hence, such policies are originated out of precedents and they become guides for future action.

External Policies: Such policies which are imposed upon business some external agencies like trade unions, government or industry associations, etc. are called external policies.

Functional Policies: Functional policies refer to the policies which are prepared for various functional areas of management. Production policy, product policy, financial plan, personnel policy, industrial relations policy are some examples of such policies.

Policies According to Organisational Levels: On this basis policies may be divided into three parts:

(i) Basic policies to be used by the top managers. (ii) General policies to be used by the top managers. (iii) Departmental policies to be used by foremen and group-leaders, etc.

Formulation of Policies : The formulation of policies takes place at various organisational levels. Some basic and important policies are developed by the top management while some are developed at middle level management level. Here are some important considerations which should bc followed in formulating the various policies:

(i) Policies should help in achieving objectives and should be based on facts, not on guess work or intuition.

(ii) To ensure successful implementation of policy, joint participation in policy-making should be encouraged. It means before formulating policies, top managers in an organisation must consult the persons who are likely to be affected by them and are supposed to implement them.

(iii) Policies should be broad, general and basic, not specific because they are a guide to thinking and action. They should not lay down the detailed procedure of doing activities.

(iv) Policies must reflect the internal and external business environment. There must be an element of stability in them. It does not mean that they must not be changed if there is a change in conditions on which these policies were based. Rigidities should be avoided to make policies realistic.

(v) Policies should be in writing and the language of the policies should be intelligible to those who are supposed to implement them.

(vi) Different policies in an organisation should support one another. They must be in conformity with and not in conflict with one another.

(vii) Policies should further general social objectives. They must not be detrimental to the interest of society, otherwise their implementation would be difficult.

(viii) Policies should be taught. Organisation members must understand them. Policies become meaningless if they are not understood by the person who are to be affected by them.

The Procedure : Procedures are clear-cut administrative specifications prescribing the chronological manner (or order) in which repetitive activity is initiated, carried forward and controlled. Thus, procedures are guides to action only. They tell how a particular activity is to be done. Hence, procedures are generally established for repetitive work so that some steps are followed each time that activity is performed. Example of certain procedures are purchase procedures, procedure of raw material issued from the store, procedure of holding meetings, procedure of recruitment of workers and so on. In fact, for every repetitive activity procedures are established because routine jobs can be performed more efficiently if one best way of doing things has been established.

Distinction Between Policies and Procedures : In this section we present the clear-cut distinctions between policies and procedures. The main points of difference are as follows:

1. Policies are guides to decision-making while procedures are guides to action.
2. Policies leave some room for interpretation and discretion but in case of procedures there is no such thing. They are more rigid and specific.
3. Policies form part of the strategies of the organisation while procedures are operational and tactical tools.
4. Policies are the basic things. They form the basis for working out the procedures.
5. Generally, policies are formulated by the top management while procedures are laid down at somewhat lower level.

Act of Forecast

Forecasting is an essential part of the process of planning. It is essentially a technique of anticipation. It provides key information and pertinent facts relating to the future. Without forecasting planning is an impossibility. Forecasting is the very basis of planning.

Forecasting refers to a systematic analysis of past and present circumstances with the aim of drawing conclusions about the future course of events. It has been defined by the management experts as follows:

"Forecasting is a systematic attempt to probe the future by inference from known facts."

—*Allen, LA.*

"Forecasts are predictions or estimates of the change, if any in characteristic economic phenomena which may affect one's business plans."

—*McFarland*

"Business forecasting refers to the statistical analysis of the past and current movements in the given time series so as to obtain clues about the future pattern of these movements."

—*Neter and Wasserman*

Thus, we see that forecasting is a systematic effort to peep into the future. No forecast can be made without a proper knowledge of current circumstances. So it implies the act of making a detailed analysis of the past and present to gain a foresight for future. By forecasting various factors, a manager gains sufficient time to formulate proper plans to obtain the maximum advantage of circumstances. Thus, forecasting becomes the process of anticipating the future course of events and trends. The following are the important characteristics of forecasting:

(i) Forecasts are the estimates for the future trends.

(ii) These estimates for future are based on the analysis of past and present circumstances.

(iii) Some systematic and scientific techniques are used for analysis of past trend and then estimating the future. A number of statistical techniques has been evolved by various experts for it.

(iv) Forecasting forces the possible changes in order to bring accuracy and exactness in decisions.

Nature of Forecasting : Forecasting is an important activity in the overall process of management. Henry Fayol has very aptly said, "If foresight is not the whole of management at least it is an essential part of it." Planning for eventualities that do not occur is obviously inefficient. Yet a failure to plan for future adversity or opportunity may have more serious consequences. Although uncertainty can never be completely overcome, intelligent and systematic forecasting can eliminate some of the difficulties. It is not an exact science but a good art, an art of reading the future course of events.

Importance of Forecasting : Forecasting is an important part and parcel of modern business management. Fayol, the father of modern management has aptly called it as the 'essence of management.' It is a real test of management foresight. The success of a business depends largely upon the skill of management in forecasting and preparing for future events. The following are some obvious facts as regards to the importance of forecasts in a business:

Importance in Planning: In business planning and forecasting have a pivotal role. It is an important aid to planning and through planning, to more effective operations. Future plans cannot be formulated without forecasting events and their relationship' to base planning decision on to solid foundation forecasting, provides key information and facts relating to the future. Most of the planning premises are merged in forecasting of one type or another. Planning without forecasting is an impossibility. Fayol has aptly observed, "The plan is the synthesis of the various forecasts—annual, long-term, short-term special, etc."

Exactness in Managerial Decision: Forecasting brings exactness and accuracy in managerial decisions. It enables a manager to probe the future economic, social and political factors that might influence his decisions and his company. It improves the quality and validity of management decisions. It enables a company to take sound decisions with reference to production, sales and financing.

Singleness of Purpose is Developed: The process of forecasting provides very valuable clues for the future actions. It brings the singleness of purpose in the minds of people working are different levels in an organisation.

Coordination is Developed: Forecasting is a common effort so it may also help to bring about unity and coordination in the plans and efforts of subordinates. It creates team spirit in the organisation. It also helps integrate all management planning so that unified overall plans can be developed in to which division and departmental plans can be merged.

Control is Facilitated: The forecasting facilitates to managerial control also. It discloses areas where control is lacking and where adequate control is necessary for efficient and effective operations of the enterprise.

It Contributes to Business Success : Forecasting contributes in small measure to the overall success of business. By forecasting various internal and external factors a business can plan to obtain maximum benefits from periods of expanding economy, and on the other hand to minimise any adverse effects when business activities slacken. It ensures better utilisation of resources by extending the frontiers of control in several directions. It steers the objectives of an organisation. It awakens management against business cycles. Thus, it contributes a lot to the success of business. But it should be remembered that forecasting does not guarantee success, but it does help in identifying the ways to success.

Significant Factors

Forecasting is essentially a technique of anticipation. It provides key information and pertinent facts relating to the future. Without forecasting, planning is an impossibility. It is the very basis of planning. Forecasting has been defined by McFarland in these words, "Forecasts are predictions or estimates of the change. If, any, in characteristics economic phenomena which may affect one's business plans."

According to James Redfield, the following are the important elements of forecasting:

Developing the Groundwork: The first step in the process of forecasting is its preliminary preparations. It involves the collection of basic information relating to the product of company, market, competition and general environment of the industry and society. Study of these facts helps not only in analysing the present position but in making future estimates also.

Estimating Future Trends : After developing the ground-work, future estimates are made as regards to the sale and production of the company. The estimate of future sales is made with the help of sales executives. In sales forecasting, the trend values are determined on the basis of calculation and anticipation.

Comparing Actual Results with the Estimated Figures : The third step in forecasting is the comparison of actual results with the estimated figures. This comparison provides an opportunity to discuss the variances, their possible reasons and further trends.

Refining the Forecasts : Forecasting is not an exact science. It is simply an estimate, so the management should always review the forecasts periodically and future trend values should be revised according to the experience gained in the immediate past.

The Limitations : Henry Fayol was the first person who propounded the importance of forecasting in business management. According to him, "A plan of an organisation is the synthesis of the various forecasts: annual, long-term, short-term or special, etc." According to Fayol, "purveyance for forecasting is the essence of managership." Without forecasting no plan can be made and without planning, no enterprise can be run successfully. So forecasts are the essential part of modern management.

But while explaining the necessity and importance of forecasting, its limitations should not be forgotten. Forecasts are only estimates of future conditions. They are not actual positions. So they can at best only give estimates of future course of events, but they can never be hundred per cent complete and reliable. The following are some important limitations of forecasts which should always be kept in mind:

1. Forecasts are not absolute truth.
2. Forecasts are based on certain assumptions.
3. The business conditions are dynamic and ever-changing. They can never be forecasted accurately.

In this chapter planning process was described at length with its various dimensions. The planning lies following inherent characteristics viz. (a) planning being an intellectual process (b) planning contributes to the objective (c) planning is a selective process (d) planning leeds to future decisions and (e) planning provides all managerial activities. Other related concepts such as policies, procedures, objectives were also defined and their highlights were provided. Towards the end the forcasting techniques, components with various related issues were presented. The important elements of forecasting process include; (i) Developing the groundwork (ii) Estimating future trends, (iii) Comparing actual results with the estimated figures and (iv) Refining the forecasts.

14

Facets of Authority

Louis A. Allen has defined authority, "As the sum of the powers and rights entrusted to make possible the performance of the work delegated". He has classified authority into three categories, namely:

(i) Authority of knowledge, (ii) Authority of position, and (iii) Legal authority.

According to him, authority of knowledge is possessed generally by the staff specialists appointed by the company. They often influence the actions of persons in line by virtue of their knowledge. Some persons have authority by virtue of their position in the organisation. Legal authority is the authority which is entrusted to a person by the law of the land. For instance, a company is a legal person and has a right to sue others according to the provisions of the Companies Act.

Different Theories

There are three different schools of thought about the sources of authority which are discussed below:

Formal Authority Theory : According to this theory, all authority originates in the formal structure of an organisation. The ultimate authority in a joint stock company lies with the shareholders. Shareholders entrust the management of the company to the Board of Directors and delegate to it most of their authority. The Board of Directors delegates authority to the chief executive and chief executive in turn to the departmental managers and so on. Every manager or executive possesses authority because of his organisational position and this authority is known as formal authority. Authority conferred by law is also regarded as formal authority. Subordinates accept the formal authority of a manager because of his position in the organisation. The subordinates are aware of the fact that if they disregard the formal authority they will be punished according to the rules and regulations of the company. The formal authority theory further states that the superiors have the right to delegate their authority. Thus, formal authority always flows from top to bottom.

Acceptance Theory : This theory states that authority is the power that is accepted by others. Formal authority is reduced to nominal authority if it is not accepted by the subordinates. The subordinates accept the authority if the advantages to be derived by its acceptance exceed the disadvantages resulting from its refusal. The subordinates give obedience to the managers because they visualise the following advantages:

(a) Receipt of financial incentives.

(b) Contribution in attaining the objectives of the enterprise.

(c) Fulfilment of responsibilities.

(d) Appreciation from colleagues.

(e) Setting of an example for others.

(f) Responsibility to leadership of superior.

(g) Moral obligation because of regard for old age, experience, competence, etc.

According to acceptance theory, authority flows from bottom to top. A manager has authority if he gets obedience from the subordinates. Subordinates obey the manager because of the fear of losing financial rewards. This theory emphasises sanctions that a manager can use and overlooks the influence of social institutions like trade unions.

Competence Theory : The supporters of this view assert that an individual derives authority because of his personal qualities and technical competence. Many persons derive informal authority because of their competence. For instance a person possesses expert knowledge in a particular subject people will go to him for guidance in that matter even though he has got no formal authority.

Decentralisation of Authority : Decentralisation of authority means dispersal of decision-making power to the lower levels of the organisation. According to Allen, decentralisation refers to the systematic effort to delegate to the lowest levels all authority except that which can only be exercised at central points. Thus, decentralisation means reservation of some authority (power to plan, organise, direct and control) at the top level and delegation of authority to make decision at points as near as possible to where action takes place.

Decentralisation is not the same thing as delegation. Delegation means entrustment of responsibility and authority from one individual to another. But decentralisation means scattering of authority throughout the organisation. It is the diffusion of authority within the entire enterprise. Delegation can take place from one person to another and be a complete process. But decentralisation is completed only when the fullest possible delegation is made to all or most of the people.

Decentralisation is distinct from dispersion. Dispersion occurs when plants and offices are located at different places with physical distance between them. Performance of work in dispersed plants and offices does not necessarily lead to decentralisation. A company may be highly centralised although its physical facilities and employees are widely dispersed and company may be highly decentralised even though all physical facilities and employees are located in a single building.

The Distinction : The points of distinction between delegation and decentralisation are given below:

(i) Delegation is a process of devolution of authority whereas decentralisation is the end-result which is achieved when delegation of authority is exercised at more than one level.

(ii) Delegation takes place between a superior and a subordinate and is a complete process. It may consist of certain tasks alone. But decentralisation involves spreading out the total decision-making power.

(iii) In delegation, control rests entirely with the superior or delegator but in decentralisation, the top management may exercise control only in a general manner and delegate the authority for control to the departmental managers.

(iv) Delegation is a must for management. Subordinates must be given sufficient authority to perform their assignments otherwise they will come to the superior time and again even for minor decisions. However, decentralisation is optional in the sense that the top management may or may not decide to disperse authority.

Factors Determining the Extent of Decentralisation : The question of the extent of decentralisation desirable, is not simple as choice between decentralisation and centralisation is very difficult, being both extremes. The following are therefore, the important factors which determine the extent of decentralisation of authority which is considered desirable for a particular organisation.

Size of the Operations: As the size of the organisation increases, more decisions have to be made at different levels and coordination becomes difficult among the large numbers of departments and the levels involved. Besides, after attaining a certain size, diseconomies of large size sets in, the decisions become slower, the extent of the paperwork increases and there is a reduction in the quality of the decisions made. Thus, as the size increases it becomes necessary to divide the large organisation into a number of semi-autonomous units.

High Costs of Decision: The more expensive or costly the action to be decided upon, decisions will be taken at the higher levels of management. Thus, the decision of whether to have another factory or not would be taken at the top levels, whilst the question of purchasing of stationery would be taken at an extremely low level.

Higher Differentiated Product Lines: The product lines in a company are very different. The extreme case being of industrial and consumer products both existing in the same company—decentralisation or divisionalisation becomes very important.

Availability of Managerial Manpower: Decentralisation of the authority requires the availability of competent managers. The organisation must provide adequate training and development facilities for managers, and decentralisation is one of the good methods of encouraging such development. A large firm can even decentralise with the objective of developing managers.

Top Management Philosophy: A subordinate generally complies his boss's orders. Thus, the whole organisation is often moulded around the character of the top management. The management philosophy of the top management determines to a large extent how much authority the managers in the organisation are willing to retain or delegate down the line.

Environmental Influences: The contingency theory of organisation stresses that an organisation's structure and functioning are dependent on its interface with the external environment.

Under dynamic or competitive market conditions and centralisation under stable non-competitive market conditions make decentralisation more important to organisation effectiveness than do stable non-competitive conditions. This is not surprising as in a seller's market an enterprise must experience little difficulty in being effective. It is only in a competitive situation that decentralisation can play a more important role, for example, in satisfying consumers (i.e., the economic effectiveness criterion) as well as organisation members (i.e., the behavioural effectiveness criterion). Again the government regulations also control the extent of decentralisation.

Nature of Expansion : The historical nature of expansion may also determine the extent of decentralisation. For example, if the company has been growing through mergers or taking over of other companies, the chances are that it will be more divisionalised, each merger constituting a separate division. Thus, the nature of the growth itself of such a company dictates greater decentralisation.

Advantages of Decentralisation : The advantages of decentralisation are discussed hereunder:

Reduction in the Burden of Chief Executive: When there is centralisation of authority in an enterprise the chief executive has to bear the entire burden of decision-making. This diminishes the time at his disposal to concentrate on important managerial functions. Decentralisation of authority reduces his burden as he delegates a part of his authority to the subordinates and thus enabling to devote more time to important functions.

Diversification of Activities: With the addition of new activities or product lines, an organisation tends to grow complex and may pose a challenge to the top executives, which can be met by decentralisation under the overall coordinating purview of the top management.

Quick Decisions: Decentralisation avoids red-tapism in making decisions as it places responsibility for decision-making as near as possible to the place where action takes place. Those close to the work situation can make reasonably quick and accurate decisions because they are well aware of the realities of the situation.

Development of Managerial Personnel: When authority is decentralised, the subordinates get opportunity of taking initiative to develop their talents, to enable themselves to develop qualities for managerial positions. They learn how to decide and depend on their own judgement and how to manage.

Improvement of Motivation: Decentralisation promotes the improvement of morale and motivation of subordinates which is reflected in better work performance. With greater opportunities of communication and leadership, the local executive can foster team spirit and group cohesion among his subordinates.

Effective Control and Supervision: The greater the degree of decentralisation, the more effective becomes the span of control. It leads to effective supervision as the managers at the lower levels have complete authority to make changes in work assignment, to change production schedules, to recommend promotions and to take disciplinary actions.

Miscellaneous Economies: In addition to the above advantages, decentralisation also achieves several internal and external economies. Internal economies include speedier communication, better utilisation of lower level and middle level executives, greater incentive to work and greater opportunities for training. These make it possible for the management to reduce the cost of production and meet competition effectively.

The Limitations

Inconsistency: Decentralisation may bring about inconsistencies in the organisation. For instance, uniform procedures may not be followed for the same type of work in various divisions.

Increased Administrative Expenses: Decentralisation increases the administrative expenses because it requires the employment of trained personnel to accept authority. The services of such highly paid personnel may not be fully utilised particularly in small organisations.

Difficult Autonomation: Decentralisation requires the product lines of the concern to be broad enough to allow creation of autonomous units which is not possible in small concerns.

Difficult Coordination: Decentralisation of authority may create problems in coordination among the various units.

Uncertainties are Difficult to Deal with: Decentralisation may not be possible because of external factors. If a company is subject to uncertainties, it will not be able to meet these under decentralisation of authority.

The Technique : Decentralisation is a special technique by which it can be effectively accomplished. The main steps in the establishment of this technique are given below:

Establishment of Appropriate Centralisation: As a first step in decentralisation, a centralised headquarters is necessary which will act as the nerve centre of the enterprise. Here plans will be formulated and communicated for the guidance of each part of the country. It will also plan an adequate organisation structure within which individual operating components can be permitted considerable latitude of action. Without such an administrative harness companies may find the individual members of the team going in different directions at the same time, which will be detrimental for the enterprise.

Development of Manager: In decentralised concerns, critical decisions have to be made at a large number of centres. This needs people who have mastered the technique of management and not simply of supervision. This poses the problem of how to develop affective managers.

Another thing to be kept in mind is that management is an art made up of identifiable skills. Hence, it is essential to reinforce training in classes by coaching them on jobs, by allowing them to make decisions and to learn through committing mistakes.

Provision for Communication and Cooperation: Decentralisation has a tendency for independence. This poses the problem of preserving the integrated character of the enterprise as a whole. In this way, provision ought to be made for communication and cooperation through coordinating executives and committees.

Establishing Adequate Controls: Autonomous managers can given free rein only so far as it will not jeopardize the purpose and integrity of the enterprise as a whole. A major problem in decentralisation, hence, is that of establishing effective control.

Key Aspects

The key aspects of the organisation, after division into different departments, are shown through organisation charts, which are graphic representation of a firm's structure. According to Leffingwell and Robinson, "An organisation chart is a plan of working relationships. It shows who is to do the work that is to be done and who is to direct and supervise the efforts of those who are to do the work." Charts reflect the organisational game plan for division of work, they give a complete and intelligent guide to company organisation, they indicate the flow of work and the responsibility for its achievement. Important aspects of the organisation for example (a) chain of command, (b) unity of command, (c) communication channels, (d) departmentation, (e) levels of hierarchy, (f) span of management, (g) division of work are shown. In a formal chart only functions and the designations of the individuals appear, visualising the organisation structure.

The Characteristics

(i) depicts the organisation's formal structure and shows only formal relationships.

(ii) does not insure good organisation or good management; merely because a chart is in existence it is no guarantee for good organisation.

(iii) essentially illustrates who reports to whom.

(iv) merely shows the designations of the individuals, thus no names appear, only functions, e.g., Sales Manager, Financial Advisor, etc.

(v) reflects a simplified and abstract model of the organisation's structure; they do not show human relationships; it is said that an organisation chart is like a snap shot; it is a static model of a dynamic, living process.

The Principles : The following principles relating to the design of an organisation chart should be kept in view:

Line of Authority should be Observed by the Top Management in Dealing with Subordinates : The executives and those at the top of the administrative pyramid should never bypass the lines of authority mentioned in the organisation chart. They should not try to go over the heads of immediate subordinates when bypassed, naturally they are humiliated. Moreover, executives who do this, cannot expect to hold subordinates responsible for the work of those under them.

Lines of Authority should be Observed by the Subordinates in Dealing with Superiors: Likewise, the subordinates should, also follow the established lines of authority. Just as the orders, under normal conditions are transmitted stepwise from superior to subordinates to the supervisors. Failure to obey the rule amounts to disloyalty and it may lead to suspicion, jealousy and non-cooperation.

Organisation Chart should Define Lines of Position of each Individual very Carefully: There should be no overlapping, nor should two persons be placed at the same position, specially when their authorities and responsibility are different.

Identical Authority or Responsibility should not Rest upon two or more Persons: The same duty should not be assigned twice. Again, none be compelled to serve two masters.

Avoidance of Undue Concentration of Duty at any Point: All persons should be acquainted with their duties and their administrative relations to others with whom they come into contact.

Organisation Chart should be Above the Personalities: Balance of organisation is more important than individuals. No position should be assigned to an individual, only because executive orders say so.

Organisation Chart should be Simple and Flexible: It should not have any complication or ambiguity. It should be so formed as to allow periodic changes that may be needed with the increase in size and nature of the concern.

The Advantages

Clear Organisational Relationships: Charts define organisational relationships clearly. They instruct employees regarding jobs assigned and show how the jobs are related to others in the organisation.

Better Understanding of Objectives: Formal charting helps executives think about organisational arrangements in an objective way. Structural deficiencies, communication gaps, fuzzy authority lines, inappropriate spans of control, overlapping positions, etc. are all brought into the limelight. If charts are not available, many of these structural defects defy identification and may prove to be costly at a later stage.

Helpful in Training: Charts are useful training devices. The specific requirements of each position in the organisation are spelt out in detail and the incumbents know in advance as to what is expected of them and prepare themselves accordingly.

Helps in Providing Useful Information: Charts provide useful information to outsiders interested in contacting the 'right person' in the organisation.

The Disadvantages

Updating is Difficult: Charts show organisational relationships at a point of time and quickly become obsolete and outdated unless revised frequently.

Fails to Depict Inner Working: Charts fail to show human relationships in the organisation. They only show the surface of the structure, not the inner workings.

A Hindrance in Team Building: Charts make people overly conscious of being superiors or inferiors, tend to destroy team feeling and give persons occupying a box on the chart too great a feeling of ownership.

Rigidity in Relationships: Formal charting introduces rigidity in relationships. Moreover, by laying the boundaries for each position, charts promote empire building tendencies. Each position holder would be interested in guarding his territories carefully and if possible, enhance by overstepping his authority. Formal charting promotes inflexible attitudes leading to conflicts between position holders.

Prohibitive Preparation Costs: The costs of preparing, disseminating, storing, updating and studying charts are prohibitive.

This chapter highlighted the concept of authority. Authority being the sum of the powers and rights entrusted to make possible the performance of the work delegated. It also presented the concepts of delegation and decentralisation along with their merits and demerits. Decentralisation of authority means dispersal of decision-making power to the lower levels of the organisation, whereas delegation is a process of devolution of authority. It also highlighted the role of organisation charts and its principles along with pitfalls and benefits. The advantages of organisation charts being (a) Clear organisational relationships (b) Better understanding of objectives (c) Helpful in training and (d) helps in providing useful information.

No organisation can be conceived without authority. Authority is attached with every position in the organisation. It is the binding force or the glue that holds the organisation together. It helps in coordinating actions in an organisation. It is, therefore, necessary for organisations everywhere and at all times.

Concept of Authority

There are numerous concepts of authority. Any person having superior knowledge in a particular field is called an authority in that field. But in the context of organisation and management, term authority has special meaning. In this context, authority is the right of superior to command and to ensure obedience of the orders from his subordinates.

According to Henri Fayol, authority is "the right to give orders and power to exact obedience."

In the words of Weihrich and Koontz, "Authority in organisation is the right in a position (and, through it, the right of the person occupying the position) to exercise discretion in making decisions affecting others."

According to Albanese, "Authority is the right of a person to issue orders and direct the behaviour of those over whom authority is exercised."

According to Robbins and Coulter,"Authority refers to the rights inherent in a managerial position to give orders and expect the orders to be followed."

In the broadest sense, authority is the formal right vested in a managerial position, to decide, to direct and to influence the behaviour of subordinates with a view to achieve organisational goals.

The Characteristics : The main characteristics of authority are as follows :

A Right : Authority is a right. This right is a type of power.

Positional Right : It is a positional right. It is vested in a position and not in an individual. When a person assumes charge of a position, he can exercise the authority. When he leaves the position, he no longer has any authority. Thus, authority remains with the position and its new holder. *[Robbins and Coulter]*

Formal : Authority in organisation is formal and legitimate.

Flow of Authority : formal authority flows from the top to the bottom of the managerial hierarchy. It flows through the process of decentralisation or delegation. Thus, every manager gets authority from his immediate superior.

Relationship : Formal authority establishes a right-duty relationship between two individuals. Those individuals are known as superior and subordinate. Superior can exercise his authority over his subordinates.

Forms of Authority : Exercising authority involves making decisions, issuing orders, taking actions, performing duties, mobilising and utilising resources etc.

Compliance : Authority implies the capacity to ensure compliance of orders and directions issued.

Guide and Influence : Authority-holder can guide and influence the behaviour against whom authority is exercised.

Binding Force : Authority is the binding force or the glue that holds an organisation together. It is essential to unite actions of organisation members. It is necessary to organisations everywhere and at all times. *[Albanese]*

Goals Achievement : Authority is granted and exercised with a view to achieve organisational goals.

Never Absolute : Authority is never absolute. It is always subject to certain rules, regulations, conditions or responsibilities.

Limited : Authority is always limited. The limit on authority is specified by the duties, responsibilities, rules, regulations, policies, procedures, budgets etc.

Objective : Authority in itself is objective by nature but its exercise may be subjective. Exercise of authority may be influenced by many factors and hence subjectivity creeps into it.

Basic to Managerial Job : Authority is basic to every managerial/job/position. Without authority, no manager can get the things done through others.

Parity between : authority and responsibility. Authority must always commensurate with responsibility. Granting authority without responsibility can create problems. Moreover, no one should be held responsible for something over which he has no authority.

Abuse or Misuse : Authority can be abused, under used and misused.

Accepted or Rejected : Authority is sometimes accepted uncritically and at other times, rejected indiscriminately. *[Albanese]*

Concept of Power

Some people regard the terms 'authority' and 'power' synonymous and do not make any distinction between the two. But, in fact, both of these are two distinct terms.

Authority is the formal right to command subordinates and ensure compliance. Power, on the other hand, is the ability of a person to influence the behaviour of others or the capacity to affect a situation. Power is neither completely formal nor informal. One can have power even without possessing power.

Distinction between Authority and Power : Power is a wider concept than authority and includes authority. Authority is, in fact, a type of power *i.e.* legitimate power. Authority is positional power whereas power is personal or individual. The main points of distinction between the two are as follows :

Meaning : Authority is a formal right vested in a managerial position to decide, to direct and to expect obedience. Power, on the other hand, is the ability to influence others or the capacity to affect situations.

Nature : Authority is impersonal and objective but power is personal and subjective.

Formal and Informal : Authority is formal in nature but power is neither completely formal nor informal.

Sources : There is only one source of authority *i.e.* the formal position in an organisation. But there are several different sources of power including legitimate power, reward power, coercive power, expert power, referent power.

Pervasiveness : Authority vests only in organisational positions. Power is all pervasive. It vests in individuals. Even an operational level employee may possess power.

Flow : Authority flows from the top to the bottom of the managerial hierarchy. It flows through the process of delegation and redelegation from superiors to subordinates. Power can flow in any direction from top to the bottom or bottom to the top.

Delegation : Authority is always delegated whereas only formal power can be delegated. Other types of power cannot be delegated.

Balance : Authority must commensurate with responsibility. Thus, there must a balance or parity between the two. However, no such principle applies to power. A person enjoying power may have no specific amount of responsibility.

Mandatory : Acceptance of authority is mandatory. The person exercising authority has a right to ensure compliance and obedience to his orders. However, the acceptance of power is not mandatory but at the free will of the individuals.

Relationship : Authority establishes right-duty relationship between the superior and his subordinates. Power need not establish such relationship.

Scope : Authority is a type of power. Hence, authority is part of the concept of power. Power is a wider concept includes authority.

The Accountability

According to Haimann, " : Responsibility is the obligation of a subordinate to perform the duty as required by his superior."

In the words of Mondy et al, " : Responsibility is an obligation to perform tasks and to account for their satisfactory compliance."

According to McFarland, " : Responsibility is the duties and activities assigned to a position or to an executive."

Thus, responsibility is an obligation of a person to perform tasks, functions and activities assigned to him.

Accountability is often used as a synonymous to responsibility. However, some experts distinguish between the two.

According to Mondy et al, " : Accountability is any means of ensuring that the person who is supposed to do a task actually performs it and do so correctly."

According to Boedecker, " : Accountability is the obligation to account for and report upon the discharge of responsibility or use of authority."

In fact, accountability is the obligation of a person to report to his superior for the actions and decisions taken or for the results achieved by him. Thus, accountability arises when a person assumes responsibility.

Accountability grows out of responsibility and goes hand-in-hand with it. *[McFarland].* When responsibility is assigned, accountability arises. The person responsible for performing certain things is under an obligation to account for it. Thus, a person liable to give account of his performance is accountable or answerable. Therefore, accountability is the obligation of a person to give account for the acts done, decisions made or results achieved by him to his superior.

It may be stated that responsibility is a personal obligation felt by a subordinate whereas accountability is the demand of a manager on his subordinates.

It is often quoted that authority is delegated, responsibility is assumed and accountability is imposed. This quotation means that authority is delegated by a superior to his subordinates. When a subordinate exercises authority it brings responsibility for him. Thus, he assumes responsibility as soon as he exercises the authority. When he assumes responsibility, accountability compulsorily imposed upon. He automatically becomes accountable or answerable to his superior for the acts done, decisions taken or results achieved by him in order to fulfil the responsibility. Thus, accountability grows out of responsibility and goes hand-in-hand with it.

Various Sources

There are three theories to explain the three different sources of authority. These theories are explained in the ensuing sub-heads :

The Formal Theory of Authority : According to formal theory of authority, authority originates at the top of the organisational hierarchy. Then it flows downward through the process of delegation and redelegation. Laws of the land and rules of the organisation indirectly give authority to the top executive. In a corporate entity, shareholders hold the ultimate authority given to them by the laws of the land. The shareholders entrust the management of the company to the Board of directors and delegate most of their powers to the Board. The Board delegates authority to the chief executive who, in turn, delegates it to departmental heads and so on. Every manager, departmental-head in the organisation, has only so much authority as are delegated to him by his immediate superior and is accountable to him alone. In this way, authority is concentrated at the top which flows downward along with the scalar chain in the organisation. It diminishes at each successive level.

Everybody holds authority by virtue of his position in the formal organisation. According to this theory every subordinate is aware of the fact that if he disregards the formal authority, he will be punished according to the rules and regulations of the organisation or laws of the land. Therefore, this authority is known as formal authority or legitimate authority. It is also known as top-down authority because formal authority flows from top to the bottom of the organisational level.

The Acceptance Theory of Authority : The acceptance theory of authority states that authority is effective only when it is accepted by others. If authority is not accepted by the subordinates, it is meaningless. Thus, the degree of effectiveness of authority is measured by the willingness of subordinates to accept it. Right to command depends upon whether or not the subordinates obey their superior. The superior can exert his authority by imposing penalty but the subordinates, if they do not accept the authority, may quit the organisation.

Thus, according to this theory, authority flows upward from subordinates to the superior. A superior is said to have authority if subordinates comply with his orders. It is, therefore, called the bottom up authority. Acceptance of orders depends upon its positive and negative consequences. Some orders may be fully acceptable while some other may be partially acceptable and still others may be totally unacceptable. But a subordinate will generally accept an order if the following conditions are satisfied :

(i) If he understands the order well.

(ii) If he believes it is consistent with the organisational objectives.

(iii) If he believes it is compatible with his own interests.

(iv) If he is mentally and physically able to comply with the order. *[Chester I. Barnard]* The acceptance theory of authority is subject to the following limitations :

 (i) This theory maintains that superior has authority if he gets acceptance from his subordinates. But a manager is unable to know in advance whether his order will be complied with or not by the subordinates. Therefore, it is said to be unreal theory.

 (ii) There is always an implied understanding that a subordinate must comply with the order of his superior and if it is so, what is meant by acceptance of authority by the subordinates.

 (iii) When a subordinate enjoys the right to confer the authority, he must also have the right to levy penalties.

 (iv) This theory totally disregards the powerful sanction and effect of social institution on the authority. Nobody can deny the impact of legal and social institution on the authority.

 (v) Authority is fundamental to the job of a manager. If it is left to the liking or the acceptance of subordinates, chaos will follow.

The Competence Theory of Authority : According to this theory of authority, an individual derives authority because of his personal competence, charisma or qualities. The competence or qualities may be in certain specific fields. Such people enjoy prestige and popularity in the society or public. The opinion or advice of such persons carries weight for the public and people readily accept their authority. Thus, these theories explain the varied sources of authority.

Extent of Authority : The authority enjoyed by a manager is neither absolute nor unlimited. It is always subject to certain limitations.

In an organisation, scope and extent of authority is maximum at the top level and minimum at the lowest level of the organisational hierarchy. It goes on decreasing at the successive lower levels of organisational hierarchy. Figure shows the scope and extent of authority at different levels in the organisation.

The Limitations : The limitations or restrictions on authority are as follows:.

Organisational Level Limitations : The amount of authority goes on decreasing at the successive lower levels of the organisational hierarchy. Thus, top executives enjoy greater authority than the middle and first-line managers.

Limitations by Organisational Policies, Rules, Regulations etc. : Organisational policies, rules, regulations, procedures, budgets, articles of association etc. impose certain restrictions on the authority of managers. Managers cannot go against and beyond them.

Legal Limitations : A manager cannot go beyond the legal framework regulating his authority. Companies Act, Income-tax Act, Sales-tax Act, FEMA are some of the laws that regulate and restrict the authority of managers.

Social Limitations : Managers run their business in social system. They, therefore, are liable to run the business while keeping in view the fundamental beliefs, usage or customs of the society.

Physical Limitations: Physical laws, climate, geographical factors etc. restrict managerial authority to a great extent. These cannot be violated by anybody.

Biological Limitations : Biological limits relate to physical and mental abilities of a human being. A manager cannot ask his subordinates to do something which is beyond his physical and mental capacity.

Economic Limitations : Economic forces like market conditions, price situation, elasticity of demand, level of competition, supply of finance and so on limit the authority of a manager.

Span of Management Limitations : A manager's authority is limited to the number of persons he supervises. A manager cannot order a person who is not under his supervision.

Thus there are some of the basic limitations to the authority of managers.

Delegation of Authority : Delegation is one of the fundamental steps in the organising process. It is essential for the existence and efficient functioning of an organisation. It is a key to effective managerial performance.

Meaning and Definition : In simple terms, delegation means dispersing or assigning authority from one manager to another. It is a means of sharing authority with another.

According to Weihrich and Koontz, "Delegation means vesting of decision-making discretion in a subordinate."

In the words of Haimman, " : Delegation of authority merely means the granting of authority to subordinates to operate within prescribed limits."

According to Terry and Franklin, " : Delegation means conferring authority from one manager or organisational unit to another in order to accomplish particular assignments."

Thus, delegation is the process by which a manager assigns his authority to his subordinates to perform certain tasks or activities assigned to them. It involves shifting of decision-making authority from one organisational level *to* another lower level.

The Characteristics : Following are the special characteristics of delegation :

1. *Process of Assigning Authority :* Delegation is a process of assigning authority to subordinates to perform certain tasks assigned to them.
2. *Shifting Decision-making Authority :* It involves the shifting or pushing of decision-making authority from one

organisational level to another lower level. Thus, it allows subordinates to make decisions.

3. Creates link-Delegation of authority creates link between two organisational levels.
4. Authorises subordinates-It authorises subordinates to act in a certain way within the specified limits. Delegation does not allow subordinates to act in an arbitrary manner.
5. Creates responsibility-It also creates responsibility of subordinates to perform the assigned tasks correctly.
6. Delegation of authority not of responsibility- Manager can delegate authority and cannot delegate responsibility because it is a personal obligation. He, therefore, himself remains accountable to his boss. However, the process of delegation creates additional authority and responsibility of subordinates. *[Robert Albanese]*
7. No reduction of authority-It does not imply reduction in the authority of superior. Both superior and subordinate can exercise the same authority because delegating superior always retains all original authority. It is something like imparting knowledge. You share with others who then possess the knowledge but you still retain the knowledge. *[Terry and Franklin]*
8. Does not discharge superior's responsibility- Delegation of authority does not imply discharge of superior's responsibility. The superior is ultimately responsible for the success or failure of delegation. It has been rightly stated that one cannot relieve oneself of any part of the original responsibility. Delegation allows only for someone else to do the work. *[Mondy et al.]*
9. Delegation out of one's authority-A manager can delegate authority out of his own authority. No manager can delegate authority which he himself does not possess.
10. Only to positions-Delegation of authority is possible only to any position in the organisation. It is never delegated to an individual.

11. Specific or general-Delegation may be specific or general. When course of action is specified, it is specific delegation. It is general delegation, when goal of delegation is specified but not the course of action.

12. Express or implied-Delegation may be expressed or implied. It may be written or oral.

13. Enhanced or withdrawn-Delegated authority may be enhanced, reduced or withdrawn at the sweet will of the delegating superior.

14. Depends on many factors-Delegation of authority depends upon several factors such as philosophy of management, abilities of subordinates, confidence of superior in his subordinates and so on.

Significance of Delegation : Delegation is regarded as a fundamental step in the process of organising. It is essential for the existence and efficient working of an organisation. Weihrich and Koontz have rightly stated that "delegation is necessary for an organisation to exist. Just as no person in an organisation can do all the tasks necessary for accomplishing a group purpose, so it is impossible for one person to exercise all the authority for making decisions in a growing organisation." Briefly, delegation of authority is essential because of the following advantages :

Key to managing-Mary Parker Follett has rightly observed that "management is getting things done through others." But no manager can get things done without delegating authority. Delegation is a prerequisite for managing things. It is a key to effective managerial performance. *[Gray and Smeltzer]*

Basis for organising process-Delegation is the basis of the organising process. Without delegation, organisation structure cannot be created. Existence and effective working of an organisation largely depends on delegation of authority. In the words of Robert Albanese, "Delegation is the process that establishes hierarchy by creating authority, responsibility, and accountability relationships between organisation members."

Quicker decisions and faster action-When matters are decided at a level higher than necessary, decisions are delayed. But through delegation of authority valuable time may be saved in making decisions. It permits to make on-the- spot decisions. Thus, delegation ensures quicker decisions which, in turn, lead to faster action.

Better Decisions : Delegation facilitates decision-making by the person who is closer to the point of implementation of the decision. Such person knows better how to do it best. Therefore, decisions made are the best possible.

Promotes Specialisation : Delegation promotes specialisation. Tasks requiring special skills can be assigned to specialists through the process of delegation.

Relieves Managers from Operative Functions : Delegation relieves managers from day-to-day operative functions. They, therefore, can devote more time to other important functions of long-range planning, policy formulation and control.

Motivates Subordinates: Delegation may lead to higher level of motivation. Persons who are given authority and responsibility by their superiors often feel motivated. Douglas Basil has observed that "delegation can be one of the management's best techniques for satisfying needs and for motivating subordinates to better performance."

Better Attitude and Morale of Employees : Delegation tends to improve employee attitude and morale. Employees with positive attitude and high morale are easier to manage and more cooperative.

Training and Development of Subordinates-Delegation helps in training and developing subordinates in the organisation. Subordinates cannot learn to perform certain things or make certain decisions unless given an opportunity. Delegating authority is, therefore, the cordinal step in developing subordinates. All the benefits of executive training programmes, seminars etc. go for naught if authority delegation is ignored. [*Terry and Franklin*]

Growth of Managerial Capabilities : Through delegation managers face and deal with wide variety of challenging situations. This, in turn, causes growth of their managerial capabilities. Ray A. Killian has rightly stated, "Art of delegation is essential to the growth of both the individual executive and the company."

Extends Managers Sphere of Responsibility : Delegation skill permits managers to extend their sphere of responsibility beyond the limits of their knowledge and energy. They can get things done better through the skill of delegation which extends their share of responsibility. Ray A. Killian has, therefore, rightly stated that "delegation is one of the most important skills of a manager to continue up the ladder of management."

Maintaining depth and continuity in organisation-Managers are taken out of an organisation through promotion, illness, resignation and business trips. Others must be able to carry on the business if the need arises. Delegation ensures this depth and continuity in organisation and can provide successors in the case of need. *[Terry and Franklin]*

Process of Delegation : Delegation process consists of certain essential and interrelated steps. Weihrich and Koontz have stated that this process involves the following four steps :

1. Determining the results expected from a position.
2. Assigning tasks to the position.
3. Delegating authority for accomplishing these tasks.
4. Holding the person in that position responsible for the accomplishment of the tasks.

Determining the Results Expected : First step in the process of delegation involves the determination of results expected from a position or subordinate. Assignment of task will be meaningful only when the subordinate clearly knows what results he has to achieve. Moreover, determination of expected results will also help in deciding the adequate amount of authority to be delegated to a subordinate. Therefore, results expected from a position must be clearly determined to make the delegation effective..

Assigning Tasks : The next step in the delegation process consists of assigning duties or functions to the position or subordinate. Duties must be clearly and precisely defined. Duties to be assigned can be described at least in two ways :

(i) In terms of activities to be performed by the subordinate.

(ii) In terms of results expected from the subordinates.

Experts are of the opinion that it is better to describe duties in terms of results expected. It is so because subordinate can know in advance in what terms his performance will be evaluated. Generally, job descriptions form the basis for assigning the duties. They establish the general categories of tasks and set the limit of a subordinate's duties. However, managers can assign the duties that are outside the subordinate's job description.

Delegating Authority : The next step in the process of delegation is delegating authority for accomplishing the tasks assigned. No subordinate can carry out tasks or duties without appropriate amount of authority. Therefore, subordinates must be given the authority necessary to carry them out. Authority consists of rights and permissions including the rights to take decisions, give directions, to take actions and to do certain things. For instance issuing orders, buying materials, selling products, hiring, firing and rewarding or penalising employees etc. are some of the rights and permissions granted to subordinates.

Creation of Responsibility : Final step in the process of delegation of authority relates to creation of responsibility. Responsibility means the obligation to carry out the duties assigned by exercising the delegated authority properly.

When authority is delegated to a subordinate, he must also be held liable to carry out the tasks and use the authority properly. Manager must, therefore, make adequate arrangements for holding the subordinate responsible and accountable for the accomplishment of tasks.

These are the four essential steps in the process of delegation. Out of these tasks, authority and responsibilities are basic to the process of delegation. These attributes or elements of delegation are like three legs of a three-legged stool, each depends on the others for support and no two can stand alone. *[Newman, Warren and McGill]*

Significant Principles

Some of the basic principles of delegation of authority are as follows :

Principle of Delegation by Results Expected : This principle states that authority should be delegated in terms of the results expected from the subordinates. The amount of delegated authority should be adequate enough to achieve the results expected. Therefore, before delegating authority, the goals and plans of expected results must be set. Moreover, these should be clearly made known and understood by the subordinates.

Principle of Functional Definition : This principle states that functions and activities of every position or subordinate should be clearly and precisely defined. This will reduce overlapping of activities. Moreover, relationship of every position with other positions should also be clearly established. A clear and precise definition of every function and relationship of every subordinate with others will greatly facilitate delegation of authority. Moreover, these functions, activities and relationships should be made known and understood by the subordinates.

Scalar Principle : This principle states that authority should flow vertically from the top to the bottom of the organisation. This will establish the hierarchy of authority and responsibility relationship. This, in turn, will facilitate organisation members to understand who can delegate to whom and whom they are accountable.

Principle of Unity of Command : This principle states that for any given activity, a subordinate should be made accountable to only one superior. Therefore, a subordinate should receive delegation only from one superior. If he receives delegations from two or more superiors, he shall be accountable to both. This will lead to a situation of confusion and conflict because no one can serve two bosses at the same time.

Principle of Parity of Authority and Responsibility : This principle requires that there should be parity between delegated authority and delegated responsibility. In other words, delegated authority should commensurate with delegated responsibility. Responsibility without sufficient authority will make the subordinate ineffective. At the same time, authority without responsibility will make the subordinate irresponsible. However, it is very difficult to know when authority is exactly equal to responsibility. But an experienced manager will find a reasonable balance between the two.

Principle of Absoluteness of Responsibility : This principle states that responsibility of superior is absolute and ultimate. Ultimate responsibility cannot be delegated by a superior. The process of delegation does not relieve the managers of any of their authority, responsibility and accountability. Therefore, it is sometimes said that authority can be delegated but not responsibility, because responsibility is a personal obligation that a subordinate owes to his boss. *[Robert Albanese]*

Principle of Residual Authority and Responsibility : This principle states that all the responsibilities cannot be delegated. Only general responsibilities can be delegated but personal responsibilities cannot be delegated. For instance, policy formulation, coordination of activities are the personal responsibilities of a manager. The manager himself is accountable to his boss for these responsibilities. If these responsibilities are allowed to be delegated, there would be no need of that manager. *[Robert Albanese]*

The Exception or Authority Level Principle : The exception principle states that managers should delegate their routine matters and retain with themselves the exceptions to the routine and overall policy matters. Thus, this principle suggests managers to develop policies and procedures to help the subordinates to carry out the routine matters. Managers should not interfere in these routine matters. However, managers should interfere in such matters only in exceptional circumstances or in the cases significant deviations from the goals and plans.

Principle of Completeness of Delegation : This principle states that whole task must be delegated but not the pieces of tasks. No one can function effectively on a task if it is an integral part of someone else's total task. Assigning of unity of command. Hence, whole task must be delegated for effectiveness of delegation of authority.

Principle of Clarity of Limits of Delegation : The limits of delegation must be clearly set and made known to the subordinates. To ensure clarity, the delegation should be written and specific.

Clarity of limits will enable subordinates to know their area of operation and to take initiative. This will also allow freedom of action to subordinates.

Principle of Communication : This principle states that there should be free flow of communication between the superior and his subordinates. They should discuss and exchange the ideas. Superior should give clear and precise instructions. Subordinates should also be- allowed to seek necessary clarifications from the superior. Subordinates should regularly keep informed the superior about the progress of his work.

The Difficulties : Many managers are found reluctant to delegate authority. Similarly, many subordinates are found unwilling to accept authority. It is because of the fact that there are many obstacles in the way of effective delegation. Those obstacles or difficulties may be discussed under the following heads :

I. Obstacles on the part of superior or delegator.

II. Obstacles on the part of subordinates or delegant.

III. Obstacles on the part of the organisation.

The Obstacles : Following are the obstacles or difficulties on the part of superior or manager that makes him reluctant to delegate authority :

Unwilling to let Go : Some managers do not delegate their authority because they are unwilling to delegate. Such managers are of the view that if they delegate their authority, their influence will be reduced. Moreover, they want to make their, presence felt everywhere. They even desire that subordinates should regularly come to them and get their decisions approved. In fact, such managers have excessive love or passion for authority. They even feel fear of loss of authority. Consequently, they are unwilling to delegate authority:

I can do it Better myself'Fallacy : Some managers have inflated sense of their own worth. They suffer from the fallacy, "I can do it better myself." They are overconfident of their own competence. Such managers, therefore, want to do the work themselves instead of the subordinates.

Lack of Confidence in Subordinates : Some managers lack confidence in their subordinates. Such managers feel that their subordinates are not trustworthy. They doubt their abilities and feel that they are incompetent to exercise authority and assume responsibility. Hence, they hesitate in delegating authority.

Feeling of Need to do Personally : Sometimes, some managers are unable to distinguish between the tasks which can be delegated and those which cannot be delegated. In such a situation, they feel that everything is important and should be done personally. They, therefore, do not delegate and do the tasks themselves.

Lack of Ability to Direct or Manage Human Resource : Some managers are not competent enough to direct, guide, train, motivate, and supervise subordinates effectively. Hence, they hesitate to delegate authority.

Aversion of Risk : Managers are ultimately accountable to their subordinates' work. Thus, managers run the risk of subordinates' failure to perform the work as required. Therefore, some managers find no point in delegating authority. They consider it better to avoid risk by avoiding delegation of authority.

Absence of Proper Control System : In some organisation, there is no proper control system which may facilitate delegation of authority. There may not be effective communication and feedback system. There may not be clear set of policies, procedures, rules etc. In the absence of proper and effective control system, managers usually hesitate to delegate authority.

Fear of Competition : Some managers are afraid that their subordinates may outperform them and consequently may become their superiors. Hence, such managers hesitate to delegate their authority.

Style of Leadership : Some managers are autocratic by style whereas some others are democratic. Autocratic managers do not want to delegate.

Unwillingness to Forebear Mistakes : Some managers are unwilling to forebear the mistakes of their subordinates. Subordinates of such managers are always reluctant to accept delegation.

The Obstacles : Sometimes, subordinates are reluctant to accept delegation of authority. In some other cases, they block the delegation process. Such situations arise due to the following reasons :

Lack of Self-confidence : Some subordinates do not dare to accept authority and responsibility due to the lack of self-confidence in them. Such subordinates do not have faith in their capabilities. They, therefore, refuse to take responsibility.

Dependence on Boss : Some subordinates find it easier and better to depend on the boss for all decisions. Such managers believe that it is easier to ask the boss what to do rather than solve the problem. Such a tendency on the part of subordinates blocks the delegation process.

Fear of Criticism : Some subordinates fear criticism for their mistakes. Such subordinates believe that greater the responsibility more the chances of making mistakes. They, therefore, like to avoid accepting authority and assuming responsibility.

Lack of Information and Resources : Sometimes, adequate information and resources needed to do the job are not available to the subordinates. In such cases, subordinates are reluctant to assume new responsibility.

Over-burdened Subordinates : Some subordinates are overburdened with work. They have more work than can do. Such subordinates are reluctant to accept further assignments.

Lack of Incentives : Sometimes, subordinates are not offered any positive incentives for assuming added responsibility. In such a situation, they might be unwilling to assume extra responsibility. They may even block the process of delegation.

Little Delegation : Sometimes, managers decide to delegate a little. This little is not enough to enable the subordinates to get the job done. Hence, they do not want to accept delegation.

Obstacles on the Part of Organisation : Sometimes, managers are willing to delegate authority and subordinates are willing to accept authority but delegation process is blocked by organisational obstacles. Such obstacles may arise due to the following reasons :

1. Inadequate planning.
2. Lack of sound policy, procedures, rules, regulation's etc.
3. Lack of sound organisation structure, particularly lack of unity of command, lack of unity of direction, lack of clear authority relationships.
4. Absence of adequate communication system.
5. Absence of proper control system.
6. Non-availability of competent managers.
7. Lack of necessary physical and human resources.
8. Lack of effective incentive system.

Guidelines for Effective Delegation : Delegation is often ineffective even though everyone admits its importance. In order to secure effective delegation of authority, following steps should be taken :

Clarify the Assignment : First of all managers should clarify what is to be delegated. Managers should clearly and precisely decide the degree of delegation of authority.

Identify the Subordinates : For effective delegation, it is necessary to delegate to right persons. Therefore, managers should identify the subordinates who are most capable of performing the task. Managers should also ensure that such subordinates have enough time and motivation to perform the task.

Clarify the Results Expected : Effectiveness of delegation will be judged from the results achieved. Therefore, managers should also clarify the results expected. Clear information of the results expected should also be given to the subordinates. Moreover, managers must try to get agreement of subordinates on the results expected.

Set Limits of Authority : Limits of authority delegated should be clearly stated. These limits should be well understood by the subordinates. Subordinates should precisely understand what is not being delegated and what is the range of their discretion. They must know from where to begin and where to stop or what is their jurisdiction.

Inform others about Authority Delegated : Managers should also inform all the concerned about the authority delegated. It should be informed that what has been delegated and how much authority has been delegated to whom.

Standards for Performance : Subordinates should also know the standards for performance of the delegated task. Standard should be specific. They should be able to encourage individual initiative, creativity and organisational loyalty.

Training and Development : Delegation requires competence on the part of both superior and subordinate. Therefore, both should be trained for better results of delegation of authority. Moreover, superior should be capable of developing skills of his subordinates.

Mutual Trust and Confidence : There should be mutual trust and confidence among all individuals involved in the process of delegation. Superior should have faith and confidence in the abilities and judgement of his subordinates. Mutual trust and confidence promote the free exchange of ideas which, in turn, lays the foundation for continuing delegation.

Freedom of Action : Once authority is delegated, the superiors should allow freedom of action to their subordinates. In other words, superiors should not interfere the routine work of the subordinates. Of course; superiors should be ready to provide advice and support to the subordinates.

Effective Communication : There should be free flow of communication between superior and his subordinates. Superiors should also give clear, precise and unambiguous directions in time. Subordinate should also feel free to contact with their superior to get guidance and necessary clarifications regarding the work problems.

Adequate Incentives : Adequate incentives should be offered to subordinates for assuming added responsibility. Monetary as well as non-monetary incentives should be provided to lure the subordinates to assume increased responsibility. Moreover, top management should create an incentive system that rewards managers for delegating their authority successfully.

Effective Control System : To ensure success of delegation of authority, effective control system is a prerequisite. Superior should set reasonable standard of performance and evaluate performance against them regularly. If the delegation is more than anticipated, superior should take necessary steps to correct it.

Willingness to Forebear Mistakes : 'To err is human.' Subordinates are human beings and will make some mistakes. Hence, subordinates should be allowed to make some mistakes for the success of delegation. Managers should be willing to forebear the cost of their mistakes. They must consider the cost of mistakes as an investment in human development.

Receptiveness : For effective delegation, managers need to develop habit of receptiveness. Managers must be able not only to welcome the ideas of others but also to help others. They must be ready to complement others on their ingenuity. *[Weihrich and Koontz]*

Willingness to let Go : A manager can effectively delegate authority if he is willing to release significant amount of authority. Therefore, managers must be willing and ready to give their authority to others without any fear of loss of power.

The Centralisation

Centralisation of authority refers to the situation in which the authority to make decisions is retained by the top management.

According to Allen, "Centralisation is the systematic and consistent reservation of authority at central point in an organisation."

According to Weihrich and Koontz, "Centralisation (as an aspect of management) is the tendency to restrict delegation of decision-making. A high degree of authority is held at or near the top by managers in the organisational hierarchy."

In the words of Henry Fayol, " : Everything which goes to reduce the role of a subordinate is centralisation."

In the words of Mondy et al, : 'Centralisation is the degree to which authority is retained by higher-level managers within an organisation rather than being delegated."

Thus, Centralisation refers to the extent to which authority to make decisions is retained by the top managers in the organisation. It is a situation which goes to decrease the role of subordinates.

Characteristics

1. Centralisation is the extent to which authority retained by higher-level managers.
2. It reserves the right to make decisions in the hands of top managers.
3. In centralised organisations, the actions and operations are regulated by the top managers.
4. In such organisations, operating authority vests with the middle managers.
5. It reduces the role of subordinates.
6. Centralisation belongs to the natural order. It is always present to greater or lesser extent. In practice, no organisation is either purely centralised or purely decentralised.
7. It undertakes close supervision and control over every aspect of the organisational working.
8. Centralisation of management authority should be distinguished from centralisation of performance and departmental centralisation. Centralisation of performance means geographic concentration in which a firm operates in a single location. Departmental centralisation refers to concentration of specialised activities, generally in one department. *[Weihrich and Koontz]*

The Advantages : Advantages of centralisation of authority are briefly discussed as follows :

Uniformity of Decisions and Actions : Centralisation permits uniformity in decisions and actions because all decisions are taken at one point.

Uniformity in Organisational Working : Centralisation facilitates uniformity in organisational working. It is so because (i) all policies, procedures, rules are framed at one point and (ii) all decisions and actions originate from one point.

Personal Leadership : Centralisation facilitates personal leadership. This, in turn facilitates quick decisions and actions which are essential for the success of every organisation.

Facilitates Integration and Coordination : In a centralised organisation (i) lines of authority are clear, and (ii) policies, decisions and directions are uniform. There is little chance of confusion among organisation members. Such situations facilitate integration and coordination of activities in the organisation.

Effective Leadership : Centralisation tends to make top managers more powerful and strong. Such powerful managers can provide effective leadership to the organisation in a dynamic and complex business environment.

Reduced Mistakes by Subordinates : Subordinates tend to make less mistakes because all the important decisions and actions are taken by top managers.

Expert Services : Centralised organisations can easily and economically avail expert services of the specialised personnel.

Closer control of Operations : Centralised organisation facilitate close control of operations performed by the lower level subordinates.

Increased Efficiency/economy : Centralisation of authority helps to avoid overlapping and duplication of activities and efforts. Top managers can utilise the resources in a most efficient way. They can hire managers with simple skills at lower levels, at lower rates of remuneration. All this leads to considerable efficiency and economy in the operation of the enterprise.

Facilitates Crisis/Emergency Management : Quick decisions, actions and the mobilisation of resources are the prerequisite for handling crisis and emergency situations effectively. Centralisation facilitates all these things. This, in turn, facilitates crisis and emergency management in an effective way.

The Disadvantages : Following disadvantages are associated with centralisation of authority :

Increased Burden on Top Managers : Centralisation of authority means all decisions and actions by top managers. This increases burden of top managers.

Delay in Decisions and Actions : Centralisation may cause delay in decisions and actions.

Weak Organisation Structure : Centralisation of authority may weaken the organisation structure because of disparities in distribution of authority.

Abuse of Power : It has been rightly said that 'power corrupts simply and absolute power corrupts absolutely.' Centralisation of authority may lead to abuse of power and corrupt the managers enjoying absolute power.

Bureaucratic and Autocratic Organisation : Over centralisation of authority fosters bureaucratic and autocratic atmosphere in the organisation. It tends to discourage initiative, enthusiasm and dynamism among the organisation members.

Weak Communication System : In a centralised organisation, system of communication tends to be weak. Free flow of communication among organisation members is generally absent. Top managers usually remain ignorant of the views, and problems of the organisation members.

Frustration in Subordinates : Centralisation may cause frustration in subordinates. It is because of the fact that they are unable to use their discretion but are forced to operate in accordance with the decisions of top managers.

Hampers Growth : Centralisation may hamper organisational growth and development. It hampers growth of middle and lower level managers. Moreover, top managers remain ignorant of real opportunities for growth.

In view of these facts, absolute centralisation should he avoided.

The Decentralisation

Decentralisation is the opposite of centralisation. It refers to a situation in which authority to make decisions is assigned at the point where operations take place.

According to McFarland, "Decentralisation is the degree to which an organisation places authority and responsibility for decisions as far down in the organisation as efficient management permits,"

According to Henri Fayol, "Everything that goes to increase the importance of the subordinates role is decentralisation."

In the words of Allen, "Decentralisation implies consistent and systematic effort to delegate to the lowest levels of all authority except that which can only be exercised at central points."

In the words of Gray and Smeltzer, "Decentralisation refers to the extent to which managerial authority is delegated or pushed downward in an organisation."

Thus, decentralisation of authority refers to the extent to which decision-making authority is widely dispersed within the organisation. In a decentralised organisation, top mangement retains authority to make certain important decisions such as setting overall objectives, strategic planning, policy formulation etc. and delegates the authority to make operating decisions at the points as near as possible where actions take place.

Characteristics

1. Decentralisation authority refers to the extent to which dispersal of decision-making authority within an organisation is made.
2. In decentralisation, authority to make operating and routine decisions is delegated at the points Where operations or actions take place.
3. In a decentralised organisation, decision-making power relating *to* functional areas are delegated to middle and lower-level managers whereas top managers retain authority to make decisions relating to setting corporate objectives, formulating policies etc.
4. In a decentralised organisation, managers at middle and lower levels have discretion in specific operational areas.
5. Decentralisation is more than mere delegation of authority. Delegation of authority means assigning authority from one person to another. On the other hand, decentralisation means dispersal of authority throughout the organisation.

Under decentralisation, top managers exercise minimum control whereas under delegation control remains with top managers.

6. Decentralisation of authority differs from decentralisation or dispersal of physical facilities. Decentralisation of physical facilities means dispersal of geographical location of factories or offices. On the other hand, decentralisation of authority means dispersal of decision-making authority within the organisation.
7. It is impossible to achieve absolute decentralisation of authority.

The Distinction

Nature : Delegation is a process of assigning authority from a superior to his subordinates. On the other hand, decentralisation is an organisational process by which dispersal of authority takes place throughout the organisation.

Process and the Endresult : Delegation is a process of devolution of authority whereas decentralisation is the end-result of the process of delegation.

Control : In delegation, immediate superior has control over the subordinates whereas in decentralisation, top managers have overall control and operating control vests with the subordinates.

Choice : Delegation is a must for management and key to organisation. Without delegation managers cannot get the things done effectively. On the other hand, decentralisation is optional. Top managers may or may not decentralise their authority.

Use of Authority by Superior : In the case of delegation of authority, both the superior and the subordinate can exercise the same authority. But in the case of decentralisation, superior cannot exercise the decentralised authority.

Responsibility : In the case of delegation, the superior continues to be responsible for the decisions and actions of his subordinates. But in the case of decentralisation, subordinates become liable for their decisions and actions to the top managers..

Dependence : Delegation is not dependent on decentralisation. It can take place even without decentralisation. But decentralisation cannot take place without delegation.

Degree of Autonomy : In delegation, degree of autonomy to subordinates is regulated by the superior. But in the case of decentralisation, the organisational departments are granted a semi-autonomous status.

Technique and Philosophy : Delegation is regarded as a technique whereas decentralisation is considered to be a philosophy of management and organisation.

Scope : Delegation is simply the process of assigning authority to subordinates in order to get things done through them. On the other hand, decentralisation is more than assigning authority to subordinates. It is both dispersal and concentration of authority within the organisation.

Relationship : Delegation establishes superior and subordinate relationship. On the other hand, decentralisation establishes relationships between organisational departments or levels.

Life Span : Delegation is a task specific and ceases as soon the task is over. Thus, it has a shorter life span. Decentralisation is an ongoing process in the organisation.

The Advantages : The main advantages of decentralisation of authority are as follows :

Reduces Burden of Top Managers : Decentralisation of authority reduces the workload of top mangers as they are free from the routine operational decision-making work. They can devote their time on more important work of strategic planning, policy formulation and so on.

Quick Decisions : It facilitates quick decisions as the decisions can be made on the spot without consulting higher level managers.

Better Decisions : Decisions are likely to be better because they are made by the persons closest to situation. Moreover, decisions are likely to be adapted to local conditions.

Better Communication : Decentralisation improves organisation's communication system. It is due to the fewer levels

of authority and lesser distance between the points of information generation and the points of action.

Training and Development : It facilitates training and development of managers at middle and lower levels in the organisation. It is because managers at these levels are allowed to make decisions and take actions independently. In this process they develop many skills and talent.

Democratic Atmosphere : Decentralisation pro motes democratic atmosphere in the organisation because of dispersal of authority throughout the organisation.

Improves Motivation and Morale : Decentralisation enables subordinates to exercise their own judgement and initiative which promote job satisfaction. This ultimately improves motivation and morale of subordinates.

Effective Supervision and Control : The greater the degree of decentralisation, the more effective is the supervision and control. Under decentralisation, lower level managers have full authority as regards operation of activities. They can change work assignment or production schedules, or can recommend promotion of the subordinates and can take disciplinary action wherever necessary. It facilitates effective supervision. Control can also be made effective by evaluating the performance of each unit in the light of predetermined standards.

Provides Flexibility : Decentralisation provides flexibility to meet changing needs at local levels.

Survival and Growth of Organisation : Decentralisation contributes to survival and growth of organisation. It is so because it creates multiple managerial centres to cope with diverse and unique situations of the organisational environment.

The Disadvantages : Following are some ot the disadvantages associated with decentralisation of authority :

Loss of Control : Decentralisation creates semi-autonomous departments in the organisation. In such an organisation structure, there is a damage that top management may lose its control over the functioning of different departments.

Difficulty in Coordination : Decentralisation may create problems in bringing coordination among the different departments of the organisation.

Lack of Uniformity : Uniformity of decisions and actions may be lacking in decentralised organisation. It is because of lack of uniform policies and procedures of different departments.

High Cost : Decentralisation of authority is likely to increase cost of administration and operation. It is mostly due to the duplication of activities, highly paid middle and lower level managers etc.

External Limitations : Sometimes, decentralisation may not be advantageous for external limitations. Growing competition, increasing complexities and uncertainties, rising cost of materials and services and so on are some of the external limitations that hampers the tendency of decentralisation.

Imbalance : It is very difficult to strike a balance between the degrees of centralisation and decentralisation. Operating functional departments demands more autonomy whereas top managers want to retain control more and more. This situation may lead conflicts between the two levels of managers.

Competition among Departments : Decentralisation may lead to unnecessary unfair competition among the decentralised departments. They may compete with each other in the market. They may even compete for a higher share of resources and facilities in the organisation.

Degree of Decentralisation : Following are the important factors that determine the degree of decentralisation of authority in an organisation.

Size and Complexity of Organisation : The size and complexity of an organisation is the strongest single factor determining the degree of decentralisation. Usually, the larger the organisation, more authority needs to be decentralised. Similarly, multi-product organisation having varying kinds of customers and varied marketing channels is likely to be highly decentralised.

History and Age of Organisation : An organisation which has grown gradually under the leadership of a particular person, is likely to be more centralised. On the other hand, organisation which has grown by acquisitions and mergers, is likely to be more decentralised. Thus, the history of organisation growth also decides the degree of decentralisation.

Philosophy of Top Management: Where the top management believes in democratic values and participative management, there will be higher degree of decentralisation. Conversely the opposite *i.e.* centralisation.

Competence of Managers : Where the competent managers are available at middle and lower levels in the organisation, there tends to be decentralisation of authority. But the shortage of competent managers would limit decentralisation.

Willingness of Subordinates : Not only the abilities but willingness of subordinates also have a bearing on the degree of decentralisation. Where subordinates are willing to assume responsibility, the organisation is likely to be more decentralised.

Geographical Dispersion of the Organisation : In a geographically dispersed organisation, operations are carried out at different locations. More the geographical dispersion, more the degree of decentralisation is beneficial. But every function should not be decentralised. Control of operational functions may be pushed down to lower levels in the organisation but control of financing function should be centralised.

Significance of the Decisions : As a general rule, the more the significant decision is to be made, it is likely to be made at the upper levels of the organisation. Therefore, the decisions which are vital to the survival and success of the organisation are centralised. For instance, the decisions involving huge investments and high risk, affecting long-term standing and good will of the organisation are made by the upper level managers. But routine decisions involving very low cost and risk are decentralised.

Impact of Decisions: The decisions that have inter-departmental or inter-divisional implications must be centralised. Authority to make decisions must be retained by upper level managers whose authority extends over more than one department.

Desire for Uniformity of Policy : Managers who want, uniformity of policy, decisions and actions favour centralisation. Where uniformity of policy is not needed, managers tend to decentralise the authority.

Desire for Independence : Where the individual or groups desire high degree of independence from the bosses, authority needs to be decentralised. Conversely the opposite.

Adequacy of Communication System : Adequate and effective communication system is favourable for centralisation of authority. It is because of the reason that top managers can get the information in time and can easily exercise centralised control. Where it is inadequate and ineffective, decentralisation of authority becomes essential.

Control System : The control system in an" organisation may also decide the degree of decentralisation. Where the available system of control is far from satisfaction, managers are unwilling to decentralise their authority. Conversely, where it is effective, degree of decentralisation tends to be greater.

Environmental Factors : Where environmental factors are comparatively static and controllable, centralisation is suitable. But if these factors are ever changing, unstable and beyond the control of managers, the organisation needs to be decentralised.

Span of Control : 'Span of Control' is also known as 'span of management', 'span of supervision', and 'span of responsibility'.

The concept of span of control refers to the number of subordinates who are directly reporting to a superior. It also refers to the number of subordinates who can be effectively and efficiently supervised directly by a manager or superior.

The principle of span of control is founded upon the premise that a manager cannot directly supervise unlimited number of subordinates. His ability to supervise a large number of subordinates is constrained by many factors including the time, knowledge, energy etc. Thus, the principle of span of control states that no manager should have more subordinates under his direct supervision than he can effective and efficiently supervise and control.

Appropriate Span : There is no consensus on a specified ideal or appropriate span of control. Management thinkers and practitioners have found that four to eight subordinates for the managers at the upper level of the organisation and eight to fifteen or more for the managers at the lower levels is the appropriate number for ideal span of, control. Urwick, for instance, has suggested that ideal number of subordinates for all upper level managers to be four while for managers at lower levels (where performance of tasks takes place) the number may be eight to twelve. Ernest Dale found that the number may range between 8 and 20.

But modern theorists believe that many factors influence the appropriate span of control. Therefore, no ideal span of control exists for all kinds of managerial situations.

Graicunas Theory of Relationships : Although it is not possible to specify the correct span of control for every situation, but number of relationships of a managerial position goes a long way in deciding the span of control. V. A. Graicunas, a French management consultant worked on this premise and derived a formula to determine possible number relationships of a manager having a given number of subordinates.

Graicunas has identified three types of superior-subordinate relationships as follows:

Direct Single Relationships : Relationships that arise from direct interaction by a manager with each subordinate. This is one-on-one relation of manager with each subordinate.

Direct Group Relationships : Relationships that arise between a manager and groups of subordinates.

Cross Relationships : Relationships that arise among subordinates themselves working under a manager.

Graicunas formulae to calculate these relationships are as follows :

1. Direct relationships = Number of subordinates.
2. Direct group relationships $= n(2^{n-1} - 1) \text{ or } n\left(\frac{2^n}{2} - n\right)$
3. Cross relationships = n(n-1)

4. Total relationships $= n\left(\frac{2^n}{2} + n - 1\right)$

Where R represents the total number of relationships.

n represents the number of subordinates reporting to the manager *i.e.* direct relationships.

According to Graicunas formula, a manager with two subordinates would create six relationships. For example, if Anta has two subordinates, Banta and Santa, the six possible relationships would arise as follows :

Direct relationships

Anta meets and talks with Banta	1 Relationship
Anta meets and talks with Santa	1 Relationship

Group relationships

Anta meets and talks with Banta when Santa is present.	2 Relationships

Gross relationships

Banta meets Santa when Anta is not present	1 Relationship
Santa meets Banta when Anta is not present	1 Relationship
	Total 6 Relationships

As per Graicunas theory, the number of subordinates increases mathematically but the number of relationships increases geometrically. Table given below shows the number of possible relationships with different number of subordinates :

Criticism of Graicunas theory-Graicunas theory has been criticised on the following counts :

1. It is based on the false assumption that all relationships arise with equal frequency. It is not so in real life situations.
2. It is based on yet another false assumption that all relationships occur with equal intensity.

3. It does not determine the exact number of relationships that exists but indicates the possible number of relationships.
4. It does not indicate the relationships that arise due to the sideways interactions such as with service departments.

Factors Determining Span of Control : Following are the factors that affect the span of control:

Ability of Manager : Ability of manager is the most important factor determining the span of control. A manager who is able, competent and well trained can effectively supervise more subordinates than ope who is not.

Ability of Subordinates : Able, competent and well trained subordinates require less supervision and less contacts with their managers. Hence, managers can go for wider span of control if the subordinates are skilled, trained and experienced.

Nature of Jobs or Tasks : If the tasks are interlocked, interdependent, complex and varied, narrow span of control is essential. But simple, routine and repetitive tasks may allow for wider span of control.

Similarity of Jobs : Span of control shall be broader if the manager is supervising subordinates performing similar jobs. Conversely the opposite.

Clarity of Delegation of Authority : When a manager has clearly delegated authority to his subordinates, the subordinates require minimum of the manager's time and attention. In such a situation, a wider span of control may be opted for. Conversely the opposite.

Clarity of Plans : Where the plans are well defined and workable, little supervision is needed in their implementation. In such a situation, managers can operate with wider span of control. On the other hand, if plans, policies, and procedures are ambiguous, subordinates may require considerable guidance. Hence, span of control has to be narrow.

Degree of Decentralisation : When the degree of decentralisation is high, subordinates can make decisions at the points of action. Hence, a superior can have larger span of control.

But in the case of centralisation, a superior is required to make many decisions. Hence, he will have to have a limited span of control. Newman and Summer states, an executive who personally makes many decisions is able to supervise fewer subordinates than one who merely provides occasional advice and encouragement.

Quality of Standards/control System : Quality of standards (control system) used for performance evaluation also determine the span of control. If the standards used are objective, wider span of control may be effective. On the other hand, if the standards are subjective and non- quantitative, narrow span of control becomes necessary.

Nature of Environment : Some managers operate in more unstable environment than the others. The managers operating in more unstable environment need to have narrow span of control. Conversely the opposite.

Communication System : Where communication system is more effective, span of control may be wider. Conversely the opposite.

Need for Personal Contacts : Sometimes, personal contacts with subordinates are essential for getting things done effectively. Where face-to-face contacts are frequently required, narrow span of control is suggested. If face-to- face contacts are occasionally required, manager can operate with wider span of control.

Level of Managers in Organisation : Level of managers in organisation is one of the most important determinant of span of control. Usually higher the level of managers in organisation, the smaller the span of control. Therefore, upper level managers, who deal with complex problems, have smaller span of control than the middle level managers. Similarly, middle level managers will require a smaller span of control than the first-line managers.

Staff Assistance : Where the staff assistance is available, manager can operate with wider span of control. It is due to the reason that manager can supervise larger number of subordinates.

Thus, it is clear that appropriate span of control for any managerial position depends on all these factors. A manager should consider these factors simultaneously while deciding the appropriate span of control.

Bibliography

Aldous, T. : *Battle for the Environment*, Collins, London, 1972.

Ashworth, G. J. : *Marketing in the Tourism Industry*, Routledge, London, 1990.

Bhatia, A. K. : *Tourism Management and Marketing*, Sterling, New Delhi, 1997.

Bhatia, A. K. : *Tourism in India : History and Development*, Sterling, New Delhi, 1978.

Bryden, John M. : *Tourism and Development*, Cambridge University Press, Cambridge, 1973.

Burkart, A.J. and Medlik, S. : *Tourism: Past, Present and Future*, Heinemann, London, 1976.

Calder, N. : *The Environment Game*, Panther, London, 1969.

Dale, E. : *Management Theory and Practice*, McGraw-Hill, New York, 1973.

Edmunds : *Environmental Administration*, McGraw-Hill, New York, 1973.

Foster, D. : *Travel and Tourism Management*, MacMillan, London, 1985.

Holloway, J. C. : *Marketing or Tourism*, Longman, Harlow, 1995.

Katler, P. : *Introduction to Marketing Management, Analysis, Planning and Control*, Prentice-Hall, London, 1975.

Laws, E.C. : *Tourist Destination Management: Issues, Analysis and Policies*, Routledge, London, 1995.

McIntosh, R.W. : *Tourism Principles, Practices and Philosophies*, Grid, Ohio, 1977.

Nicholson, M. : *The Environmental Revolution*, Penguin, London, 1972.

Pearce, Sales, J. : *Travel and Tourism Encyclopedia*, Blandford, London, 1959.

Richards, G. : *Tourism and the Economy*, University of Surrey, Surrey, 1972.

Seth, P.N. : *Successful Tourism Planning and Management*, Cross Section Publications, New Delhi, 1978.

Tull, D. S. : *Marketing Research: Measurements and Methods*, Prentice-Hall, London, 1993.

Wahab, Salah : *Tourism Management*, Tourism International Press, London, 1975.